The Best American Short Plays

2009–2010

The Best American Short Plays

2009–2010

edited with an introduction by
Barbara Parisi

APPLAUSE THEATRE & CINEMA BOOKS
An Imprint of Hal Leonard Corporation

The Best American Short Plays 2009–2010
Edited with an intoduction by Barbara Parisi

Copyright © 2011 by Applause Theatre & Cinema Books (an imprint of Hal Leonard Corporation)

Published in 2011 by Applause Theatre & Cinema Books
An imprint of Hal Leonard Corporation
7777 West Bluemound Road
Milwaukee, WI 53213

Trade Book Division Editorial Offices
33 Plymouth St., Montclair, NJ 07042

Printed in the United States of America
Book interior by UB Communications

ISBN 978-1-55783-763-9 [cloth]
ISBN 978-1-55783-762-2 [paper]
ISSN 0067-6284

www.applausebooks.com

To William and Gloria Parisi,
Rochelle Martinsen,
and my husband—
Michael Ronald Pasternack

contents

foreword

Size matters.

How long have we lived under the dark umbrella of this old saying? A long time is the answer, in case you're continuing to read this, and it was getting annoying even before the ink had time to dry after the first time somebody wrote it. "Well, of course it matters but not very much" is the proper response to it, at least from my point of view. In fact, if anything really does matter, the correctness of a thing is a whole lot more important if you ask me. Big or small, getting it right is the real task at hand.

I love writing short plays for the challenge of it; trust me, it's not for the money. The only thing smaller than the plays themselves is the profits you see from a night of one-acts at a local theater. The freedom to explore, however, is priceless. Theater is still the home of the possible as far as I'm concerned—if you can imagine it, then it can happen. Writers are free in this abbreviated form to explore through character and genre and dialogue and structure in a way that is frowned upon in longer works, at least from a commercial standpoint. Better safe than sorry. Not so, though, when it comes to shorter works in the medium—long mono-logues are as welcome as a wordless interlude or the briefest of dramatic interactions between actors. Some of my favorite words by people as diverse as August Strindberg and Caryl Churchill are contained in their shorter plays—read *The Stronger* or *Three More Sleepless* sometime and you'll see why.

Short plays are playgrounds for the minds of playwrights, and I continue to go there not just for practice but because I really love the neighborhood. It may be harder to produce a play that's only four minutes long, but it can be an extremely liberating experience to write one. Don't get me wrong: it feels pretty terrific to write a full-length play as well, but the demands of getting it all in there in just a handful of pages is a challenging and extremely rewarding experience.

These days many of our mothers and fathers have fallen out of the cliché of wanting us to grow up to be doctors and lawyers—they leave the decision to us, knowing it's so damn scary out there in the world and so hard to be brave and do what you want that many of us will settle for the first good job that comes along. We gain security through terror and fear and we don't let ourselves dream any more (or if we do have dreams they remain only that and nothing more). Theater is the place where we can still make dreams become a reality, but it's not for the weak of heart. You have to be a little crazy and strong and bighearted to write something down and then show it to people—people who are more than willing to laugh at you and bring you down and then blog or tweet about it afterward. Do not believe them. In fact, don't listen to the good or bad reviews because they are only an opinion—one opinion out of many and the only people in the crowd who didn't pay for their tickets. Why trust them? Listen to your own heart and your own mind; you know when you've done good work or not. No matter what anyone else says, inside you know the truth.

Writing is a key that unlocks not just this world but a vast multitude of worlds—as far and wide as your own imagination will take you. If you've never done it, you should try it. If you already do it, keep right on doing it and trying to get that work published or produced or in front of anybody who'll take the time to read it or listen to it. Don't be afraid and start small if you need to—short plays are a great place to begin. I used to only write short plays and comedy sketches because I couldn't stop writing until I finished something—it was a little like *The Red Shoes* and kind of scary. I'm better now, but I still love the idea of brevity where plays are concerned and seeing what you can cram into only a few pages. Give it a try. I dare you.

And remember: size does matter, but not very much (and sometimes smaller is definitely better).

—Neil LaBute
March 2011

introduction
by Barbara Parisi

As editor of my sixth edition of Best American Short Plays, I have found myself reading many, many one-acts, discovering new playwrights, and being interviewed by theater journalists. I have had the pleasure of being reviewed by theater book critics, talking with successful playwrights and going to annual one-act theater festivals. The journey for me has been exciting. In the introduction to this edition, I have focused on the importance of subtext in one act playwriting.

In real life people rarely say exactly what they mean. Subtext refers to the unspoken thoughts and motives of characters. It is used to imply controversial subjects. And it is a tool used in narrative to explicitly make the reader aware of the message in the dialogue. Subtext can be humorous and is used as a method of inserting social or political commentary. Dramatic irony created through the use of subtext develops strong characterizations.

Through subtext the audience understands what characters really think and believe. In the Playwriting Seminars, Richard Toscan states:

> In well-written dialogue, subtext seldom breaks through the surface of the dialogue except in moments of extreme conflict. At other times, it colors the dialogue. . . . There's nothing there except lines of dialogue.

If they're sketched correctly and *minimally*, they will give the audience the illusion that these are "real people," especially if the lines are spoken by real people—the actors are going to fill a lot in. So a large part of the technique of playwriting is to leave a lot out.

Subtext gives the performers something to do. If you let your characters tell each other everything they think or feel, actors can't do what they're trained to do. Actors can reveal through gesture, intonation, and expression the real essence of a character.

In dialogue, subtext is very important. Although subtext is hidden, the audience can read between the lines to understand the true motivations of the characters through implicit, rather than explicit meaning. As a playwright, the best way to learn how to write dialogue is to listen to conversations. Spoken dialogue is full of fillers, such as "um" and "uh." Remember, the shorter the play, the less opportunity you can have for character development and subtext. Playwrights need to understand how to create strong subtext so actors can create strong characterizations in the development of a good one-act play.

As you read through this edition, see if you can sense how playwrights use subtext. In my last five editions, I have explored definitions of one-act plays and defined themes, plots, characterization and titles. As in the past, I have asked the playwrights to express their theme, plot, and inspiration for writing their one-act plays.

Red Light Winter
Adam Rapp

Escaping their lives in Manhattan, former college buddies Matt and Davis, Brown college English grads, take off to the Netherlands and find themselves thrown into a bizarre love triangle with a beautiful young prostitute named Christina. But the romance they find in Europe is eventually overshadowed by the truth they discover at home. This play of sexual intrigue explores the myriad and misguided ways we seek to fill the empty spaces inside us.

In reviewing *Red Light Winter*, Charles Isherwood said:

> Mr. Rapp is here exploring a wider range of human emotion and writing with a new sensitivity to match his natural gift for crackling, hyper-articulate dialogue…Matt…is the kind of guy who has somehow skidded through his twenties with all of his adolescent awkwardness rigidly in place.…[His] hunger for a physical intimacy that will allow him to escape the echoing corridors of his mind is persuasively drawn in Mr. Rapp's writing.

In an interview about *Red Light Winter* on SFGate.com, Jessica Werner Zack asked Mr. Rapp: "You're known for exploring some pretty dark subjects and circumstances. Does *Red Light Winter*, which is really about unrequited love, feel like a departure for you?"

Mr. Rapp responded by saying: "It was a departure. I always avoided the big emotional themes because I figured our greatest writers had already covered them so well and I wanted to be new and original. But once I decided to give it a try, it quickly wrote itself."

Mr. Rapp's inspiration for the play came as he started thinking about and experience he had had in Amsterdam with a friend who had recently gone through a breakup. Mr. Rapp had the idea to get him a prostitute to help him reconnect with the world. Engaged in theatricality, he developed this idea in *Red Light Winter*.

In Curtain Up, a theater review website, Simon Saltzman noted: "In an interview, Rapp stated that there was a lot in the play that he was drawing upon that was personal. For his sake, let's hope it didn't go that far. It is, however, the sense of torturous reality that propels this unsparingly gritty and graphic drama."

Who You Got to Believe
Charlene A. Donaghy

It is human nature to hold on to and fight for home, to cling to hope and belief, yet sometimes the connection of these is threatened by outside forces. For slightly touched, elderly Kathleen, who returns to New

Orleans four and a half years after Hurricane Katrina, a set of forlorn concrete steps epitomizes home. With stubborn resolve she refuses to leave. She is visited by tenderhearted, elderly Ray, who has been helping rebuild New Orleans. He pleads to get her to safety as they struggle with their hope, belief, and the true meaning of home.

New Orleans is my second home and muse. My soul and my writings are tied to that steamy, decadent, dirty, injured, haunted, beautiful city. With this play, I put the sadness of loss, and the anger at the government, of post-Katrina New Orleans into words. I craft Kathleen and Ray as true souls of New Orleans, those people who embrace New Orleans's spirit, who define her eccentricities, who know her deep gumbo of cultures, as well as her flaws, and ferociously defend and love her despite her failings.

Ella
Dano Madden

Sometimes I know the exact inspiration for my plays. *Ella* is a bit more difficult to track. The simplest answer is that I wrote this play for my friend Kianné Muschett. Kianné has an incredibly kind and generous spirit that inspires people to do nice things for her. We became friends in graduate school and I decided to write a play for her. Thus was born the character of Ella. I knew Ella was running away from something and I kept seeing visions of her sculpting, but the story didn't truly take hold until I remembered one of the most unusual holidays of my life. During this holiday, I found myself far from my own family on what felt like another planet. I met a young man who was trapped in an incredibly violent and oppressive environment. I wondered if he could ever escape. I feared that he wouldn't. As I remembered this experience, the character of Cutter was born. When Cutter entered into Ella's world, the story followed.

Ella is on the run after a life-changing tragedy. She is an artist who no longer knows how to sculpt. She is desperate to leave her past behind. A nineteen-year-old, white, gator-hunting farm boy named Cutter is the last person she needs to help her get her life back on track. At least that's what she thinks.

Ella is more personal for me than many of my plays. I'm drawn to the idea of strangers who are dealing with tremendous loss finding each other for a moment. I often think about the people who pass through our lives briefly and then leave, never to return. What is the impact they have on us? How can they change our trajectory?

This Is Your Lifetime
Jill Elaine Hughes

I wrote my one-act comedy *This Is Your Lifetime* for two reasons: one, for an actress friend of mine who wanted a piece written just for her to perform in a women's performance art festival, and the Marissa character is modeled on her somewhat; and two, to respond in a critical yet entertaining manner to one of the strangest (and least confrontable) manifestations of misogyny in our society—feminine-hygiene product advertising. The actress for whom I originally wrote the piece never performed it—in fact, she got involved with another *man's* theater company and then became too busy to do women's theater. But I decided to promote the play for production without her anyway. And it seems doing so was the right move, because less than two months after finishing the final draft, the play had already received two production contracts, along with rave reviews from the actresses and directors involved. It has gone on to have several productions across the United States.

Each and every woman who has read or seen this play has said almost the same thing—"This play describes *exactly* how I feel whenever I watch television."

I am a well-educated, intelligent feminist. And an artist. But that doesn't mean I don't enjoy reading the occasional bodice-ripper novel or watching the infrequent trashy made-for-TV melodrama. I think nearly all American women—even the strongest, smartest, and most liberal among us—have a few "guilty pleasures" that would make our college women's studies professors blush, maybe even brand us as traitors.

And for millions of American women, that "guilty pleasure" is the Lifetime Network.

The Lifetime Network's slogan is "Television for Women." I used to watch Lifetime frequently, especially when I was out of work following the 9/11 attacks, holed up in my apartment in a deep depression that I alleviated with a combination of Sara Lee cherry cheesecake and Lifetime Network movie marathons. Since I couldn't afford health insurance at the time, the Lifetime Network's often schlocky programming provided me with a means of escape that probably worked better at elevating my mood than Prozac ever could.

On the one hand, we feminists can decry contemporary women's programming as sexist, shallow, and unrealistic. Many other derogatory adjectives could certainly apply as well. But there is one thing that can't be denied about the Lifetime Network, and women's television programming in general—at least right now.

Lots of women *watch* it. Furthermore, lots of women *love* it.

They love it so much, they won't give it up, no matter how much Gloria Steinem might tell them it's unhealthy. This is a phenomenon the makers of feminine hygiene products understand very well. Far too well. The manufacturers of such medically unnecessary (and borderline dangerous) products like disposable douches, vaginal perfume sprays, and pantiliner "deodorant" powders (as well as the Madison Avenue ad execs making the commercials) know that if they buy commercial airtime on Lifetime, they will have a captive audience. The women addicted to their guilty-pleasure movies and coma-of-the-week miniseries will have no choice but to watch. And maybe, just maybe, laugh at themselves in the process.

Pair and a Spare
Avi Glickstein

Pair and a Spare begins with one man innocently mistaking another for someone he knows. The man leaves and the matter seems settled. But the men—One and Two—will soon play out this scenario over and over until one of them reaches a breaking point. Inspired by a similar, real-life encounter, the story of the play is the story of the people we ride in the same train car with every day, the people who are always *also* at our coffee shop, the people we see in stores or parks or on the street every weekend—all of the people who are part of our lives, but aren't. It's the story of those quick interactions we have every day that, without our knowledge, can mean more than we think. How we are almost completely ignorant of our own effect on others. Not how we see but how we are seen. As it developed, the play became an encapsulated and sad—but strangely funny—portrait of a person for whom a daily anonymous connection becomes very, very personal. Perhaps you'll recognize yourself in it. Perhaps not. But, almost certainly, you will *be* recognized.

The Trash Bag Tourist
Samuel Brett Williams

In 2005, shortly after Katrina hit, I returned home to Hot Springs, Arkansas. A friend picked me up at the airport, and she immediately began telling me stories about the Katrina victims who the town was "supporting." She claimed they were "stealing from Wal-Mart" and "raping little boys."

My stepfather, a social worker, is the county administrator for Arkadelphia, Arkansas. He assured me that no one was being raped and Wal-Mart was not being robbed daily. He said the town had been generous to a degree—they were willing to house the New Orleans refugees for six months, but then they were going to have to return to Louisiana.

I was fascinated by my friend's racism and by the town's generosity—generosity with a time limit.

Then my stepfather went on to tell me about people who were "faking it." They were claiming to be Katrina victims, but they were actually just the local homeless. My stepfather said they were checking social security numbers, and if anyone in the shelter was not actually from New Orleans, then they had to turn them out.

My stepfather is the best man I know. He said it was destroying him to have to do this.

I was fascinated by how my hometown could say that a certain type of victim needed help, but others (victims to circumstance, poverty, etc.), well, it wasn't their time—and it probably would never be.

I immediately began work on the play that is now called *The Trash Bag Tourist*.

Michole Biancosino (my director/dramaturg/hero/inspiration) helped me develop this piece in a basement theater at Mason Gross School of the Arts (Rutgers University). If it weren't for her patience, talent, and world class BS detector, this play would not exist.

My only hope for this play is that it forces you to ask the same questions I found myself asking back in 2005 when I returned home to Arkansas.

The Date
Joan Lipkin

The inspiration for *The Date* derives from my preoccupation with communication and the inevitable misunderstandings that occur as we lurch awkwardly toward connection. Courtship, in particular, strikes me as nothing so much as an adult version of "Mother, May I?" Take two steps forward, screw it up, take one step back.

The Date began as a writing exercise for a larger piece. I was commissioned to write a play to be performed at Washington University in St. Louis by college students, a play that would reflect their concerns. One of the issues that came up in many conversations was courtship in the age of AIDS. I realized that none of them had ever lived in an era before safe sex. I wondered how that might impact two men who were attracted to each other.

As I began to write a scene, which eventually made it into the play *Stories from Generation X (Y, Z . . .)*, I realized that I was not writing for college students. The voices in my head were the voices of my peers. Voices that were historically affected by the AIDS epidemic. Voices in which a new tentativeness was palpable.

The two men I created as characters in the play touch me deeply. I am so moved by certain burdens of socialized masculinity, especially for gay men who—rightly or wrongly—do not have the convenience of certain heterosexual conventions on which to rely. The play is deeply rooted in gay male experience and yet has universal application.

The beginning of most relationships is often alternately exhilarating and agonizing, regardless of gender or sexual orientation. When does something begin? Is there a single decision or moment? Or rather, does a relationship depend on a series of explorations: tentative, bold, then tentative again as people decide what they are willing to risk. Beginnings are thrilling in their newness, but I imagine that in the best of circumstances, we begin over and over again.

A finalist for the Heidemann Award at Actors Theatre of Louisville, *The Date* has been produced at The Gate (London), the Provincetown Theatre, Unity Fest (New York City), Theatre Out (Santa Ana), and Washington University in St. Louis.

Death Comes for a Wedding
Joe Tracz

Death Comes for a Wedding grew out of the Kennedy Center's playwriting intensive, which taught dramatic structure via fairy tales. I wanted to write a play that felt like it came from that same oral tradition, and I've always been fascinated by the Greek myth of Persephone, the "bride of Death" forced to marry the lord of the Underworld. As in the myth, my bride, Beth, is an unwilling sacrifice linked to the harvest (plus she has her own Greek chorus of playground girls). But Beth wants more out of life than getting married and dying, so she enlists the aid of the oldest woman in town to escape the engagement. The play's theme is that life changes the way you look at things, including death. What I like about a lot of folk stories that personify Death is that he's not really a bad guy—it's all in the timing and perspective. Here you have a young woman who's not yet ready for her ending, and an older woman who's lived a full enough life to welcome it. Beth will die someday, too, but like the Old Woman, and unlike Persephone, she gets to live it up in the world first.

Seven Card Draw
created by Daniel Gallant

Seven Card Draw is an evening of darkly comic tales about risk and reward.

It marks the second collaboration among a group of seven authors who have used their words and wit to support endangered theatrical venues.

In 2007, I organized a benefit production to help save the historic Thirteenth Street Repertory Theatre from demolition. This production, entitled *Five Story Walkup*, featured never-before-produced short plays and monologues focused on the theme of home. Authors John Guare, Neil LaBute, Daniel F. Levin, Quincy Long, Clay McLeod Chapman, Laura Shaine, and myself contributed new dramatic works to the show. Thanks in part to the success of *Five Story Walkup*, the Thirteenth Street Repertory Theatre still stands today. The short works that constitute *Five Story Walkup* were subsequently published in the Applause Books anthology *The Best American Short Plays 2007–2008*. The authors of *Five Story Walkup* are proud that our first benefit production helped preserve a historic home of experimental theater. In 2010, we gladly lent our words to benefit a new home for multiarts performance: *Seven Card Draw* raised funds to help complete the construction of Dixon Pace's new venue in Manhattan's Lower East Side.

The works in *Seven Card Draw* cover a wide range of styles and subject matter. John Guare's monologue, *What It Was Like*, describes life in 1970s Manhattan, when the author was living in John Lennon's former apartment and watching the city fall apart while building his own theatrical career. The prolific Quincy Long contribution, *The Huntsmen*, is a short play in which a lawyer discovers that his son may have committed a violent crime and must decide whether to protect or prosecute. Laura Shaine's *Beware of Waiter* is a dark screwball comedy in which a young urbanite couple visits an eccentric restaurant and meets a waiter who is secretly obsessed with an endangered species. From monologist Clay McLeod Chapman comes *undertow*, in which a tow-truck driver makes a chilling discovery. Daniel F. Levin conjures a haunted historical reenactment in *What Really Happened, Starring Abraham Lincoln*. Neil LaBute's *Totally* features a young woman who exacts stunning vengeance against her disloyal spouse. And in my short work, *Determined to Prove*, a sheepish young man uses a Shakespeare monologue to pull off an elaborate con.

Both *Five Story Walkup* and *Seven Card Draw* grew out of collaborations among theater artists at the 92nd Street Y's Makor Center, where I served as the director of theater programming before joining the Nuyorican Poets Cafe (where several of the works in *Seven Card Draw* were developed). Special thanks are also due to the HB Playwrights Unit, the Actors Studio, the Cornelia Street café, and Actors and Writers for their roles in developing the pieces that eventually became *Seven Card Draw*; to Michael Gallant, who provided original music for *Seven Card Draw* as well as *Five Story Walkup*; and to the sensational cast, crew, and directors who helped bring these short works to life at Dixon Place.

The Best American Short Plays

2009–2010

Red Light
Winter

Adam Rapp

Adam Rapp

Adam Rapp has been the recipient of the Herbert and Patricia Brodkin Scholarship; two Lincoln Center le Compte de Nuoy Awards; a fellowship to the Camargo Foundation in Cassis, France; the 1999 Princess Grace Award for Playwriting; a 2000 Roger L. Stevens Award from the Kennedy Center Fund for New American Plays; a 2000 Suite Residency with Mabou Mines; the 2001 Helen Merrill Award for Emerging Playwrights; and Boston's Elliot Norton Award. He was short-listed for the 2003 William Saroyan International Prize for Writing for *Nocturne* and received the Jeff Award for Best New Work in 2005 for *Red Light Winter*.

His plays include *Ghosts in the Cottonwoods* (Victory Gardens; The Arcola, London); *Animals and Plants* (American Repertory Theatre); *Blackbird* (The Bush, London; Pittsburgh City Theatre; Off-Broadway at Edge Theater); *Nocturne* (A.R.T.; Off-Broadway at New York Theatre Workshop); *Stone Cold Dead Serious* (A.R.T.; Off-Broadway at Edge Theater); *Finer Noble Gases* (26th Annual Humana Festival of New American Plays; Off-Broadway at Rattlestick); *Faster* (Off-Broadway at Rattlestick); *Trueblinka*.

His first feature film, *Winter Passing*, starring Ed Harris, Will Ferrell, and Zooey Deschanel, which he wrote and directed, premiered at the 2005 Toronto International Film Festival. A graduate of Clarke College in Dubuque, Iowa, Rapp also completed a two-year playwriting fellowship at Julliard. He lives in New York City.

··· production note ···

Red Light Winter was originally produced in Chicago, Illinois, by the Steppenwolf Theatre Company on May 30, 2005. It was directed by Adam Rapp; sets were designed by Todd Rosenthal; costumes by Michelle Tesdell; lights by Keith Parham; and sound by Andre Pluess and Ben Sussman. The production stage manager was Kerry Epstein. The assistant director was Joanie Schultz. The cast was as follows:

MATT   Christopher Denham
DAVIS   Gary Wilmes
CHRISTINA   Lisa Joyce

Red Light Winter was subsequently produced in New York City by Scott Rudin, Robyn Goodman, Stuart Thompson, and Scott Morfee at the Barrow Street Theatre in January 2006. It was directed by Adam Rapp; sets were designed by Todd Rosenthal; costumes by Michelle Tesdell; lights by Keith Parham; and sound by Eric Shim. The production stage manager was Richard A. Hodge. The cast was as follows:

MATT   Christopher Denham
DAVIS   Gary Wilmes
CHRISTINA   Lisa Joyce

characters

MATT, thirty

DAVIS, thirty-ish

CHRISTINA, twenty-five

setting

Amsterdam and New York City

• • •

···scene 1···

[*A nondescript, inexpensive hostel room in Amsterdam's Red Light District, not too far from the train station. Two made twin beds, one upstage center, one downstage right. Tall, blank walls, with a small shelf over the downstage-right bed. A small lamp hangs from the shelf. Also on the shelf is a paperback dictionary and random toiletries. On the upstage wall, three coat hooks. A door leading to a hallway. An offstage bathroom just outside the door. Above the upstage bed, a window overlooks the street below. There are two duffel bags, whose contents are half unpacked. There is a desk next to the window. On the desk, a laptop computer, some pens. It is winter. MATT is seated at the desk. He is thin, boyish, a little nervous, slightly unkempt, an insomniac. His dress is somewhat nondescript. His pants are just pants. His shoes are just shoes. He wears a long-sleeved thermal undershirt under a plain brown T-shirt. He is peering at his computer screen. He has been this way for a long time. It is early evening. The light from the hostel sign spills in weakly through the window. After a moment, MATT pushes away from the desk and stands. He stares at a hook on the wall. He then walks to the center of the room, paces a bit, removes his belt while pacing, stops, stands very still. He pulls on the belt a few times to test its weight-bearing possibilities. He turns to the desk, studies it for a moment, crosses to the chair, centers it to the desk, and aligns his computer and pens symmetrically. He then turns the desk lamp off, considers this light, turns the lamp back on. He crosses back to the center of the room, feeds the belt through the buckle, and loops it over his head and around his neck. He tugs on the end of the belt a few times, creating a noose, which produces a few gagging sounds. With the belt noosed around his neck, he then approaches the wall, forces a belt hole over the hook, squats so that the belt is stiff with tension, breathes extremely rapidly for a moment, and then lifts his feet, attempting to hang himself. The hook breaks and MATT crashes to the floor just as the sound of keys jingling on the other side of the door can be heard. MATT desperately undoes the belt from around his neck and stands very quickly, hiding the belt, just as the door opens. DAVIS enters with the flair of a high-energy kung-fu movie. He performs a series of kicks and punches, making kung-fu noises—a typical DAVIS entrance. He is standing on one of the beds and the overhead room light is on now as he punctuates his entrance. He leaves the door open. He is broad-shouldered, handsome, clean-shaven, confident, a charmer. He*

*wears conservative, casual attire and a smart winter coat. Throughout the following,
DAVIS crosses to the shelf above his bed, grabs deodorant, applies it, gets a clean
pair of underwear out of his bag, stuffs it in his pocket. MATT remains standing,
awkwardly holding on to the belt.*]

DAVIS   You're missing all the fun, bro. This place is a trip. It's totally
familiar but dreamlike at the same time. The cobblestone
streets. The velvet curtains in the sex windows. Cyclers riding
their three-speeds into crowds of pedestrians. Silver mimes
pop-locking for spare change. It's like a fucking Tim Burton
movie or something.

[*From the shelf DAVIS grabs a cylinder of some sort of scented aerosol
musk, sprays a few clouds into the air and walks into them. When
DAVIS isn't looking, MATT works the hook back into the wall.*]

There's this homeless guy over by the Anne Frank museum
who I swear I've seen in the East Village. He wears a lab
coat. Pushes a duck around in a shopping cart. Same coat.
Same duck. Bits of electric tape in his beard. It's like some
slightly refracted parallel reality.

MATT   It's the heroin.

DAVIS   What heroin—I haven't done any heroin.

MATT   No, some guy in Paris told me there's this, um, sect of addicts
that revolves between the East Village, Zurich, and
Amsterdam. They follow the quality stuff around. This dealer
supports their habit pro bono for talking up the product in
the streets. Flies them business class from city to city. He's
revered as this like total holy man.

DAVIS   Talk about direct marketing.

MATT   The guy with the duck probably is the same guy from the
East Village.

DAVIS   You know who I'm talking about?

MATT   Yeah, bits of electric tape twisted in his beard. He used to hang out by the ATM at Banco Popular and like quote Schopenhauer all the time. I think his name is Saigon.

DAVIS   Yeah, Saigon. That's the guy.

[DAVIS *spritzes* MATT *with the cylinder of musk.* MATT *flinches and lowers his computer screen.* DAVIS *crosses to the door.*]

It's such a fucking trip. It makes the world feel so small. I mean, migrating marketeering junkies, who would've thought? By the way—[*He points to someone who has been waiting in the hall.*]—this is Christina.

[*He beckons her in.* CHRISTINA *enters. She is beautiful, pale, somehow lost. She wears a too-thin coat; a sweater underneath, with a coffee stain; a knit hat; a scarf; and mittens, and she carries a large baglike purse. Despite the dark makeup, her eyes make you forget what day it is. She is generally quiet, but when she does speak she uses a French accent.*]

Christina, Matt.

[MATT *stands, approaches her. They shake.*]

CHRISTINA   Nice to meet you.

MATT   Nice to meet you.

[*They watch each other for a moment and then* MATT *crosses to his bed, where he attempts to gracefully kick his underwear, socks, and used towel out of sight.* DAVIS *removes* CHRISTINA's *coat.* MATT *attempts to cross back to the desk, but* DAVIS *cuts him off at the pass and* MATT *backs up and sits on the downstage bed.* DAVIS *sits with* CHRISTINA *on the upstage bed. An awkward pause.* DAVIS *shoots* MATT *a look to urge him on.*]

So, how is it out there?

DAVIS   Cold. But it's weird. You don't feel it as much here.

MATT   You might want to lay off the space cakes.

DAVIS   No, I'm serious. Temperature-wise it's as bad as New York but it feels somehow milder. Even when the wind hits you, it's sort of soothing.

[CHRISTINA *removes her scarf and hat and bends down to place them in her bag.* DAVIS *shoots* MATT *a look as if to say, "What the hell are you doing? Don't be such a geek."* MATT *quickly rises and crosses back to his desk, sits.*]

How's the writing going?

MATT   It's going.

DAVIS   Matt's a playwright. I don't know how to say that in French. *Plum de drama* or whatever.

MATT   *Le dramatiste.*

[*To* CHRISTINA.]

Is that right—*le dramatiste?*

CHRISTINA   Yes. *Le dramatiste. L'auteur.*

DAVIS   Christina's from Paris. She's been in Amsterdam for how long now—five years?

[CHRISTINA *holds up three fingers.*]

Trois, right. Before that she lived in the Latin Quarter and worked at one of those Australian bars.

[*To* CHRISTINA.]

Matt and I were freshman roommates in university.

[*To* MATT.]

Christina's a singer.

MATT   Cool. What kind of stuff do you sing?

CHRISTINA   Nina Simone. Sara Vaughan. Billie Holiday. Judy Garland.

DAVIS   Back in Paris she had a weekly cabaret gig at some bar called—what was it called again?

CHRISTINA   Polly Magoo's.

DAVIS   Say it again.

CHRISTINA   Polly Magoo's.

DAVIS   Say it again.

CHRISTINA   Polly Magoo's.

DAVIS   [*Under his breath.*] Oh, my god—

MATT   I know it.

DAVIS   You do?

MATT   Last week we walked past it like four times.

DAVIS   No shit?

MATT   Yeah, we actually went in for a minute, but you wouldn't stay because you said it looked seedy. Dark floorboards. Ancient wooden booths. Old lady with bad teeth behind the bar.

DAVIS   Right. Polly Wants a Crackpipe Magoo's. Where they scowl at you if you're over five-foot-six and exhibit even the slightest modicum of North American decency.

[DAVIS *stands suddenly.* MATT *stands as well.*]

Excuse moi...

[*Substitute a smattering of bad faux French.*]

Faire pipi.

[DAVIS *exits to the bathroom, closes the door. MATT sits.*]

[MATT *and* CHRISTINA *sit in silence. There is some fraternity party–like shouting from another hostel room.*]

MATT   It's weird how everyone here sounds like they're from Madison, Wisconsin . . . You must meet a lot of annoying Americans. I mean, we blow into town, smoke all your pot, drink all your Heineken . . . You must get like, *"Merde! Beaucoup des frat boys! Courons aux montaigne . . . "*

[CHRISTINA *touches the coffee stain on her sweater, and then removes her hat and then her sweater. Bare-breasted now, she reaches into her purse, produces a V-neck T-shirt and some deodorant. MATT turns away during the nudity. She applies the deodorant, slips into the new shirt, stuffs the sweater in her bag.*]

CHRISTINA   May I have a cigarette?

MATT   You may, but no. I mean, I don't . . . I'm sort of a part-time smoker. I ran out. But Davis'll have some. He bought a carton of Camel Lights at the duty-free at KFC—I mean, JFK. Soft packs, I think they were.

[*An awkward pause.*]

So you're, um, really pretty.

CHRISTINA   Thank you.

MATT   Sure. No problem.

[*The sound of the toilet flushing.* DAVIS *returns from the bathroom with one of his signature kung-fu entrances. He is now holding a large, well-made café joint.*]

DAVIS   Shall we?

[*He lights the joint, smokes, passes it to* CHRISTINA. *She takes a hit, passes it to* MATT.]

MATT   I better not.

DAVIS   Oh, come on, man.

MATT   No, I really shouldn't.

[*To* CHRISTINA.]

I'm still on these antibiotics. *Les medicaments* . . . I got like this infection thing a month and a half ago. Back in New York. This bacteria strain. In my intestines. *Les intestines.*

DAVIS   Matty-boy was in pretty bad shape for a minute there.

MATT   Yeah, I lost a bunch of weight. Couldn't keep anything down. It's this thing called giardia. You get it from drinking, um, fecal water. Like water that's contaminated from people's, uh

[*He makes a vague gesture involving his bowels.*]

[DAVIS *makes a farting noise like a French horn.*]

Well, you know . . . Usually you get it camping. I got it from this restaurant on East 4th Street.

DAVIS   It's also known as "beaver fever."

[*He laughs.*]

Every time I hear that, I imagine fecal beavers. Like this fleet of giant beavers unloading schooner-size turds in some glacial lake.

[*He laughs.*]

I also imagine the beavers actually made out of feces. Like sculpted or whatever. And then, of course, there's the classic adolescent poontang thing. "Beaver fever!"

[*Over the following,* DAVIS *crosses to* MATT, *who is sitting on the desk now. He sits next to him and pushes* MATT *off the desk and toward* CHRISTINA. MATT *winds up sitting on the bed next to* CHRISTINA.]

Like hundreds of undergraduate males going apeshit for pussy. Like needing it so bad they affect an actual fever. Can't you just see it? Overcrowded infirmaries. Campus-wide sedation. Twenty-year-old undeclared, blue-balled males moaning into the night like cows.

CHRISTINA Cows?

DAVIS Yeah, cows. Boob milk.

[DAVIS *thinks this is the funniest thing he's ever said in his life and laughs until his laughter expires.*]

Actually, when you come to think of it, the fecal beaver thing really doesn't make much sense because "fecal" and "fever" aren't exactly what you'd call smoking homonyms.

[*To* CHRISTINA.]

You probably have no idea what I just said.

MATT Yeah, that was pretty layered.

CHRISTINA What is "beaver"?

DAVIS God, I love Frog chicks. The accent, the intrigue.

MATT Um. A beaver is like this sort of hefty aquatic rodent with a flat tail. And buck teeth.

DAVIS Think extra-large sewer rat with a canoe oar sticking out of its ass.

[DAVIS *imitates a buck-toothed, extra-large sewer rat with a canoe oar sticking out of its ass. He pulls the invisible canoe oar out of his ass and canoes across the room doing some sort of clichéd Native American Indian chant. He sits on the other bed, smokes the joint, and passes it to* CHRISTINA. *She takes it, smokes.*]

Smokin' in Amsterdam. Two guys and a girl.

[*To* MATT.]

Aren't Frogs cool when they smoke? I mean, we Americans smoke like we have glaucoma or like our fucking eyelashes are on fire or some shit, but Frogs, man. It's like it's an aperitif or this preamble to sex or something.

MATT   Oh, by the way, can Christina have a cigarette?

DAVIS   What are you, her handler?

MATT   Um. No.

DAVIS   Did I miss the telekinetic interplay?

MATT   She asked me for a cigarette while you were in the bathroom.

DAVIS   But what.

MATT   What.

DAVIS   You said—

MATT   I didn't say but.

DAVIS   I know, but you wanted to. But what.

MATT   Nothing.

[*Awkward pause.*]

DAVIS   What, did something happen when I was in the bathroom?

MATT No.

DAVIS Really.

MATT Nothing happened. Forget it.

[*Awkward pause. Awkward glances.*]

DAVIS You sure nothing happened when I was in the bathroom?

MATT Davis, chill.

DAVIS Christina?

MATT Nothing fucking happened. She wanted a cigarette and I didn't have any!

DAVIS Because you don't smoke.

MATT Just drop it, okay, fucker?!

[MATT *rises, crosses back to the desk, sits in the chair.* DAVIS *reaches into his pocket, removes a soft pack of Camel Lights, produces two cigarettes.*]

DAVIS Would ye like a cigarette, Christina?

[*She nods.* DAVIS *hands one to* CHRISTINA, *puts the other in his mouth so that it is paired with the joint now. He produces a lighter, lights her, lights himself, and smokes the cigarette and the joint simultaneously.*]

CHRISTINA You look like a walrus.

[*He smokes both again to entertain her in a walrus sort of way and then whispers something in her ear. They share a laugh.*]

MATT What.

DAVIS Nothing.

[*They laugh.*]

MATT   What's so funny?

DAVIS   It's just you keep holding on to that belt like you're gonna...

MATT   [*Standing quickly.*] Like I'm gonna what?

DAVIS   I don't know. I just think Christina and I should be prepared if there's gonna be some sort of spontaneous flogging ritual.

    [MATT *opens the desk drawer, puts the belt in the drawer, closes it, then sits.*]

    Now what were we talking about before?

MATT   Um. My giardia.

DAVIS   Right. Matt's giardia. Shall we continue to pursue that scatological subject matter—no pun intended wink-wink—or opt for a new theme?

MATT   Where's the pun?

DAVIS   What?

MATT   You said no pun intended.

DAVIS   I actually said no pun intended wink-wink.

MATT   Right. I guess I missed the pun.

DAVIS   Subject matter.

MATT   I don't get it.

DAVIS   Well, think about it, Herr Wunderkind, there's subject matter and then there's the matter that's been like napalming out of your anus for the past six weeks. Get it?

MATT   I do.

DAVIS   Makes sense?

MATT   It does. Witty.

DAVIS   IQs are skyrocketing all around.

[DAVIS *rises, grabs the ashtray from the windowsill, crosses to the corner by the door, smokes for a moment.*]

CHRISTINA   Has your health improved?

MATT   Yeah, everything's pretty much cleared up now. I mean, no more, you know...

DAVIS   Septic disasters?

MATT   Right.

DAVIS   Exploding green feces?

MATT   Thanks, Davis.

DAVIS   [*Crossing back to the bed opposite* CHRISTINA *with the ashtray.*]
You should've seen it, Christina, it was really sort of bizarre. The violent verdant volume that this skinny fucker could produce—

MATT   You're being an ass, dude.

DAVIS   [*Mock indignant.*] What.

MATT   Violent verdant volume?

[DAVIS *laughs, takes another hit from the joint, passes it to* CHRISTINA.]

CHRISTINA   No, thank you. I am very stoned.

DAVIS   Good.

[*To* MATT, *looking at* CHRISTINA.]

She's so pretty, isn't she, Matt?

MATT   Um, very much so, actually, yes.

[*Suddenly the sound of distant church bells.* CHRISTINA *turns and looks out the window behind her.* DAVIS *makes some silly gesture to* MATT, *somehow trying to urge* MATT *on. The bells cease and* CHRISTINA *turns her attention back to the room.*]

[*To* CHRISTINA.]

The bottom line is that I'm still finishing the antibiotics and I'm not supposed to drink or take drugs.

DAVIS   Dude, I totally understand the no-drinking thing but smoking pot's not gonna like mutate with the antibiotics in some weird way. If anything, it'll probably be good for the nausea.

MATT   I know, I just...

DAVIS   You just what? The little instructions from the pharmacy say no barbiturates and no alcohol.

MATT   I'd rather not risk it.

DAVIS   Pot is technically a hallucinogen, right, Christina? *Le hallucinacion?*

MATT   Next subject, please.

[DAVIS *suddenly does a horse imitation, pulling his lips out and clucking through his teeth. He punctuates it with a titanic whinny.*]

DAVIS   *Les cheveux d'amour.*

MATT   *Cheval.*

DAVIS   *Cheval, cheveux*, what's the difference.

MATT   Well, actually, *cheveux* is hair and *cheval* is horse. Based on your little performance, I think it's a safe bet to say that you were intending to say the horse of love, not the hair of love.

DAVIS   And what if I wanted to say the hairy horse of love? . . . Christina, Matt can read Latin. And he can quote Robert Frost poems and the various statutes of Aristotelian poetics. And his SAT scores were just. Off. The fucking. Charts!

[MATT *shakes his head.*]

CHRISTINA   [*To* MATT.] What is your drama about?

MATT   It's actually about a young train engineer.

CHRISTINA   Oh.

MATT   You know what that means?

CHRISTINA   Yes.

MATT   Cool.

DAVIS   . . . Well, tell her more.

MATT   [*To* CHRISTINA.] You really want to know?

CHRISTINA   I am curious, yes.

DAVIS   *S'il vous plait, mon canard. Mon champignon. Mon fromage—*

MATT   Shut up, Davis.

[*To* CHRISTINA.]

It's about this rookie train engineer. On his first time out at the front of this huge freight line hauling some

environmentally toxic combustible fuel, this '69 Buick
Electra 225 stalls on the tracks ahead of him. He puts the
train into emergency, but it takes a mile and a half to stop a
freight train because of all the impending megatonnage, so
the young engineer can't stop in time and he hits the car,
which is populated by a family of four. The Buick is severed
in half and a young mother and her infant daughter who were
in the backseat are killed instantly. Like blown to pollen. The
father and their little boy live—the father unscratched, the
boy barely makes it—and years later, through a series of
letters, the train engineer, pretending to be some sort of
generic representative of the railroad, anonymously contacts
the father and they correspond a bit, and the engineer road-
trips to their home in Pittsburgh, and the little boy is seven
now but he's a mental vegetable from the accident, and the
train engineer gives the father a bunch of money that he'd
been saving and the father takes it, and a half a dozen or so
Juenglings later—that's a local Pittsburgh beer—the
engineer confesses his true identity, and after an awkward
moment or two they make their peace, and then the train
engineer asks if there's anything else he can do to help, and
the father asks him to kill his son. Well, to like remove his
oxygen mask when he's sleeping, because at night the boy
forgets how to breathe sometimes because of cognitive
malfunctions or whatever and he has to wear this like free-
flowing Lucite oxygen mask. And the engineer does it. He
removes the mask and kills the kid . . .

DAVIS Dark fucker. Tell her the title.

MATT Oh, it's called *Speckled Birds* but I'm not married to that yet. I
might call it *Roundhouse Winter* instead. A roundhouse is this
like donut-shaped depot where they house and switch
locomotives . . . Did that whole thing make any sense?

[CHRISTINA *nods.*]

MATT I didn't speak too fast or anything?

CHRISTINA No. I understood.

MATT Cool. Sometimes I speak too fast.

DAVIS When Matt was a kid he stammered.

MATT And when Davis was a sophomore in college he got busted masturbating in the basement of the reference library with a pair of women's pantyhose noosed around his neck.

DAVIS Yeah, you like half pass out right when you start blowing your load. It feels pretty fucking groovy, you should try it sometime.

[*Pause.*]

CHRISTINA Your drama sounds very sad.

MATT It's sort of a tragedy, yeah.

DAVIS What's your hero's name again—Halifax?

MATT Hallux.

DAVIS Yeah, Hallux. How do you spell that?

MATT Um. H-a-l-l-u-x.

DAVIS Hallux.

MATT What, you have a problem with it?

DAVIS I don't know. "Hallux the Railroad Man." It just sounds made up or something.

MATT It's not made up.

DAVIS   Oh. Is it an actual name?

MATT   I mean, not like Larry, but it's a word.

DAVIS   It is?

MATT   Yeah.

DAVIS   Huh. What's its origin?

MATT   Latin.

DAVIS   And it means...?

MATT   It means ankle.

DAVIS   You sure about that?

MATT   Pretty sure, yeah.

DAVIS   Like sprain-your-ankle, ankle?

MATT   Like the chancellor of Dickville broke his ankle sticking his foot in his mouth, yeah.

DAVIS   I don't know, Matt.

MATT   Well, what does it mean?

DAVIS   I'm gonna go out on a limb and say big toe.

MATT   Big toe.

DAVIS   Yeah, big toe.

MATT   Like he-stubbed-his-big-toe, big toe?

DAVIS   Like the mayor of Spermtown had a hard time pulling his big toe out of his recently ravaged ass, yeah.

[MATT *tosses the dictionary to him.* DAVIS *catches it.*]

MATT Look it up.

DAVIS Should I?

MATT Go ahead.

DAVIS I mean, I wouldn't want to humiliate you in front of Christina or anything.

MATT I'll take my chances.

DAVIS Christina, Matt's what we in the world of letters call a wordsmith. A lover of language. He's a bit of a pedant, too, but we'll talk about that at our next cultural enrichment summit. The truth is he's a damn good playwright. Outside of a small, vaguely attended, weeklong showcase at this place called La Mama that feels more like a community center for recovering glue huffers than a theater, he hasn't had a single production, bless his heart. But he keeps plugging away. Old Sisyphus himself.

MATT Sisyphus?—

DAVIS Pushin' that rock. But there is light at the end of the old Hershey Highway as he recently got this award for being burgeoning or something. What was it called again?

MATT Why?

DAVIS Why?

MATT Don't.

DAVIS Don't what?

MATT Just don't.

DAVIS   Come on, nerd, brag a little.

MATT   [*To* CHRISTINA.] He loves doing this.

DAVIS   You got an award for being burgeoning. You got paid like ten grand. Own that shit.

MATT   Own your ass, buttfucker.

DAVIS   Oh, we shan't go there, shan't we.

[*Pause.*]

MATT   [*To* CHRISTINA.] It's called the Hayden Gray Tharp Award for Emerging Playwrights.

[*To* DAVIS.]

Emerging, not fucking burgeoning.

CHRISTINA   Congratulations.

MATT   Thanks.

DAVIS   Matt's been emerging for so long methinks he's setting some sort of record. He's like the Olympic gold medalist for emerging playwrights. But we shall overcome, as they say.

[*Awkward pause.*]

CHRISTINA   I very much like the title of your play. *Speckled . . . Birds?*

MATT   Yeah, *Speckled Birds*. It's actually sort of a double entendre.

DAVIS   [*To* CHRISTINA, *with bad French accent.*] Double entendre.

[CHRISTINA *holds up two fingers, nods.* DAVIS *holds up two fingers as well and then, when* CHRISTINA *turns her attention to* MATT, *at some point over the following,* DAVIS *performs a bit of cunnilingus between his parted fingers for* MATT'*s benefit.*]

MATT   You see, the, um, windshield of any train engine collides with a lot of birds. So there's lots of spots or speckles. *Les oiseaux pointillés*. Which doesn't totally make sense because the title would suggest that the actual birds are speckled, speckled being the descriptive qualifier, not the windshield of the train engine, but I'm not so worried about that. It's also the name of this amphetamine that railroad men take to stay awake. Amphetamine. Well, that's actually called speckled bird. It's used only in the singular.

DAVIS   Why don't you just call it *Hallux*, colon space, *The Tragic Ode of a Young Everyman's First Day on the Railroad*?

MATT   Why don't you close your mouth and spare us the manure slide.

DAVIS   Oooh, red rover, red rover, send Matty right over.

[MATT *rises very quickly, as does* DAVIS, *but* MATT *thinks better of it, or at least he pretends to for a moment.* DAVIS *gloats to* CHRISTINA *a bit and then* MATT *goes in for the kill but* DAVIS *very swiftly puts him down, with* MATT'*s arm forced up behind his back. With his other hand,* DAVIS *forces* MATT'*s head into the carpet.*]

Ooh, you damn bastard, your tiger style is no good here!...Tap out...Come on, tap out.

[MATT *hits the floor with his hand and* DAVIS *releases him.* MATT *rises off the floor, clearly humiliated, and moves to sit in the desk chair, but* DAVIS *swipes it away and uses it like a lion tamer to force* MATT *to sit next to* CHRISTINA.]

Christina, I keep trying to get Matt here to cross back over into fiction, but he insists on slumming in the theater like some sort of third-class peasant. In university he was a damn good short-story writer. He was like a young Raymond Carver.

[*When* MATT *is properly seated,* DAVIS *puts the chair in the hallway and closes the door, then crosses to the desk, sits on it.*]

MATT   I can't stand Raymond Carver.

DAVIS   Oh, that's right, you're one of those Henry Miller hos.

MATT   Miller was a genius. Carver was all craft and no substance.

DAVIS   I'm sorry but Carver could've written Miller under the table on any day of the week.

MATT   What, like ready, set, write?

DAVIS   Like pound for pound Carver was a better writer. Period.

MATT   The biggest difference between Carver and Miller, besides Carver's obvious lack-of-style-passing-off-as-minimalism, is that Carver was a writer and Miller was an author.

DAVIS   Yeah, a gob of spit and all of that. How fucking sexy.

MATT   Davis, in another twenty years, they're gonna forget all about Raymond Carver and his little tales of suburban paralysis. And a hundred and twenty years after that, in some Parisian basement along the Seine, there will be an anticapitalist literary preservationist group binding Henry Miller bibles with thread spun from the intestines of poets. They'll be hand-sewing the spines. Knitting every signature. Each completed volume will be anointed like a sacrament. No one could juxtapose the decay and grace of our humanity better. The fury with the joy. Miller turned sewage into poetry. His language was ecstatic. You could feel the velocity with which he wrote flying across the page. Carver wrote constipated, mediocre claptrap from the kitchen table of his upstate suburban home.

DAVIS   So Carver was constipated. I guess that would make Miller
         the literary equivalent of what—giardia?

MATT   [*To* CHRISTINA.] I just love how these young editors pull
         their first acquisition out of the slush pile and they suddenly
         think they're Maxwell fucking Perkins.

DAVIS   Hey, that novel I pulled out of the slush pile hasn't done too
         badly. You even liked it, Mister Literary Fucking Litmus Test.

MATT   I'll admit it's a good novel.

DAVIS   The other day you said it was a great work of art.

MATT   I did?

DAVIS   I swear, Christina, the God of Frog strike me as I'm standing
         here. In a rare moment of artistic armistice, on the platform
         of the Gare du Nord, while waiting to board the train to
         your lovely Amsterdam, Mattyboy here turned to me and
         said that the novel I had acquired for my company out of the
         slush pile was a great work of art. Not a great novel, story, or
         composition. A great work. Of art.

MATT   I just said that so you would help me pay for my train ticket.

DAVIS   Oh, bullshit. You know you loved that book.

MATT   It's a good novel. You did some very nice work on it, Davis.
         Made the dedication page and everything. I'm sure our
         brothers and sisters at Brown University are very proud.

[MATT *suddenly rises, moves to the window, tries to open it. It doesn't budge. He
tries again.*]

DAVIS   It won't open.

         [MATT *continues trying.*]

I think they actually nail them shut.

[MATT *continues struggling.* DAVIS *makes he-man sounds, throws in another French-horn fart for good measure.* MATT *struggles with the window for another moment, gives up, then crosses to the door and goes out into the hallway.*]

Tune in next week, ladies and gentlemen, when our hundred-and-fifty-two-pound lactose-intolerant hero puts a Barcelona chair through the window of his hotel room. Will he free himself from the clutches of despair? Will he ever be able to escape his own noisome body odor and gastrointestinal impediments? Don't miss our next exciting episode. Aaaaand commercial...

[MATT *returns with the chair, sets it at the desk, crosses back to the door, slams it, sits in the chair.*]

What about you, Christina? Who's your favorite scribe?

CHRISTINA   What is scribe?

DAVIS   Writer.

CHRISTINA   I very much like this person Harry Potter.

DAVIS   Of course you do!

CHRISTINA   He is extremely smart. And boyishly handsome.

DAVIS   Well, whattaya know, Frogs love Harry Potter too! They weren't even interested in one of the most celebrated new literary American novels of last year, but they get their panties in a knot for Harry Fucking Potter. That's so, I don't know, reverse xenophobic.

MATT   That doesn't even make any sense.

DAVIS   Why not?

MATT   Because J. K. Rowling isn't American.

DAVIS   She's not?

MATT   No.

DAVIS   Where is she from—Nova Scotia?

MATT   She's English.

DAVIS   Well, I say amen to Harry Fucking Potter! And I'd say it in Frog if I knew how to say it.

MATT   *Tu es un poisson salopé.*

[CHRISTINA *laughs.*]

DAVIS   What does that mean?

MATT   Nothing. What you said. About Harry Potter.

[CHRISTINA *laughs some more, then covers her mouth.*]

DAVIS   You ever read Henry Miller, Christina?

CHRISTINA   Yes.

DAVIS   In Frog or American?

CHRISTINA   In English. He is very popular in Paris.

DAVIS   Which one did you read?

CHRISTINA   *Tropic of Cancer.*

DAVIS   You like it?

CHRISTINA   I liked it very much, yes.

DAVIS   You ever read any Raymond Carver?

CHRISTINA   I do not know this person.

MATT   [*Standing.*] My point exactly. The rest of the world thinks he's provincial.

[DAVIS *stares at* MATT *until he sits back in the chair.* CHRISTINA *rises, shoulders her purse.* MATT *and* DAVIS *rise as well.*]

CHRISTINA   Please excuse me for a moment.

[CHRISTINA *exits to the bathroom with her purse.* MATT *crosses to his bed, pretends to adjust the pillow.*]

DAVIS   So what do you think?

MATT   About what?

DAVIS   About Christina.

MATT   She's nice.

DAVIS   That's it—she's nice?

MATT   I like her.

DAVIS   She's fucking beautiful, bro.

MATT   Yeah, she's pretty.

DAVIS   A hundred and fifty fucking oyros pretty.

MATT   Oyros? What is that, like Funyuns?

DAVIS   You're still up for this, right?

MATT   Sure.

DAVIS   Sure?

MATT   Yeah, it's cool.

DAVIS   You don't sound too excited.

MATT   No, I just...

DAVIS   What?

[MATT *sits on the bed, starts to cry.*]

Oh, no, don't start this shit again.

[MATT *cries.*]

Fuck.

[DAVIS *crosses to* MATT *on the bed, hugs him, attempts to give comfort.* MATT *holds on for dear life, calms down after a moment.*]

You okay?

[MATT *nods, still getting it together.* DAVIS *sits next to him.*]

Look, Matt, you need this.

[MATT *nods, struggles for a moment.*]

You sure you're okay?

MATT   Yes.

DAVIS   Because she's not gonna want to even touch you if you're blubbering all over yourself. Frog chicks don't like that.

MATT   Stop calling her a Frog.

DAVIS   She knows I'm kidding. She likes it.

[MATT *almost loses it again.*]

If you start crying again, I'm gonna kick your ass. You're thirty years old and you're gonna fucking do this. So stop feeling sorry for yourself and get your shit together.

[MATT *gets himself together, grabs the dictionary, crosses to the desk with it, starts to arrange his pens and things.*]

By the way, she shaves her pussy.

MATT   She does?

DAVIS   Clean as a car seat.

MATT   How do you know?

DAVIS   Because I know. She showed it to me.

MATT   Why?

DAVIS   It's what they do. To assure the clientele that they don't have venereal warts or yeast or whatever.

MATT   Did you mess around?

DAVIS   We made out.

MATT   You made out?

DAVIS   Yeah. So what?

MATT   Jesus, Davis.

DAVIS   Jesus what?

MATT   Nothing. I just... forget it.

[MATT *crosses to his shelf, removes his toiletries, and starts to place them in his traveling bag, which is under his bed.*]

DAVIS   I had to earn her trust. She wouldn't come back with me unless I proved that I didn't have dubious intentions.

[*From his travel bag,* MATT *removes a moth-eaten cardigan sweater and puts it on. He then removes his shoes, and uses the cylinder of musk spray that* DAVIS *had used at the top of the act to deodorize his socked feet.*]

MATT   So you like made out made out?

DAVIS   Yeah, we French kissed. With tongue and such. I felt her up a little too.

MATT   Like her tits?

DAVIS   Yeah, her tits.

MATT   Are you gonna tell Sarah?

DAVIS   This has nothing to do with Sarah. Why, are you?

MATT   Of course not. But—

DAVIS   But what?

MATT   Well, you're sort of like engaged.

DAVIS   What, are you judging me?

MATT   No.

DAVIS   Good. Because that would suck. Ye holy disciple of Henry Miller.

MATT   I'm not judging you.

DAVIS   Just remember, let him that casts the first stone . . .

[MATT *puts his shoes back on, ties them.*]

MATT   So she shaves it?

DAVIS   She does indeed, my skinny white brother.

MATT   And you like that?

DAVIS   I do, yeah. It's like a cold cut or something.

[MATT *shoves his travel bag back under the bed, crosses to the door, almost opens it to check the hall, thinks better of it.*]

MATT   So you made out with her and felt her up where—in like one of those display windows?

DAVIS   Pretty much. I mean, she closed the curtain.

MATT   It sounds like some oversized terrarium.

DAVIS   It was a little room. Shag carpeting. Queen-sized bed. Mirror ball hanging from the ceiling. Little space heater off to the left. Portable cassette player resting on the headboard.

MATT   Music?

DAVIS   She played Waits.

MATT   *Bone Machine?*

DAVIS   *Small Change.*

MATT   Good album.

DAVIS   It's a great fucking album and she's a great fucking girl. She was the best-looking one in all the windows.

[MATT *walks over to the shelf over the bed, turns off the small lamp.*]

MATT   So what—you just like walked up to her?

DAVIS   She called me over.

MATT   Like over a PA?

DAVIS   No, she beckoned me.

MATT   How?

DAVIS   She waved.

[DAVIS *demonstrates the wave.*]

MATT   Wow.

DAVIS   I know, right?

MATT   That would be cool.

DAVIS   It was totally cool. I mean, I got the feeling that she really wanted me. Don't get me wrong, I know there's like hundreds of people every day who she probably suckers like that, but I really felt singled out. And that's how it'll be for you, too. She'll make you feel special...Just think of those legs wrapped around you.

[DAVIS *uses* CHRISTINA'*s coat to demonstrate and has a little fun miming sex with her.*]

MATT   Does she like, um, know—

DAVIS   Why she's here? Of course she does. We talked about it.

MATT   She probably thinks I'm some sort of freak.

DAVIS   I just told her you were shy. Frog chicks dig shy. She likes you, I can tell.

MATT   You really think so?

DAVIS   You should see the way she was looking at you.

MATT   When?

DAVIS   When you were talking about your play. And during that load of shit about Henry Miller. She was all over it.

MATT   Really?

DAVIS   I swear.

MATT   So what, you'll like leave?

DAVIS Yeah, I'll leave. She'll be all yours.

[DAVIS *hands* CHRISTINA's *coat to* MATT. *He holds it for a moment and then hangs it on one of the three coat hooks on the upstage wall.*]

MATT Where will you go?

DAVIS I'll go to Café Space Cake, eat a flooginflaffin. Gaze at the architecture.

[MATT *thinks a moment.*]

MATT Was she . . . ?

DAVIS What, a good kisser?

MATT Yeah.

DAVIS She's fucking solid, bro. I mean, I didn't see fireworks or anything, but she's legit. And her body's killer. Dominant legs. Perfect tits. Heart-shaped ass. No weird moles or anything. She tried jerking me off too, but I couldn't get it up.

MATT So she, um, felt you up too?

DAVIS A little, yeah.

MATT Why couldn't you get it up?

DAVIS I don't know. I think it was the combination of all the shrooming and the idea of you being with her. I sort of wanted her to be—I don't know—fresh for you or something.

[MATT *quickly crosses to his laptop, seizes it, crosses to the bed, reaches under it, removes a computer travel bag, puts the computer in it, shoves the bag back under the bed.*]

And besides, she wanted to put this like three-ply, industrial-strength condom on me. It would've been like getting a massage in a snowmobile suit. But she's feral, bro.

MATT   Really?

DAVIS   Yeah. As in ferocious. I mean, I felt bad. She really wanted me to get off. After I pulled the plug she felt so guilty she actually tried to give me my money back.

[MATT *rises, starts pacing, periodically picking a piece of lint or two off the floor.*]

MATT   You didn't take it, did you?

DAVIS   Of course not. I let her tea-bag my nuts for a few minutes, though. She felt better after that.

MATT   [*Stopping dead in his tracks.*] She tea-bagged your nuts?!

DAVIS   That actually felt great. But it was also [*Insert ridiculous faux French word*]. Because, like I said, I was sort of preparing to give her to you. So in some weird way it was like you were tea-bagging my nuts.

[MATT *stands, paces again, starts clicking his pen.*]

MATT   So she's pretty into this stuff?

DAVIS   She's a fucking pro. But not insensitive. She really understands the value of a job well done. Oh, and while she was—

MATT   Tea-bagging your nuts?

DAVIS   Yeah, exactly, while she was tea-bagging my nuts she started meowing.

MATT   Come on.

DAVIS   I swear to you, Matt, she meowed.

MATT   Like a cat?

DAVIS   No, like a fucking hammerhead shark. Of course like a cat.

MATT   Wow.

DAVIS   See?

MATT   That's weird.

DAVIS   Yeah.

MATT   But in a good way.

DAVIS   In a totally good way.

MATT   She really is pretty.

DAVIS   Stop pacing. You're gonna throw your back out or something.

[MATT *stops pacing.*]

And jettison that pen, man.

[MATT *stops clicking his pen, places it on the desk.*]

[*Proffering the joint.*]

You sure you don't want a hit of this? It's incredible.

[MATT *shakes his head, starts to fix his hair.* DAVIS *rises off the bed, crosses to the door.*]

What the fuck is she doing in there, retiling?

[MATT *starts to tuck his sweater into his pants.* DAVIS *crosses to him, untucks* MATT'*s sweater, removes it, and untucks his thermal under-shirt and T-shirt and hangs the sweater on one of the three coat hooks on the upstage wall.*]

So here's the plan: I'll stick around for a few more minutes, just to make sure everything's on the up-and-up, and at the appropriate moment I'll make a graceful exit and leave you two alone . . . So everything's cool, right?

MATT   Yeah, everything's cool. You got any gum?

DAVIS   No, why? Your breath stinks?

MATT   My mouth tastes funny.

DAVIS   Breathe on me.

MATT   Why?

DAVIS   Just breathe on me.

MATT   No, that's weird.

DAVIS   Come on, I'll tell you if you have bad breath.

            [DAVIS *leans into* MATT. MATT *hesitates, breathes on him.*]

            You're fine.

MATT   Are you sure?

DAVIS   Yeah, just make sure to brush your teeth before the fireworks
            begin.

            [MATT *bolts for his bag, removes a tube of toothpaste just as*
            CHRISTINA *enters.* DAVIS *nudges him, urges him to stand, then
            sit, then stand, then sit.* CHRISTINA *turns to them after she closes the
            door. She is now wearing a long red dress, and her hair is up. She is also
            wearing nice earrings and heels. She looks beautiful.* MATT *and*
            DAVIS *sit,* MATT *still holding the toothpaste but not realizing it.*]

            Whoa.

MATT   Wow.

DAVIS   We were wondering what was taking you so long.

CHRISTINA   If you will allow me, I would like to sing a song.

DAVIS   Like a song song?

CHRISTINA   Yes.

> [*To* MATT.]

> Would that be okay?

MATT   Totally. Yeah. It'd be great.

CHRISTINA   Okay. Picture blue light and a piano.

[CHRISTINA *closes her eyes. After a moment she opens her eyes, begins to sing. She sings beautifully. She is mesmerizing.*]

CHRISTINA   [*Singing.*]

> In the time that it shall take to move your body
> In the time that it shall take to lure you home
> I'll find a willow tree and sleep beneath its branches
> And in its bark I'll carve my heart's most private poem
> Thirty years shall I require to pick the lemons
> Thirty more to draw the flowers from the grove
> A drop of vodka from the soil of ancient Russia
> A pinch of sea salt from the shores of our lost cove
> It's a long way to the bottom of the ocean
> The lonely mermaid braids a starfish through her hair
> Her sailor drowned twelve years ago near Zaragosa
> And counting oysters never soothed her slow despair
> It's the pearl that I long for
> The pearl that I long for
> The pearl that I long
> To hold near
> It's the pearl that I long for the pearl that I long for
> The pearl that I long for
> My dear

[CHRISTINA *remains suspended in the song for a moment, then comes out of it. An awkward silence. Then . . .*]

DAVIS   That fucking rocked!

CHRISTINA   Thank you.

DAVIS   Whose tune is that?

CHRISTINA   It's one of mine.

DAVIS   You wrote that?

CHRISTINA   I composed it on the piano at Polly Magoo's.

DAVIS   I say we call up Interscope, get her a record contract, right, Matt?

MATT   It's a beautiful song, Christina.

CHRISTINA   I am very pleased that you liked it.

DAVIS   Great stuff. I mean, I have no idea what it's about as the imagery jumps around and the themes start to blur a bit but I really dig it.

CHRISTINA   It's about unrequiet...

MATT   Unrequited love?

CHRISTINA   Unrequited love, yes.

DAVIS   Huh. That's funny, I didn't get that.

CHRISTINA   I'm sorry.

DAVIS   No, don't be. Just maybe add a line or two to underscore your subject matter. I'm a firm believer in organizing the information for your audience so they're like in on it. I mean, Rome wasn't built in a day-care center.

[*Awkward pause.*]

MATT Did you write that in English?

CHRISTINA I did, yes.

MATT Because the lyrics are really cool.

DAVIS Yeah, the lyrics, the phrasing, the imagery!

CHRISTINA Thank you.

MATT I especially liked the deep-sea stuff: the mermaid and the oysters and all that. Going from this sort of spinal love tree to the bottom of the ocean. It's a pretty cool journey.

DAVIS Phantasmagoric.

MATT Yeah, totally surreal. And the rhyme scheme is cool too. Home and poem. And, um, hair and despair. And that off-rhyme coupling of ocean and Zaragosa. Really subtle but affecting. And your voice.

DAVIS Yeah, what a voice! It's like Paula Abdul meets Coretta Scott King or some shit.

MATT You have a really beautiful voice.

CHRISTINA Thank you.

[*Another awkward pause.* CHRISTINA *remains standing.*]

DAVIS [*Standing suddenly, going for his coat.*] Well, boys and girls, this bad little camper is gonna go hunting for a few hours of quote-unquote Amsterdamage.

[MATT *stands.* DAVIS *removes a pack of Camel Lights and his Zippo lighter and sets them on the desk.*]

Let her have as many of these as she'd like.

[DAVIS *gathers his coat, crosses to* CHRISTINA. *He goes to a knee, takes her hand, kisses it, chastely.*]

Madame.

[*Rising.*]

It was very nice to meet you, Christina. Enjoy the rest of your evening.

[DAVIS *starts for the door.*]

CHRISTINA   Davis.

[*He stops, turns. They face each other for a moment. Things get sort of awkward.*]

DAVIS   Oh, fuck me. Did I forget to pay you?

CHRISTINA   No, you paid.

DAVIS   You want American dollars instead of oyros?

CHRISTINA   No. I was wondering if I could have your address in New York.

DAVIS   Why, are you gonna like invoice me for add-ons?

CHRISTINA   I'd like to send you something.

DAVIS   Oh. What.

CHRISTINA   My music. I have a CD. From Paris.

DAVIS   Cool. Sure thing.

[DAVIS *crosses to the desk, grabs* MATT'*s notebook, tears out a clean sheet, writes the address on it with* MATT'*s pen, folds the paper in half. Before he turns back he spots the dictionary, opens it up, fingers to a spot.*]

Hallux. It's a noun and it reads and I quote: The inner or first digit on the hind foot of a mammal; in man, the big toe...

[DAVIS *closes the dictionary, sets it back on the desk, crosses to* MATT, *reaches into his pocket, removes a condom packet, places it in* MATT*'s hand.*]

Lambskin.

[DAVIS *then crosses to* CHRISTINA, *hands her the piece of paper. She takes it, and he kisses her on either cheek and she hugs him good-bye, holding on a little too long.* DAVIS *pats her on the back and breaks from the hug.*]

Bon suar, then.

CHRISTINA   Good-bye.

[DAVIS *exits. The door closes.* CHRISTINA *stands there for a moment, somehow paralyzed. She then crosses to the upstage bed, sits, and starts to cry.* MATT *watches her for a moment, tries to move toward her, hesitates, then opens the door and exits to the bathroom. The sound of a tap running.* MATT *returns with a plastic cup of water, hands it to her. She drinks.*]

I feel so stupid.

MATT   Don't.

CHRISTINA   That was humiliating.

MATT   What, your song? No, it was really beautiful. I'm serious.

[*He crosses to the cigarette pack and Zippo lighter, gets a cigarette, crosses back to her, gives her a cigarette, lights it. She smokes. He crosses to the desk, sits in the chair.*]

CHRISTINA   When he came to visit me he was so nice. And just now he was so . . .

MATT   Asshole-ish?

CHRISTINA   Yes. When we were together he was so gentle.

MATT Yeah, Davis told me you guys fooled around a little.

CHRISTINA Yes.

MATT Like what did you do? If you don't mind me asking.

CHRISTINA We made love.

MATT Oh. You made love.

CHRISTINA Yes. Is that bad?

MATT No, it's just, um, well, weird.

CHRISTINA Why?

MATT Oh, no reason. I mean—How many times, if you don't mind me asking?

CHRISTINA Three times.

MATT He paid for three times?

CHRISTINA He only paid for one, but I could not bring him to orgasm, so I gave him two more sessions for free.

MATT Oh. So can I like ask a question?

CHRISTINA Of course.

MATT I know this isn't a court of law or anything, and it's probably none of my business, but if he didn't come, how did you like, um, demarcate each session?

CHRISTINA What is demar…

MATT Demarcate. How did you distinguish or like measure it?

CHRISTINA Because I orgasm.

MATT   Three times?

CHRISTINA   Yes.

MATT   It must have been pretty special.

CHRISTINA   It was strange. We got very close. We talked. We told each other things.

MATT   Like what?

CHRISTINA   Personal things. About my life. About his life. About his sadness.

MATT   His sadness?

CHRISTINA   Yes. Davis possesses very much melancholy. He talked about his mother. The treatments and the cancer.

MATT   His mother, the treatments, the cancer. Really.

CHRISTINA   Yes.

[*She looks for the ashtray. It's on the other bed.* MATT *crosses to it and hands it to her, crosses downstage right.*]

MATT   So let me get this straight. You guys quote-unquote made love three times.

CHRISTINA   I wanted four, but he wouldn't stop talking about you.

MATT   What did he say?

CHRISTINA   How important you are to him. And how he felt strange making love because he wanted to introduce me to you. He cares about you very much.

MATT   Oh, no doubt... So are you like all smitten with him or something?

CHRISTINA   What is smitten?

MATT   Love. Are you in love with him?

CHRISTINA   I don't know. Just now when he was leaving, I suddenly felt like I would never see him again and it made me feel very sad.

MATT   Well, you probably won't . . . See him again, I mean.

[CHRISTINA *turns away, smokes for a moment.* MATT *crosses back to the desk.*]

Christina, as a human being or whatever, I feel I should say something. And this isn't intended to burst your bubble, or like cock-block him because he really is like a brother to me, but Davis's mother is alive and well. She actually teaches comparative literature at Brandeis. And regarding his melancholy, the only angstrom of quote-unquote sadness that I've ever been privy to was the time when he cried because he wasn't named a Rhodes scholar.

[CHRISTINA *puts her cigarette out and reaches into her bag and removes a small snow globe of the New York City skyline. She shakes it and watches it snow for a moment.*]

What's that?

[*She hands it to him.*]

Did Davis give you this?

CHRISTINA   It's beautiful.

MATT   Yeah, he bought this at a gift shop near the train station in Paris.

CHRISTINA   I was very moved to receive it.

MATT   I'm sure.

CHRISTINA   I wish to someday go to New York.

MATT   Well, you should come visit.

[*He hands the snow globe back to her. She stares at it for a moment, then puts it in her bag.*]

So regarding this whole thing, we don't have to like, um, do anything if you don't want to. I mean, you seemed pretty upset there and I wouldn't want you to feel like obligat—

CHRISTINA   It's okay. I would like to be with you.

MATT   Really? I mean, I can't guarantee you like orgasming in triplicate.

CHRISTINA   That's not important.

[*Awkward pause.*]

MATT   More water?

CHRISTINA   No, thank you.

MATT   Another cigarette?

[*She nods. He gives her another cigarette, lights her, then sits on the other bed.*]

So before we continue, I have to say something. And I might be totally off base here.

CHRISTINA   What.

MATT   You're not French, are you? I mean, you might be, right? But I'm almost totally sure that you're like this very talented imposter. So you can like stop the routine. I won't tell anybody. I mean your accent is spot-on perfect, and the slight lack of knowledge of English vocabulary is very subtle and authentic, i.e., your purported ignorance of words like smitten and demarcate and, um, scribe, but you sort of blew it when you sang. I mean, you have this totally like mellifluous voice or whatever, and your song really is affecting—it's just that there was a moment or two there where you suddenly sounded really Midwestern. I'm from Illinois, so I have these like Des Plaines River Valley superpowers... I mean, if you want to continue in like character or whatever it's fine with me.

[*Suddenly a cell phone starts ringing. CHRISTINA goes into her bag, removes it, stands, and faces the corner for privacy, answers.*]

CHRISTINA   Hello? Oui...Oui...Oui...No...No...

[*She hangs up.*]

MATT   Who was that?

[*She turns to face him.*]

CHRISTINA   [*Dropping the accent, American English now.*] Albert.

MATT   Your boyfriend?

CHRISTINA   My husband.

MATT   You're married?

CHRISTINA   It was arranged. He's gay, lives in Paris.

[MATT *offers her the upstage bed to sit on. She hesitates, but gathers her things and does so. He crosses to the desk, leans against it over the following.*]

MATT   Did you like get paid a lot of money to marry him?

CHRISTINA   Enough to buy an apartment here. He has dual citizenship.

MATT   How often do you see him?

CHRISTINA   We spend about six months out of the year together. Go to art openings. Fancy dinners. Cocktail parties. We hold hands and rub noses, put on a show for his colleagues.

MATT   What does he do?

CHRISTINA   He's a lawyer.

MATT   You met in Paris?

CHRISTINA   I was performing at this bar. After my set he sent me a note. He was hot. Dressed well. Smoked Nat Shermans. We started hanging out. It was weird, I totally thought he was straight. But we never slept together. A few weeks later he made the offer. His lover stopped by at the end of the meeting, and we shook hands. It was all business.

MATT   What if you...

CHRISTINA   What if I what.

MATT   I don't know. Like meet someone.

CHRISTINA   I meet people every day.

MATT   No, but I mean like what if you meet someone and... well, you know... Like what happened with Davis.

CHRISTINA   It doesn't happen.

MATT   Right.

[*She smokes. He moves the chair closer to her, sits.*]

MATT   So where are you from, anyway?

CHRISTINA   Baltimore.

MATT   Oh, I would've guessed like Green Bay or something.

CHRISTINA   My parents are from Madison. We moved to the East
Coast when I was seven.

MATT   So why the facade?

CHRISTINA   I don't know. It's easier somehow.

MATT   For your job?

CHRISTINA   It's just easier.

MATT   So this is pretty weird.

CHRISTINA   Why?

MATT   I don't know. You were doing this whole character thing.
Mysterious French ingenue. It's like you just came out of the
stage door and you're suddenly sort of normal.

[*She stands.*]

CHRISTINA   If you want me to go, I'll go.

[*He stands.*]

MATT   No, stay.

[*She sits. He sits.*]

MATT   So how did you wind up in Paris?

CHRISTINA   I was in school. I did a semester abroad and never came
back.

MATT   What were you studying?

CHRISTINA   Theater.

MATT   So you're an actress.

CHRISTINA   I was, yes.

MATT   Where'd you go to school?

CHRISTINA   Bard.

MATT   What year did you go abroad?

CHRISTINA   I was a sophomore.

MATT   Wow. You were young... What was the last play you did?

CHRISTINA   Fucking *Oklahoma*. But it was pretty experimental. It was set in a small engine-repair shop and all the townspeople were part machine.

[*They share laughter.*]

So Davis works in book publishing?

MATT   Yeah, he's recently become this like hot-shit editor. He pulled this book out of the slush pile. A total random discovery. It was named a *New York Times* Notable Book and got all these rave reviews. Davis got promoted pretty quick after that and now he's on this fast track. He'll probably have his own imprint before he turns thirty-five.

[*Standing.*]

If you want me to go find him, I totally will. He's probably over at that café with the foosball tables. At school he used to play people for money. He'd even take 'em on two-on-one. And he's a helluva dart player too. The guy has the genes from some like super race. And he has this great apartment in the Village. Brick walls. East-west exposure. Flower pots on the window ledges. A Bowflex. I'll seriously go get him if you want me to.

CHRISTINA   Stop acting like him. You were doing better as yourself.

MATT   Right.

[*He sits.*]

CHRISTINA   So Davis told me it's been a while since you've been with anyone.

MATT   Yeah, it's been a while.

CHRISTINA   How long?

MATT   Um, like three years. Three and a half, actually.

CHRISTINA   Why?

MATT   I don't know. I was sort of in love with this girl. We were living together. She met some guy. Moved out. I took it pretty hard. Depression set in. I stopped doing my laundry. Drank a lot of Robitussin. Got addicted to online bridge. I guess I sort of lost my confidence after that. Davis would set me up with people. Nothing really ever felt right. For a while he actually thought I might be gay.

CHRISTINA   Are you?

MATT   What, gay? No way. I mean, at least I don't think I am.

CHRISTINA   Have you ever been with a man?

MATT   Well, in high school I had this huge crush on the captain of the football team.

CHRISTINA   Really?

MATT   That was a joke.

CHRISTINA   Maybe you should explore it.

MATT   No, I prefer women. Like I'm looking at you right now and I'm totally like balls-to-the-wall attracted to you...

CHRISTINA   But?

MATT   There's no but, really. I just sort of...I don't know what it is.

CHRISTINA   Can you get an erection?

MATT   What?

CHRISTINA   Are you impotent.

MATT   A perfectly legitimate question, Christina, but check it out, I get these like totally ferocious morning boners every day.

CHRISTINA   What was her name?

MATT   Who, the girl I was in...her name was Sarah. We dated for like two and a half years. Lived together for a few months. And then things got weird.

CHRISTINA   How did things get weird?

MATT   I don't know. They just did...If you want to know the truth, she sort of fell in love with Davis. And now they're together, actually. It was pretty fucked up for a while, but it's cool, now.

CHRISTINA   Are you still in love with her?

MATT   Who, Sarah? No. No way. She's a fucking cunt.

CHRISTINA   Are they in love?

MATT   Um. Yeah. They are. They're sort of perfect for each other. Davis actually bought that snow globe for her. Because of the skyline. It's the new, like post–September eleventh version.

[CHRISTINA *stands and turns away.*]

That's when Sarah and I split up and she and Davis, well, got together. It's really hard to find new skyline stuff in New York. I mean, they have key chains and like T-shirts and stuff, but they all have images of the Twin Towers or bands of light where they would be still standing or whatever.

[CHRISTINA *turns to him.*]

He's not who you think he is, Christina. Whatever happened between you two. It wasn't real. I know that probably sucks to hear...

CHRISTINA   So how many women have you been with?

MATT   Well, not many, actually.

CHRISTINA   Are you a virgin?

MATT   No. I mean, it's a staggeringly low number of women. Like two, if truth be told.

CHRISTINA   Who were they?

MATT   Well, I was with Sarah. A lot. Like every day.

[CHRISTINA *crosses to the upstage bed, sits.*]

And I was with this other girl back in college who liked this haiku I wrote about a pair of pajamas.

CHRISTINA   Come here.

MATT   What do you mean?

CHRISTINA   I mean, come here. Sit next to me.

MATT   Like join you on the bed?

CHRISTINA   Yeah.

[MATT *hesitates, rises, sets the chair in front of the desk, crosses to her at the bed, sits. He starts bobbing up and down a bit.*]

MATT   The beds here are pretty firm. Good for bouncing...

CHRISTINA   Kiss me.

[*He stops bobbing.*]

MATT   Are you sure?

CHRISTINA   Yeah.

MATT   Do you really want me to, or is this like some sort of pity-the-nerd exercise?
       [*She pulls him into her. They kiss for a moment. They stop.*]
       Was that okay?

CHRISTINA   It was nice.

MATT   Is my breath...I mean, I could—

CHRISTINA   Your breath is perfect.

MATT   Oh, cool.
       [*He folds into himself.*]
       So, can I kiss you again?

CHRISTINA   Do you want to?

MATT   I do, yeah.

CHRISTINA   So do it.

[*He leans into her and they kiss again. It lasts a little longer. When it ends,* CHRISTINA *stands, starts to take her dress off.*]

MATT   That's a great dress.

CHRISTINA   Thanks.

MATT   Really, really great. Very, um, flattering, etcetera, etcetera.

CHRISTINA   The zipper gets caught at the top. Will you help me undo it?

MATT   Sure.

[*He stands, takes a step toward her, reaches toward the zipper, stops, closes his eyes.*]

Um, I think I should say some things.

CHRISTINA   What?

MATT   I'm an insomniac... I haven't slept in over six weeks... And I was going to kill myself tonight.

CHRISTINA   Open your eyes.

[MATT *opens his eyes.*]

Why?

MATT   I don't know. I was just sitting there. In that chair and... I just wanted everything to stop... I used my belt. I actually had it rigged to a hook on the wall and I had started to, um... hang myself... when you guys came in... And now I'm glad I didn't do it... I just needed to say that, Christina. I'm glad you came in.

[*They look at each other for a long moment and then she turns around again. He moves to her, unzips the dress. She crosses to the light, turns it out. Only the light from the window now. She lets her hair down, steps out of the dress. She stands naked before him for a moment, then helps him undress, removing his shoes, his shirt, his pants, his socks, until he is naked too. She then takes his hand and leads*] *him to the bed. They sit before each other and* MATT *draws the covers over his shoulders. She licks her hand and then masturbates him for a moment. She removes the condom from the packet and puts it on his erect penis. He touches her face and she pulls him on top of her. They kiss for a moment and then he inserts his penis and they start to slowly make love. It quickly picks up speed. It is brief but something real passes between them. After* MATT *comes, he collapses on top of her, and falls instantly asleep.* CHRISTINA *stares out for a moment, and then pushes him off of her, gets out of bed, and dresses at the foot of the other bed. She gathers her things and crosses to where her dress fell to the floor. She picks it up, considers it, and then crosses to the chair and lays it across the arms of the chair. She then reaches into her bag and removes a small portable cassette player. She sets it on the desk, watches* MATT *sleep for a moment. She grabs* DAVIS's *cigarettes and lighter that were left on the desk, puts them in her bag, and quietly exits, closing the door behind her. After a moment,* MATT *wakes as if he was dreaming that he was falling. He sits up in bed, disoriented. He looks around, then reaches down, removes the condom, places it on the windowsill. He gets out of bed, crosses to the door, opens it, looks out into the hallway. He then sees the dress laid over the arms of the chair. He takes it, pulls it into him, holds it for a moment. He then spots the cassette player, presses Play. Tom Waits's "Tom Traubert's Blues" plays. He sits holding the dress as lights fade to black.*]

• • •

···scene 2···

[A year later. Dusk. MATT's *small nine-by-twelve-foot domicile in the East Village. A twin bed, up against one wall. The bed is made. On the floor beside the bed, several stacks of books as well as a few stray items of clothing that never found their way to the laundry bag. A small kitchenette with a half-fridge, a short countertop, a single cupboard, a portable stove top, a sink, and other space-saving items. Above the sink, a window facing an airshaft. Against one wall, over the twin bed, a homemade library fashioned from planks of wood, a phone-slash-answering-machine unit on the bottom shelf. A few pictures and postcards of literary titans arranged on the wall: Henry Miller, John Fante, Jim Carroll, Frederick Exley, Arthur Miller,*

Bertolt Brecht, and Raymond Carver. In black Sharpie ink, there is a large X scrawled over Carver's face. Next to the bed, a slightly cluttered desk containing a few paperback novels, a dictionary, a bottle of sleeping pills, a laptop computer, a cheap manual-feed printer, a few bottles of various liquid antihistamines, a Kleenex box, and the portable cassette player from the end of act I. Between the desk and the bed is a closet, whose door is closed. Downstage of the desk is an electric space heater. The room is generally neat, but the enormous volume of books gives it a congested, almost claustrophobic quality. MATT is seated at the desk. He is dressed in corduroy pants, a thick sweater, and wool socks. There is an afghan throw draped over his shoulders. He is writing. After a moment, he stops and checks the space heater, fidgets a bit, blows into cupped hands, returns to his computer. He writes for a bit and then stops again. He looks out the window, rises off the chair, goes for the Kleenex box, sees that it is empty, exits the room, and returns moments later with a wad of toilet paper that he uses to clean the dust off his computer screen. He presses a button on the portable cassette player. "Jitterbug Boy" from Tom Waits's Small Change *plays. He listens for a moment and then presses Stop, rewinds it, listens again. He does this twice, then sits there, blank. He reaches for the sleeping pills, undoes the top, fingers into the bottle, and removes two pills, arranges them next to each other on his desk. A knock at the door. MATT quickly stops the cassette player, freezes. Another knock. MATT puts the pills back in the bottle, sits very still. A woman's voice calls out from the other side of the door.*]

VOICE   Hello?

[MATT *doesn't respond.*]

VOICE   Davis, is that you?

MATT   No. Davis isn't here.

VOICE   Oh. Are you sure?

MATT   Yeah, I'm positive.

VOICE   Are you one of his roommates or something?

MATT   Um. No.

VOICE   I'm sorry to bother you but I was led to believe that Davis lives here.

MATT   He doesn't.

VOICE   Well, this is the address he gave me.

MATT   He's never lived here.

VOICE   But you know him, right?

[MATT *doesn't answer, rewinds the cassette player.*]

I said, you know him, right?

MATT   I do, yeah.

VOICE   Well, can you tell me where I might be able to find him?

MATT   Who are you?

VOICE   A friend.

MATT   [*Standing.*] A friend from where?

VOICE   I met him last winter. I'm just passing through town and I was hoping to say hello.

MATT   Did he know you were coming?

VOICE   No. I wanted to surprise him.

MATT   How did you get in the building?

VOICE   The front door was open. Is he in there or something? . . . Hello?

MATT   Yeah.

VOICE   Did you hear me?

MATT   I heard you. He's not here.

VOICE   Do you know where I might be able to find him?

MATT   I'm not sure. I mean, it's Saturday night. Most people have plans.

VOICE   It doesn't seem like you have any plans.

MATT   What?

VOICE   I said, it doesn't seem like you have any plans.

MATT   I'm working.

VOICE   On what?

MATT   Nothing. I'm just working.

VOICE   Mysterious . . . Mysterious work being done behind a mysterious door.

MATT   Look, if you want to leave Davis a message, I'll be sure he gets it the next time I see him.

VOICE   Can I maybe get his phone number?

MATT   I'm not sure that's such a good idea.

VOICE   Why?

MATT   Who are you?

VOICE   Why don't you just open the door?
[MATT *starts to open the door, hesitates.*]
Please? It's fucking cold as shit out here.

[MATT *opens the door.* CHRISTINA *stands in the entrance. She is dressed in several thin layers under a thin coat. She wears the same hat, scarf, and gloves she wore in act I. She also carries the same baglike purse. She is very cold, shivering. She looks paler, a bit gaunt, perhaps thinner.*]

CHRISTINA   Thanks. It looks like someone broke the window to the fire escape.

MATT   Yeah, it's been that way for almost a year now. They put plastic over it but it keeps getting ripped down.

CHRISTINA   It's colder in the hall than it is outside.

MATT   One of the many benefits.

CHRISTINA   Benefits of what?

MATT   I don't know. Of, um, low-income, um, housing, I guess.

[MATT *watches her for a moment. He falls to the floor. Gathers himself, stands.*]

CHRISTINA   Are you all right?

MATT   I'm fine. I just... I'm fine.

CHRISTINA   ... Can I come in?

MATT   Um, sure.

[*He steps aside. She enters. He closes the door, turns the room light on.*]

CHRISTINA   [*Looking around the room.*] So you live here?

MATT   I do, yeah.

CHRISTINA   It's so small.

MATT   You mean cozy, right?

CHRISTINA   Cozy, sure.

MATT   Small is so, I don't know, reductive or whatever. Cozy makes you feel like you're getting more bang for your buck.

CHRISTINA   No, it's nice. How much do you pay?

MATT   Two-eighty-five a month.

CHRISTINA   Cheap.

MATT   Yeah, for the East Village it's not so bad. The bathroom-in-the-hall thing can get a little tedious. And there are only two outlets, so you develop this like emotional dependency on extension cords, but you get used to it...I apologize in advance about the heat. It goes out like every other day, thus augmenting is necessary.

CHRISTINA   I can't get over how small it is.

MATT   It actually has its benefits. Keeps things simple. Prevents you from buying too much shit. It's sort of like a return to campus housing, but without the RA's...And the overqualified maintenance crew...And the, um, good-looking Banana Republic chicks...

CHRISTINA   Are all these books yours?

MATT   Yeah. I like having them around me. Makes it feel like less of a POW torture chamber.

CHRISTINA   You've read them all?

MATT   Most of them. Except for the Curious George omnibus. Totally impenetrable and overblown...

[*Awkward pause.*]

CHRISTINA   [*Extending her hand.*] I'm Christine.

MATT   Um, I already know you.

CHRISTINA   You do?

MATT   Yes, actually.

CHRISTINA   [*Retracting her hand.*] Oh. We've met?

MATT   You could say that, yeah. Except last time I was, um, introduced to you, you were using the name Christina. With like an "a" on the end. I assume that's a variation.

CHRISTINA   I prefer Christine.

MATT   What, like depending on what side of the Atlantic you're on? ... You seriously don't remember me?

CHRISTINA   I'm sorry, lately my memory sucks. Where did we ... ?

MATT   What, meet?

CHRISTINA   Yeah. Was it in Paris? Or, wait, are you that guy I sat with on the train to Copenhagen? The guy with the thumbs?

MATT   No, that wasn't me.

CHRISTINA   Are you sure? Because on the train to Copenhagen I sat next to this guy and he had these triple-jointed thumbs. It was creepy. He could make them like stick in these weird positions. He had a zittier face, but the resemblance is sort of uncanny...

MATT   Um, we met in the Red Light District, actually. A year ago. At the Crown Hotel. Davis was with you in the windows or whatever you call them and brought you back to our room. The three of us hung out for a while. And then Davis left and we, well, I mean, you and I, um—

CHRISTINA   Oh. Wait. You were the friend.

MATT   Yeah, I was the friend . . . I still am the friend. Referring to someone in the present tense can be surprisingly good for his or her self-esteem.

CHRISTINA   I'm sorry.

MATT   No, don't be. It's cool . . .

CHRISTINA   What's your name again—Colin?

MATT   Colin?

CHRISTINA   Yeah, Colin.

MATT   Like Copenhagen Colin?

CHRISTINA   Come on, seriously. It's Colin, right? Or something like that.

[MATT *doesn't respond.*]

Brian?

[MATT *doesn't respond.*]

Clarke.

[MATT *doesn't respond.*]

Milt.

MATT   You're getting warmer.

CHRISTINA   Shit.

MATT   Matt.

CHRISTINA   Matt, right.

MATT   Milt?

CHRISTINA   I had the *M* right.

MATT   Do I look like a fucking Milt?

CHRISTINA   No, you look like a Colin...I'm kidding. You look like a Matt.

[*Awkward pause.*]

MATT   Here, sit down.

[*He wipes the dust off his desk chair. She sits.*]

CHRISTINA   Matt, right. You were the one who...

MATT   Who what?

CHRISTINA   No, nothing. I just remember you had that problem. With your kidneys or something.

[*He grabs a milk crate next to his small refrigerator, sets it down, sits.*]

MATT   It was my, um, intestines, actually.

CHRISTINA   That's right. You had some sort of disease.

MATT   Bacteria infection.

CHRISTINA   And you wouldn't drop acid.

MATT   Smoke pot.

CHRISTINA   Right, you wouldn't smoke any pot because you were like all depressed and on Prozac or something.

MATT   Actually, I was sort of depressed at the time. But the drug I was on is called Flagyl. And it's an antibiotic. I had this thing called giardia.

CHRISTINA   Oh, shit—that was you?

MATT Yeah, that was me—the sexy giardia guy.

CHRISTINA Wow. That's so weird, right?

[*Awkward pause.*]

So how've you been?

MATT I've been good. Pretty good, yeah.

CHRISTINA Good. Your bowel problems are behind you, I'm assuming.

MATT Intestinal. Yeah, they're pretty much behind me. In more ways than one...How've you been?

CHRISTINA I've been good.

MATT Cool.

CHRISTINA Hey, didn't you used to wear glasses?

MATT Glasses? No.

CHRISTINA Are you sure? Like those little round ones?

MATT I've never worn glasses. I'm sure people think of me as wearing glasses. I mean, I'm not exactly what you'd call the like Lorenzo Lamas of the East Village or whatever, but I'm proud to say that throughout my thirty-one-year reign as King of Nerdville I have miraculously managed to remain ophthalmologically unchallenged.

CHRISTINA There's something about you that's different...Is your hair longer or something?

MATT No, my hair's pretty much the same. I might've put on a little weight. When I met you I had just lost like twenty pounds. Because of my, um...

CHRISTINA   Bacteria problem?

MATT   Yeah, that.

CHRISTINA   No, now I remember—it's totally coming back to me. You were still sort of—

MATT   Convalescing?

CHRISTINA   Exactly. You and Davis were traveling together. You guys were in Paris and then you came to Amsterdam. You're an actor.

MATT   Writer.

CHRISTINA   That's right. You were working on some article.

MATT   Play.

CHRISTINA   I mean, play. It was about a train wreck, right?

MATT   Well, sort of, but not really.

CHRISTINA   No, it was about a train wreck, I'm almost positive. It had geese in the title.

MATT   Birds.

CHRISTINA   I mean, birds.

MATT   It was called *Speckled Birds*.

CHRISTINA   Yeah, *The Speckled Bird*.

MATT   *Speckled Birds*. In the plural. And no *The*.

CHRISTINA   Sorry.

MATT   No, don't be. I just have this like neurotic, control-freak thing with titles. I'm sort of anti-article. No A's or An's or

The's. The article in the title is so, I don't know, like Ernest Hemingway or something.

[*She takes her hat off.*]

CHRISTINA Did you ever finish it?

MATT What, *Speckled Birds*? No.

CHRISTINA Why not?

MATT I don't know. I guess I sort of got like derailed.

CHRISTINA Oh.

MATT But I started something new. Single set. Three characters. Lights up, lights down—that kind of thing.

CHRISTINA Well, that's cool.

MATT Yeah, with playwriting there's lots of false starts. Ill-fated first acts, etcetera. I blame it all on Shakespeare. He stole all my ideas like three hundred years before I was even born. He futuristically ruined my career...

[*Standing now.*]

Hey, would you like some tea or something?

CHRISTINA You don't have any coffee, do you?

MATT No, I can't do coffee. I mean, I could totally go out and get you some if you want. Ever since the episode—

CHRISTINA With your intestines?

MATT Yeah, I sort of try and steer clear of all the major diuretics now. I can't even look at apple juice. Tea's easier on my...

CHRISTINA Intestines?

MATT   If I hear that word again, I'll probably turn into some like genitally void Nerf puppet.

CHRISTINA   Sorry.

MATT   But seriously, if you want, I'll totally brave the elements and go out and ferry you a Frappuccino. There's this whole like constellation of Starbucks within a five-block radius.

CHRISTINA   No, tea is good. Thanks, though.

MATT   All I have is Earl Grey. Is that okay?

CHRISTINA   It's fine.

[MATT *crosses to the kitchenette, fills a tea kettle with water, starts the portable stove top, prepares tea bags in mugs, etc.*]

MATT   So where'd you fly in from?

CHRISTINA   Paris.

MATT   How was it?

CHRISTINA   I slept through most of it. But it was weird. When we started circling over JFK, they almost wouldn't land the plane because of all the snow.

MATT   Yeah, it was coming down pretty hard earlier. We're supposed to get another big storm tonight. Like multiple inches... You flying back out tomorrow?

CHRISTINA   No, why?

MATT   Oh, no reason. It's just that before I let you in you said you were passing through town.

CHRISTINA   I am.

MATT   Where you heading?

CHRISTINA   I was gonna take a train to go visit my parents.

MATT   They're in Baltimore, right?

CHRISTINA   How did you know that?

MATT   You told me. Back in, um…when we met.

CHRISTINA   I told you that?

MATT   You did, yes.

CHRISTINA   That's weird.

MATT   The whole night was sort of weird, actually.

CHRISTINA   What else did I tell you?

MATT   How you were going to Bard and wound up staying in Paris when you were studying abroad your sophomore year. And how you were performing at some bar in the Latin Quarter and you met this gay lawyer with dual Dutch and French citizenship who you wound up marrying because he gave you a lot of money or whatever and you spent X amount of months doing your thing in Amsterdam and X amount of months like posing as his wife in Paris.

CHRISTINA   I wasn't posing as his wife. I was his wife.

MATT   Oh, right. But he was gay, so it was sort of an act, right?

CHRISTINA   A marriage is a marriage.

[*Awkward pause.*]

MATT   You also told me about how you used to be an actress. And that the last play you were in was some postmodern version of *Oklahoma* that was set in a lawn-mower repair shop and everyone was half bionic or had like Duracell batteries sticking out of their backs or something.

CHRISTINA   Wow. You know a lot of shit about me.

MATT   I could go on and on, actually. I have a memory like a ... very nerdy elephant.

CHRISTINA   I remember your play and your chlamydia—

MATT   Giardia.

CHRISTINA   Yeah, that. For some reason I can remember that stuff really clearly... but other things...

MATT   I came in like point four seconds. I think it's a safe bet to assume that it wasn't one of your most unforgettable experiences, Christina.

CHRISTINA   Christine.

MATT   I mean, Christine. I'd be willing to like mortgage my books on that. Well, if you could actually mortgage books... I hadn't been with a woman in over three years. I don't blame you for not remembering.

[*Awkward pause.*]

CHRISTINA   So have you been with anyone else?

MATT   What, since I was with you? Of course.

CHRISTINA   Really?

MATT   Yeah, why?

CHRISTINA   You just looked left. When people look left, it means
        they're lying.

MATT   According to who?

CHRISTINA   I learned it from an old acting teacher.

MATT   And which way do they look when they're telling the truth.

CHRISTINA   Up.

[MATT *looks left. He looks up.*]

MATT   So I totally just lied. But it's a choice.

CHRISTINA   To be celibate?

MATT   Sort of, yeah.

CHRISTINA   Keeps things simple?

MATT   Yeah, simple, sure ... So you're on your way to Baltimore?

CHRISTINA   My train leaves tomorrow, yeah.

MATT   Where are you staying? Tonight, I mean.

CHRISTINA   I'm not sure yet.

MATT   Well, you're more than welcome to ... I mean, it's not exactly
        the St. Regis, but ...

CHRISTINA   Thanks.

MATT   How long will you be down there?

CHRISTINA   Sort of indefinitely. It depends, I guess.

MATT   On what.

CHRISTINA   On a lot.

[*The tea kettle starts to whistle. MATT crosses to it, turns it off. He pours the boiling water into the mugs.*]

MATT   Milk or honey?

CHRISTINA   No thanks.

[MATT *crosses back to* CHRISTINA, *hands her a mug of tea, then realizes he has forgotten to give her anything to set it on and gives her some random paperback novel as a saucer. He then sits on the end of the bed. They sit in silence for a moment, warming their hands.*]

You wouldn't happen to have a cigarette, would you?

MATT   I don't smoke ... That was Davis.

[CHRISTINA *sips her tea.*]

So how long has it been?

CHRISTINA   Since what?

MATT   Since you were on this side of the pond.

CHRISTINA   Almost six years.

MATT   Whoa.

CHRISTINA   What?

MATT   Nothing. It's just ... Well, that's a long time to be away.

CHRISTINA   Yeah, I was gonna come back a few times, but I sort of got sucked into performing. And then 9/11 happened ... And then I got married.

MATT   Are you close to your parents?

CHRISTINA   Not really.

MATT   You don't stay in touch?

CHRISTINA   We did for the first year or so. But they were pretty pissed that I quit school.

MATT   Do you have any brothers or sisters?

CHRISTINA   No.

MATT   Is that going to be like weird?

CHRISTINA   What.

MATT   To see your parents?

CHRISTINA   It will be, yes.

MATT   Do you mind me asking why you're going home?

CHRISTINA   I just thought it was time.

MATT   Cool.

CHRISTINA   And I'm sick.

MATT   Oh...What, like sick sick?

CHRISTINA   Yeah.

MATT   Should I not ask?

CHRISTINA   I have AIDS.

MATT   Oh. Shit...Wow, I'm really sorry, Christina. I mean Christine.

[*She starts to cry.* MATT *is paralyzed for a moment, but manages to move to her. He comforts her awkwardly. After a minute, he quickly crosses to the kitchen and seizes a roll of paper towels. He tears off a few sheets, crosses back to* CHRISTINA, *hands them to her.*]

CHRISTINA   Thanks.

[*She wipes her face, blows her nose.*]

I can't believe I'm fucking crying.

MATT   No, totally cry all you want. There's plenty of Bounty.

[*He awkwardly comforts her again for a moment, attempts to touch her face but retracts his hand, then grabs a garbage can instead, setting it next to her for easy paper-towel disposal.*]

How long have you known?

CHRISTINA   About a month.

MATT   Jesus. You must be . . .

CHRISTINA   Yeah.

MATT   People live a long time with it now. I mean, they have all of these new treatments, right?

CHRISTINA   I guess. But you have to be able to afford them.

MATT   What about your husband?

CHRISTINA   What about him?

MATT   Can't he help you?

CHRISTINA   He won't.

MATT   But isn't he like legally responsible?

CHRISTINA   He was, yeah.

MATT   I mean, what happened to "for better and for worse" and all that?

CHRISTINA   It was too embarrassing for him. He divorced me on grounds of adultery. Things got ugly and I lost my work permit.

MATT   You told your husband you were sick and he turned you out?

CHRISTINA   After I got the results I went to his firm to tell him and he started making calls right there at his desk.

MATT   What a fucking asshole.

CHRISTINA   I don't blame him, really. I mean, who wants a fucking trophy wife with AIDS?

MATT   But still. That's so, I don't know... low... Do you know how you got it?

CHRISTINA   No.

MATT   Don't you have protected sex?

CHRISTINA   I always make my partners wear condoms.

MATT   Did you ever have like a blood transfusion?

CHRISTINA   No. The only thing I can think of is I did heroin a few times with this guy from Zurich, but the needles were in these fucking hermetically sealed packets... I don't know how I got it. That doesn't even matter. The fact is I got it.

MATT   How did you find out?

CHRISTINA   At a routine checkup at my gynecologist.

MATT   Do you have any money?

CHRISTINA   I used my last three hundred dollars getting here.

MATT   What's your plan for Baltimore?

CHRISTINA   I'm just gonna get on the train.

MATT   That's illegal, Christina.

CHRISTINA   Christine.

MATT   I mean, Christine. The fucking Amtrak police will totally throw you off the train. Can't your parents wire you some cash?

CHRISTINA   I haven't spoken to them in over five years.

MATT   So now would be a pretty good time, don't you think? I mean, you're not calling to like ask to borrow the car or something... Can't you get treated in Paris?

CHRISTINA   Albert and I weren't married long enough for me to get full citizenship. So I lost my medical eligibility.

MATT   But they can't refuse you treatment, can they? I mean, they wouldn't throw you out on the street.

CHRISTINA   I just felt like I needed to come back.

[CHRISTINA *rises and crosses to the kitchen, stares out the window. The phone rings.* MATT *doesn't answer it. It rings twice and then his answering machine picks up.*]

MATT'S VOICE   Hey, it's Matt. Please leave a message.

[*A beep.*]

DAVIS'S VOICE   Yo, Matt, it's me. I think I left my cell phone over there last night. I'm heading downtown to meet Sarah later and I was wondering if I could stop by to pick it up. If you get this message, give me a call on my land line. All right, bro. Hope the writing's going well. I'll see you later.

[*The answering machine beeps again. A silence.*]

CHRISTINA   That was Davis, wasn't it?

MATT   Yeah, actually, it was.

CHRISTINA   Are you gonna call him back?

MATT   Not right now.

CHRISTINA   You should call him back. I mean, he needs his phone, right?

MATT   He'll probably stop by.

[*She crosses to her purse, sits in the chair.*]

Look, Christina—

CHRISTINA   Christine.

MATT   I mean, Christine. I'd like to help you.

CHRISTINA   How?

MATT   I don't know. I only have a few hundred dollars in the bank but I'll totally get you that train ticket. It can't be more than fifty bucks.

CHRISTINA   It's seventy.

MATT   Fine. Seventy bucks, that's nothing. We'll go to Penn Station together. I'll put you on the train.

CHRISTINA   I'd feel weird taking your money.

MATT   You can't afford not to. Look, you don't even have to pay me back. It's only seventy dollars. I just started this temp job that pays like twenty bucks an hour. And as far as having a place to stay tonight, you can totally crash here. I have this like polystyrene yoga mat thing. I can sleep on the floor.

CHRISTINA   [*Half joking.*] What, you don't want to sleep with me?

MATT   No, I totally want to sleep with you, Christina. I mean,
        Christine. I just…I don't know…I think you should be
        comfortable, that's all.

[CHRISTINA *hands the paper towels back to* MATT.]

CHRISTINA   Would you mind if I took a shower?

MATT   Not at all. It's in the hall. There's a clean towel on the shelf
        in the closet.

        [*She rises. He does as well, crossing to the kitchen to give her some space.
        He might put something in a cupboard. Hanging on the inside of the
        closet door is* CHRISTINA's *red dress from the end of act I. She has to
        move the chair to enter the closet and doesn't see it until she comes out
        with the towel. She closes the door. She is suddenly lightheaded, has to sit
        on the bed.*]

        You okay?

CHRISTINA   I'm fine. I'm just a little lightheaded. It was a long
        flight.

[*She stands.*]

MATT   Have you like eaten?

CHRISTINA   I couldn't eat the plane food.

MATT   You must be starving. Maybe I should go get something.

CHRISTINA   Not yet.

MATT   Oh. Why?

CHRISTINA   Wait till I finish my shower.

MATT   Okay.

CHRISTINA   I'd feel safer.

MATT   Then I'll totally stay right here... The shower's, um, down the hall to your left.

CHRISTINA   Thanks.

MATT   Sure.

[*She turns and exits. As soon as the door is shut,* MATT *spots* DAVIS*'s cell phone next to a lamp. He opens it, shuts it. A knock on the door.* MATT *puts the cell phone back.*]

CHRISTINA'S VOICE   It's me.

> [MATT *opens the door.*]

> Can I borrow some soap and shampoo?

MATT   Of course.

> [MATT *hands her a large bucket containing shower supplies.*]

> It takes a minute for the hot water to kick in.

CHRISTINA   Hey, thanks again.

MATT   You're welcome.

CHRISTINA   You're really sweet.

MATT   I, well, um, thanks. Thank you.

> [*She turns and exits down the hall.* MATT *shuts the door, turns, and in a whirlwind panic he kicks drifts of laundry under his bed, removes his sweater, replaces it with a clean shirt, throws things away, deodorizes the room with Febreze spray—he Febrezes just about everything in sight—attempts to straighten up the kitchen and wave the heat from the space heater into the room. He then quickly goes to the cupboard, removes a toothbrush and a tube of toothpaste, brushes his teeth in the sink with Olympic velocity, smells his armpits, reaches back into the cupboard, removes some deodorant, applies it very quickly, checks his*]

reflection in the mirror, fixes his hair, puts a baseball hat on, takes it off, and then almost passes out. He sits on the bed for a moment, almost starts to cry. He tries to make himself stop by punching his leg repeatedly. He stops crying. MATT *then seizes the phone. He dials, waits.*]

[*Into phone.*]

Hey, Davis, it's me. I, um, got your message. You might not get this, but what I wanted to say was that, yeah, you did leave your cell phone over here. It's on my bookcase, actually. But tonight might not be the best time to come over. I mean, you can totally give it a shot but I'll most likely be out. I've been sort of feeling cooped up lately and I was thinking about going to check out a movie. So tomorrow might be better. All right . . . Hey, Sarah. Later.

[*He hangs up, spots* CHRISTINA'*s bag, crosses to it, opens it, removes the snow globe that* DAVIS *had given* CHRISTINA *back in Amsterdam.* MATT *shakes it, stares at it for a moment, then puts it back in her bag. Suddenly,* MATT *seizes the phone again, dials, waits.*]

[*Into phone.*]

Hey, Davis, it's me again. I just wanted to let you know that I decided that I'm definitely gonna go check out a movie. I mean, I'm just sitting ere, waiting for the snow . . . again. So don't waste your time stopping by. I'll give you a call tomorrow.

[MATT *hangs up, then turns to* CHRISTINA'*s bag again. He fixes it so that it doesn't look tampered with.* CHRISTINA *re-enters. Her hair is wet and she is dressed in the same clothes.*]

Was there any hot water?

CHRISTINA   Uh-huh.

MATT   No shower-room-floor surprises? At least once a week someone leaves this totally unnameable like supple mass in the corner . . .

[*He watches her for a moment.*]

CHRISTINA What?

MATT Nothing. You're just so pretty.

[*Awkward pause.*]

You can hang the towel on the hook on the door.

[*She hangs the towel. He takes the bucket from her, puts it away. She crosses to her purse.*]

Here, take the bed.

[*She sits on the bed. He sets the afghan beside her. She puts her hat on. He then positions the space heater so that it is closer to her, waves some heat toward her.*]

You look like Jean Seberg. With your hair under your hat like that.

CHRISTINA Who's that?

MATT Oh my god, you don't know who Jean Seberg is?

CHRISTINA No.

MATT She was an American actress who starred in this 1960 French New Wave film called *Breathless*. It was directed by Jean-Luc Godard and written by François Truffaut. In French it's called *À bout de souffle*. It's an amazing movie. Like one of those ones that change your life or whatever. Jean Seberg played this sort of lost American girl living in Paris who's in love with this car thief, Michel. Michel is played by Jean-Paul Belmondo and he's this like total Humphrey Bogart wannabe, but in a cool way. All they do is steal cars and make love, but Michel shoots this cop and then they're fucked and they try to escape to Italy. In 1983 they did this cheesy American remake with like Richard Gere. It was set in Vegas instead of Paris and they're trying to get to LA instead of Italy. It was sort of an all-time low in American filmmaking. Jean Seberg didn't wear a hat but she had short hair. The legend goes that after she had starred in these two flops, *Saint Joan* and this other French film called *Bonjour tristesse*, Godard like saw her at a café in Paris and got all spellbound and asked her to be in his movie. She was originally from Marshalltown, Iowa . . . She was really beautiful, so it's like a high compliment.

CHRISTINA   Thanks.

MATT   I can't believe you don't know that film. After *Breathless* came out, like hundreds of thousands of women cut their hair short. She totally inspired this whole new look. She was married four times. Later she sort of freaked out and moved to LA and joined the Black Panthers. Some people believe that the FBI was actually after her. When she was forty-one she like OD'd on barbiturates. They found her dead in a Paris suburb.

CHRISTINA   So did it change your life?

MATT   What—*Breathless*?

CHRISTINA   Yeah.

MATT   Not really. I mean, it definitely should have. I'll probably go see it again at some point. This theater in the West Village revives it every so often.

[*Pause.*]

CHRISTINA   So what's your new play about?

MATT   You really want to know?

CHRISTINA   I do, yes.

MATT   It's actually about two friends who go to Amsterdam. They both sleep with the same, um, girl.

CHRISTINA   And what happens?

MATT   Well, one of them sort of falls in love with her and he can't seem to get over it.

CHRISTINA   Is the girl—

MATT   She's a prostitute, yeah.

CHRISTINA   I was actually gonna ask if she's in love with one of them.

MATT   Oh. She is. But not with the right one. One of them is a bit quiet and nerdy, and the other one is sort of dickish and macho. The quiet, nerdy one is in love with her but he isn't really her type. And the dickish, macho one is her type, but he's not interested in her. At some point the dickish, macho one gives her this like Fabergé glass egg thing that changes colors—it's sort of like a mood egg. He buys it as a joke and sort of unloads it on her because he can't fit it in his suitcase and she takes it the wrong way.

CHRISTINA   She thinks it actually means something.

MATT   She does sort of, yeah.

CHRISTINA   That's sad.

MATT   It is sad. But it's funny too. In like a sad way.

CHRISTINA   How does it end?

MATT   Well, you see, that's the part that's screwing me up. I'm like three-quarters of the way through it and the double unrequited love thing totally works but I can't figure out the final movement. The hypotenuse of the love triangle never quite gets completed because they're all like star-crossed or whatever. And beyond that, it's not conventionally structured because there are these like songs in it that sort of come out of nowhere. Not to say that there isn't at least some semblance of organic logic at work. The female character used to be this famous torch singer in Istanbul. Sometimes to communicate she has no recourse but to sing. And other times she functions as this like five-a.m. vision in the quiet, nerdy guy's head. Don't get me wrong, it's not a musical. And it's not like Brechtian or whatever. It's just what it is. I mean, what it definitely isn't is your typical Aristotelian, three-act, architecturally sound type of thing. It's not what they call a well-made play. It's more of this like half-remembered dream or a spell or a haunting or something. If anything, it's an un-well-made play. And my instincts are to let it sort of fade out, to like resist the big clichéd, melodramatic ending.

[*Sitting on the bed now.*]

But I keep writing into this like weird corner of confrontation and emotional apocalypse. Where the girl and the quiet nerdy guy who she doesn't love wind up alone and like go round and round about why they should and shouldn't be together and then peace is achieved after some totally cheesy song about mermaids trapped under calving icebergs or whatever.

CHRISTINA   And all of this happens in Amsterdam?

MATT   In Amsterdam, yeah. In one night. Lights up, lights down. But real life never works like that, right? . . . I mean, it really doesn't, right?

CHRISTINA   Maybe you should just let it fade out like you said.

MATT   Maybe.

> [*Awkward pause.*]

I'm not writing an act break into it. I don't think the audience should be let off the hook. But these days everyone wants an intermission so they can sell shit. Like chocolate-covered espresso beans and thirty-dollar T-shirts with pictures of Tony Kushner eating a banana.

> [*A silence.*]

I better go get us some food.

> [*He crosses to his winter coat, starts to put it on.*]

CHRISTINA   Hey, Mark?

MATT   Matt.

CHRISTINA   I mean, Matt. Sorry.

MATT   What.

CHRISTINA   Why are you being so nice to me?

MATT   Look, Christine or Christina or whatever your name is, I feel I have to say something. And I have no idea how this is going to come out, so please don't freak out and stone me to death or kick me in the balls or like projectile vomit from boredom...

CHRISTINA   Okay.

MATT   How to start... Let's see... Um, since we were together last January I haven't been able to like stop thinking about you. I mean, it was easily one of the biggest things that's ever happened to me. I know that like sexually speaking at least it was this totally uneventful blip of antimatter for you, but I'm pretty convinced that despite my inept, like desperate sexual brevity or whatever that something real passed between us. Even if for a moment. And I know you remember it—you fucking have to—because I'd never known that feeling before. And when that kind of thing happens there has to be at least a shred of mutuality at play, even if it's like point seven percent. You like walked out of your dress. And then you helped me take my clothes off. And then you took my hand and led me to the bed. It was…Well, it was more than the sex, way more than that. You were like kind. And it helped me. It helped me so much, Christina. In ways that I'd need like the twelve thousand semitones of dolphin language to articulate. And I'm sure that with all the guys or johns or clients or whatever you call your rotisserie of men that most of the time it's just a series of these like fast, pound-of-flesh experiences for you, but that's not what happened for me. It wasn't this like anecdote that American guys go over there to collect. They eat a few space cakes and fuck a window whore and get a tattoo of like a dagger or a yin-yang sign or a fucking stallion getting struck by lightning. That's not what it was about for me. It was way bigger than that. And it was way bigger than a play or a paperback novel or like some precious cultural artifact or whatever. It was bigger than anything I could ever fucking write about. I mean, I spend most of my time in my head, like trapped with my own fucking terrible, spiritually corrosive thoughts. And sure, I know a lot of people suffer and have constant nightmares and mental illness and horrible crushing madness or whatever, but for some reason, it's not easy for me. To be with those thoughts, I mean. And sometimes disappearing seems like the only fucking answer. Just like ending it, you know? I used to wish that I could make a painting of a dog eating spaghetti or like write a haiku or a fucking play that would push those thoughts out of my head permanently, but I could never figure it out...But after I met you I...I don't know, I just felt like I could sort of be in the world again. And it made things in my head, I don't know...like slow down for a while. And I don't even know why. I mean, I hardly know you, but at the same time I do. Something happened in that room in Amsterdam. And I know this is going to sound like some totally New Age Carlos Castaneda psychic cookbook or something, but sometimes I close my eyes and send you thoughts. I'll be like, "Hey, Christina. I hope you're doing well. I hope everything's going good for you in that city you live in...Stay safe, okay?...I love you." And I've been doing this thing lately where I imagine what you were like as a little girl. In Baltimore or whatever. Like flying a fucking kite or smashing chocolate cake on your coloring book or making a lemonade sign or eating crayons under the patio furniture or whatever.

CHRISTINA   I never had patio furniture.

MATT   So I'll nix the patio furniture. We can make it a picnic table.

CHRISTINA   And my name's not Christina.

MATT   So there's a vowel change. Christine's just as pretty.

CHRISTINA   It's not Christine, either.

MATT   Oh. Well, what is it?

CHRISTINA   Annie.

MATT   Annie?

[*She nods.*]

MATT   So I can adjust to that...I suddenly feel like you should show me your ID or something.

        [CHRISTINA *reaches into her bag, removes her passport, opens it. He looks at it for a moment.*]

        Are you really from Baltimore?

CHRISTINA   Aberdeen.

MATT   And you're really sick?

CHRISTINA   Yes.

MATT   So I'll start calling you Annie, it's a minor adjustment...And I'll tell you one more thing, because what the hell I've already said too much, and then I'll shut up and go get us some food.

CHRISTINA   What?

MATT   I sleep with your dress. The red one that you changed into that night in Amsterdam. You left it in our room. I was going to return it to you the next day but I couldn't. I rolled it up in a towel and like absconded with it. I actually sleep with it, Christina. I mean, Christine. I mean, Annie. Because it has this smell. Like sesame oil and hairspray and frozen cigarettes. And there's this faint clove thing going on too.

        [*He starts to turn the covers of the bed down.*]

        I like tuck it into the bed every morning and—

CHRISTINA   It's hanging in the closet.

MATT   You're right, it is hanging in the closet. It's totally hanging there, you know why? Because I fucking put it on last night. I actually put on your red dress because I wanted to feel what it was like to be inside you again. I actually slept in it and it was like we were holding each other or like slow-dancing or something. That kind of slow-dancing where you hardly move and you just sort of lean up against each other because you need the other person that fucking bad. And I couldn't wait for tonight. Till I got tired. I take these pills now to help me sleep and I was going to take them earlier than usual because I couldn't wait to be inside you again. You see, because sleeping is the one thing I look forward to anymore. Because I get to be with you. And then tonight there's this knock on my door and here you are... I'm sorry, I'm totally rambling. And now my hands are like shaking. What are you hungry for anyway—you want a cheeseburger?

[CHRISTINA *nods.*]

Cool. Anything else? Fries? A pickle?

[*She shakes her head. He pulls a hat out of his coat pocket, puts it on, stands there for a moment.*]

Was that okay? All that stuff that I just spewed?

CHRISTINA Sure.

MATT Because I'm glad I told you.

CHRISTINA Me too.

MATT So I'll be right back... Are you gonna be okay?

[*She nods.*]

Are you warm enough?

[*She nods.*]

Cool. Then I'll just go then.

[MATT *crosses to the front door, starts to open the door, stops, turns back.*]

So don't, um, like leave, okay?

[MATT *exits.* CHRISTINA *removes the afghan and crosses to his makeshift closet. She opens the closet door, removes the red dress, pulls it off its hanger, stares at it for a moment. Then she undresses, puts the dress on, crosses to the kitchen, uses the small mirror to fix her hair. She pinches her cheeks to give some color to her face. She stands before the mirror for a long moment. There is a knock at the door. A* MALE VOICE *can be heard.*]

VOICE Matt?

[*More knocking.*]

Hey, Matt!... Come on. Wake up, nerd, I need my cell.

[*Suddenly, the door flies open kung-fu style.* DAVIS *is standing in the entrance. He is wearing nice clothes, a good leather jacket.*]

DAVIS Hi.

[CHRISTINA *stands there.*]

Is Matt around?

[*She shakes her head. He enters, closes the door.*]

He's not?

[*She shakes her head.*]

Really.

[*She nods.*]

Do you know where he is?

[*She shakes her head.*]

Was he here earlier?

[*She nods.*]

How long ago did he leave?

[*She holds up ten fingers.*]

Ten minutes ago?

[*She nods.*]

What are you supposed to be, like a prom mime or something?

CHRISTINA   [*With a French accent, from now on.*] He just left.

DAVIS   Oh. Is he coming back?

CHRISTINA   I think he is, yes.

DAVIS   Do I know you?

CHRISTINA   We met last winter.

DAVIS   We did? Where?

CHRISTINA   Amsterdam.

DAVIS   Oh. Really?

CHRISTINA   You don't remember?

DAVIS   I don't, no. I mean, I met a lot of people in Amsterdam.

CHRISTINA   Well, I remember you very well.

DAVIS   Wait, were you that guide at the Anne Frank museum? The one in the corduroy jumpsuit who kept calling the attic a fucking garret?

CHRISTINA   No.

DAVIS   You sure?

CHRISTINA   I am positive.

DAVIS   Oh, wait a minute. Fuck me with a curling iron, you're that chick who threw a plate of Swedish pancakes at me.

CHRISTINA   No.

DAVIS Yes.

CHRISTINA No.

DAVIS Yeah. Because I called you a Dutch cunt.

CHRISTINA I'm not Dutch.

DAVIS No, I know. You're actually from Brussels or you're like Czech or Hungarian or something. But I called you a Dutch cunt and you threw that plate of Swedish pancakes at me and this very menstrual-looking Rorschach of strawberry sauce went all over this gabardine cowboy shirt I bought in Spain. Later we made out in the bathroom of that café with all those Marx Brothers pictures on the walls. Groucho's or Harpo's or fucking Flippo's or whatever it was called.

CHRISTINA I met you at the windows.

DAVIS Oh. You mean you're that whore?

CHRISTINA Yes.

DAVIS No shit?

CHRISTINA Christina.

DAVIS Yeah, Christina. Matt fucked you.

CHRISTINA So did you.

DAVIS Did I?

CHRISTINA Yes.

DAVIS Really? Wow. I must have been really fucking stoned or something because I can't place it. Was I good? Just kidding.

Um, I actually came by to grab my cell phone. I don't have to have some like international Frog search warrant to get by, do I?

[*He crosses to the kitchen, starts hunting, grabs the milk that* MATT *had left out for tea, sniffs at it, drinks a slug.*]

So how are you? *Comment allez-vous? Ça va bien?*

CHRISTINA   I'm good, thank you. And you?

DAVIS   I'm fucking happy as a handshake. Just trying to beat the snow. We're in for a pretty big storm tonight...

[*Crossing to the mini-fridge with the milk.*]

Hey, do you ever get snow in Amsterdam?

CHRISTINA   Sometimes, yes. But it...how do you say—disappears?

DAVIS   Melts?

CHRISTINA   Yes. It melts very quickly. And the channels rarely freeze.

[*From the mini-fridge he removes a squeezable bottle of ketchup, removes the milk cap, squeezes some ketchup into the milk, puts the milk cap back on, sets the milk and the ketchup back in the mini-fridge.*]

DAVIS   Yeah, I can't quite imagine anyone ice-skating there. Stoners on skates.

[DAVIS *moves to the bed. From a crate, he flings a few pairs of underwear behind him. He looks under the bed. He sifts through* MATT's *various piles of things.*]

So how long are you in New York for?

CHRISTINA   Not long.

DAVIS   Just passing through?

CHRISTINA Yes.

DAVIS Business or pleasure?

CHRISTINA Pleasure.

DAVIS Plaisir. Hey, if you're looking for clients I have a couple of lonely friends I could probably set you up with. Big, beefy guys with bad hair. Smart fuckers, though.

CHRISTINA No thank you.

DAVIS *Non merci.* Are you still hooking?

CHRISTINA No.

DAVIS What, you had some sort of come-to-Jesus moment or something? A little too much viscosity down low?... Viscosity is this friction thing that happens in sports cars. High engine viscosity. It's an old Quaker State commercial. Or maybe it's Pennzoil... Oh, right. Wrong country. Sorry.

[DAVIS *crosses to* MATT*'s desk, starts rooting through his stuff, picking up papers, etc.*]

Look at all this shit. Used Kleenex. Mylanta. Robitussin. Benadryl. It's like a fucking supply depot for insomniac, tubercular neurotics.

[*Touching the books.*]

A Fan's Notes. Crazy Cock. Ask the Fucking Dust... You know he reads the same authors over and over again? John Fante, Frederick Exley, Henry Miller. How ironic, right? I mean, these guys lived crazy lives. They were these demented, alcoholic, promiscuous fucking apes who had syphilis and got crabs and fell asleep in dive bars and camped on people's sofas and Matt like cloisters off in this monastic cell like some malnourished warlock and picks lint out of his navel and stares out the window for several hours a day. You'd think he'd take a little stock in his heroes. Let it rip every once in a while. I can't even get him to go to the fucking movies with me anymore.

CHRISTINA   Maybe he is just shy.

DAVIS   Maybe he's just a big fucking pussy who thinks too much. The guy needs to stop living in his head. He's really starting to lose touch.

[DAVIS *crosses back to the kitchen, takes a clean dishrag, stuffs it down his pants, puts it back on the kitchen counter.*]

So how'd you track him down, anyway?

CHRISTINA   It was a mistake.

DAVIS   Oh yeah? How's that?

CHRISTINA   I was looking for you.

DAVIS   Really?

CHRISTINA   Yes.

DAVIS   I don't get it.

CHRISTINA   In Amsterdam I asked for your address.

DAVIS   And I gave you Matt's?

CHRISTINA   Yes.

DAVIS   God, I'm such a dick, right?

[DAVIS *crosses back to* MATT's *desk, turns up* MATT's *computer screen, touches the touch pad. The screen is illuminated. He reads.*]

What the fuck is this freak writing now?

[*Scrolling down.*]

He's got some character named Davison. Hmmm, I wonder who that could be?

[*While reading.*]

So why were you looking for me, anyway—do I owe you money?

CHRISTINA   I missed you.

DAVIS   Davison, Matthews, and Yildiz? What is he writing, a fucking autobiographical klezmer musical? I can just hear the dueling accordions.

[*He starts to type.*]

CHRISTINA   Do you have a cigarette?

DAVIS   No.

CHRISTINA   Did you quit smoking?

DAVIS   No... Fucking things are seven bucks a pack now.

[DAVIS *continues typing.* CHRISTINA *starts to gather her things. She doesn't bother putting anything on; she simply gathers them in her arms and starts for the door.*]

Walrus.

[CHRISTINA *stops dead in her tracks.* DAVIS *then reaches into his jacket pocket, removes a pack of cigarettes, offers her one. She sets her things down by the door, crosses to him, accepts the cigarette. He produces a lighter, lights her. He takes one for himself, lights it. They smoke.*]

CHRISTINA   What did you type?

DAVIS [*Reading off the screen.*] I typed, Dear Matt-slash-Matthews, comma, If you're going to use the platform of your art to lampoon your friends, comma, perhaps it's high time to revisit your chosen vocation, full stop. I would be happy to take some Polaroids of myself in a Speedo, comma, pubes a-bursting, comma, so you can hang them on the door of your two-and-a-half-foot refrigerator, full stop. This way you wouldn't have to write an entire eighty-four-page play in order to make an ass of your best friend, full stop. You might also want to get a little craftier with your character names, full stop. Quote, Davison, unquote, and quote, Matthews, unquote, is about as subtle as an erect horse cock bobbing along the cliffs of the Costa Brava, full stop. Also, comma, your dialogue is starting to sort of suck, full stop. I would advise revisiting some Eugene O'Neill, comma, or might I recommend William Inge, comma, or even Li'l Abner, full stop. Return, return. Yours in editorial sleuthing, comma, return, return, Davis-slash-Davison, return, return. P.S., full stop. I deleted a few lines that sucked, full stop. And I found my cell phone, full stop.

[*He lowers the laptop screen.*]

Pretty good, right?

CHRISTINA [*Almost losing the accent.*] Why do you pretend to be so cruel?

DAVIS What?

CHRISTINA You're not a cruel person.

DAVIS Really.

CHRISTINA You are kind and I know this to be true.

DAVIS You do, do you?

CHRISTINA   Yes.

DAVIS   Interesting.

CHRISTINA   You are only sad.

DAVIS   I'm sad? What is this, some sort of Christian youth group intervention?

[CHRISTINA *goes into her purse bag, removes the globe he had given her during their first encounter. He crosses to her.*]

What's that?

[*Taking it from her.*]

Yeah, this is that piece of shit I bought at that knickknack shop in Paris. I didn't feel like taking it on the plane. That shop was brilliant. They had like David Hasselhoff action-figure dolls with bulges.

CHRISTINA   You are not a cruel person, Davis.

DAVIS   What, you think you know me?

CHRISTINA   I do, yes.

DAVIS   Well, I'll tell you something, Chiquita or Chitaqua or whatever your name—

CHRISTINA   Christina.

DAVIS   I'll tell you something, Christina. You're an idiot. You think you know me because I let you tea-bag my nuts for a few minutes? Because I stuck my finger up your ass while I fucked you like the whore you are?

CHRISTINA   We made love.

DAVIS   We made love. I was fucking bored and I felt sorry for you!

[*He drops the snow globe in the trash. She turns away, then turns back to him, her fists clenched.*]

Oh, what. You're gonna hit me? . . . Go ahead. Hit me.

[*She suddenly hugs him, holding on for dear life. He pushes her to the floor. She comes back to him, trying to kiss him. He stops her, pushes her away. She tries again. He seizes her arm, a momentary struggle, and then he pulls her close and they begin making out, which moves to the bed. It is very passionate for a moment. They are both aroused and relieved. She kisses him. He turns away. She kisses him again. After a moment,* DAVIS *pulls her off the bed, sweeps the books off of* MATT's *desk, turns her around, hikes her dress up, and folds her over* MATT's *desk. He takes his pants down, spits in his hand, rubs her, and starts to take her from behind. They both get lost in it. It might be the best and worst thing they've ever felt. After several thrusts,* DAVIS's *cell phone rings. Still inside* CHRISTINA, DAVIS *covers her mouth and answers his cell.*]

Hi, honey . . . Yeah . . . Yeah . . . I'm over at Matt's . . . Yeah, I just got it. I left it on his bookshelf. He probably used up all my minutes, the little leech . . . Oh, I'm a little out of breath, I just ran up the stairs. I'll meet you there in about twenty minutes . . . I love you too.

[DAVIS *hangs up, uncovers her mouth. She is devastated. He thrusts a few more times, comes, stays inside her for a moment, and then pulls out. He pulls his pants up, stands there for a long moment.* CHRISTINA *remains folded over* MATT's *desk, her face down.*]

Well, that was weird . . .

[*Using the afghan to wipe his hands.*]

I should probably go wash my dick, right? . . . That was a joke . . . So I better go . . . If you see Matt, tell him I came by . . . Are you okay?

[*She doesn't respond.*]

I didn't hurt you, did I?

[*She doesn't respond.*]

Cool . . . I'm not a good person, Christina.

[*She doesn't respond.*]

Well, good luck then. *Bon suar. Au revoir.*

[DAVIS *exits, closing the door.* CHRISTINA *slowly lifts herself off the desk, sits in the chair, in shock. She spots her old portable cassette player, presses a button. Tom Waits's "Jitterbug Boy" plays. She listens. Just as he starts singing, she presses Stop, sits in silence. She then spots the bottle of sleeping pills, considers them for a moment, takes them in her hand, and then rises off the chair, crosses to the door, her dress half-zipped, opens the door, exits toward the fire escape, leaving the door open. In the window we can see that it has started to snow. Moments later,* MATT *enters, carrying a few deli bags of groceries and takeout food. He sets the groceries down on the milk crate, looks around the room. He opens the door, exits to the shower room. Moments later, we see him quickly pass by the doorway, toward the fire escape. He re-enters, closes the door, and crosses to the closet, opens it, stares at the hanger that was holding the dress, removes his hat. After a moment, he slowly crosses to the desk and sits. He presses a button on the portable cassette player. Tom Waits's "Jitterbug Boy" resumes from where* CHRISTINA *had stopped it. Lights fade as the snow falls across the window.*]

• • •

Who You Got
to Believe

Charlene A. Donaghy

Charlene A. Donaghy

Charlene Donaghy's play, *Who You Got to Believe*, has been in the Association for Theater in Higher Education New Play Development Workshop in Los Angeles. Her play, *Trinity*, received a finalist award in the New Orleans Saints and Sinners Literary Festival. Her other writings have been honored by the Writers' Workshop of Asheville, North Carolina, and featured in numerous publications including *In the Eye: A Collection of Writings*. Charlene holds a master of fine arts in writing for stage and screen from Lesley University in Cambridge, Massachusetts, and a baccalaureate of arts in creative writing and literature from Vermont College. She is the Director of Production for the Provincetown, Tennesee Williams Theater Festival and a stage manager at various venues. Charlene teaches writing and stage management and is a member of the Dramatists Guild, the Association for Theatre in Higher Education, the Association of Writers and Writing Programs and the Playwrights' Center. She is a breast cancer survivor, resides in Connecticut, and her second home, the magical city of New Orleans, is and forever will be the muse for her art.

characters

KATHLEEN, Caucasian woman in her late 60s

RAY, African American man in his early 60s

time

A spring night. 2010.

setting

New Orleans, LA. A short set of distressed concrete steps surrounded by tall weeds is illuminated at center stage. Near the stairs is a pile of moldering trash items, including a handkerchief, a dog collar, and old Mardi Gras beads.

• • •

[*At rise: The lights come up as* KATHLEEN *slowly wanders in from stage right. She is noticeably disheveled. She is humming "When the Saints Go Marching In." Thunder is heard in the distance. She stops abruptly at the steps, her humming immediately cuts off. She looks about, bewildered.*]

KATHLEEN I's home.

> [*Looks around, walks downstage of steps.*]

Living room.

> [*Turns slowly, shocked, confused at what she does and does not see.*]

Kitchen? Bedroom?

> [*Crosses to the pile of items, pokes with foot, picks up an old handkerchief, looks at it, sniffs, trying to recognize it.*]

Don't smell like me no more. Smells older than me. If that even be possible.

> [*Shakes out the handkerchief, stuffs it into her bosom, pokes pile, and spots something, focuses, picks up the dog collar. She strokes it, shakily touches it to her heart.*]

Mojo?

[*Wanders as if searching.*]

Mojo!

[*Beat as she places the dog collar around her wrist.*]

You prob'ly long gone, you. I didn't want to leave you. I sorry. I sorry. I keep lookin' for you...maybe you comes home to me. That's what I hopes, anyways.

[*Walks around the pile, picks up several strands of old Mardi Gras beads, and places them around her neck.*]

My place...my home...my steps.

[KATHLEEN *hums "When the Saints Go Marching In" and looks around, lost.* RAY, *in dirty work clothes and light rain jacket, carrying a well-worn small cooler and a stepladder, enters. He stops a few feet from* KATHLEEN, *looks around, following her eyes.*]

RAY   Where y'at?

[*Moves closer to her.*]

Hey, chére, I say where y'at? You okay?

[*Sets cooler down.*]

It's fixin' to rain, be gettin' dark soon. This ain't no safe place for anybody to be in the dark, alone, not no more, anyway. You got someplace to go? You got people?

KATHLEEN   People gone.

RAY   You got a house? Place to stay, keep you dry?

KATHLEEN   They told me I would...but I don't.

RAY   Who they?

[RAY *crosses away from* KATHLEEN, *opens and places stepladder, then crosses back to* KATHLEEN.]

KATHLEEN   All of 'em. They all say it. We gonna take care of you, Miss B. Don't you worry now, we give you money and food and we fix your home right fast. I bet they say it to you, too.

RAY   People say lot a things, chére.

KATHLEEN   This ... this is my home ... what's left of it. Now I own me a nice set a steps.

[*Sits on the steps, caressing them.*]

Don't you think these steps is nice?

RAY   They nice enough, far as steps goes, but not a place for you to be settin' all by yo'self.

KATHLEEN   They the best steps in the world. They my steps, this my neighborhood.

RAY   [*Looks around.*] Was, one time, surely was.

KATHLEEN   Is! Is! What you doin' out here in my place, you, anyways, bothering me? I ain't doin' nothin'.

RAY   I volunteer cleaning up. You know, same things we been doin' around here goin' over four years now.

KATHLEEN   I don't know nothin'. They ship me off to some place in Utah. Pretty country out there, but what a old Cajun woman like me goin' to do in Utah, alone, with no Mojo to keeps me comp'ny? I got no good andouille to cooks jambalaya with, no Mormon ever heard of boudin, and they think I's fixin' to be crazy when I asks for a po'boy dressed. No idea what that is, them.

[RAY *chuckles. He opens his cooler, takes out a half po'boy sandwich, and passes it to* KATHLEEN. *She looks from it to* RAY. *She takes a strand of beads from around her neck and hands it to* RAY. *He nods in appreciation and places it around his neck.* KATHLEEN *then takes a few bites of the po'boy while looking about.*]

I ain't askin' for much, no, me. I keep goin' all my life bein' one-woman maid, one-woman cook, one-woman dressmaker, I don't like no handouts, me. I's only had to take care a myself my whole life. Me and Mojo.

[*Pets the dog collar on her arm, then eyes* RAY *up and down, assessing him.*]

Never met a man I could stand more than a few years, and I ain't got no use for children. Least that's what I tells myself after the doctor took out my insides. Neighbors all gone now, so just me, alone, wondering why it been four years, goin' *past* four years, why the only thing settin' here now be these concrete steps?

[*Pause—looks lovingly at steps.*]

They nice steps, though, don't ya think?

RAY   They nice. But they not a safe place to be, chére, and we gonna be gettin' wet soon. Storm clouds on the way.

KATHLEEN   Storm already rolled in. Rolled out. Rolled over us.

[*Lights up on stepladder.* KATHLEEN *rises, crosses to it, and climbs a few rungs.*]

I had me a hurricane protection policy. Cuttin' me a hole in the roof . . . right about here. Just big enough for my head to fit through so I could breathe. Young coast guard boy flies in a big old helicopter come saves me.

[*Sounds of helicopter and lapping water.*]

I hears ya good enough. And I can see ya a little. I'm not blind.

[*Beat.*]

Young man, I's in my attic. My house is flooded. Do I look alright?

[*Beat.*]

This hole not big enough for me. And what about Mojo here? You got to get us both out, you know.

[*Beat as dog barks.*]

Don't you say Mojo ain't comin' with me, you. I won't have it. He my bébe.

[*Beat as dog barks.*]

Well, if'n you goin' to open it up more, we be stepping back a bit. You best hurry up. Water's risin'.

[RAY *shakes his head.* KATHLEEN *descends, crosses to concrete steps, sits: the stepladder lights, helicopter, and water sounds fade out.* RAY *sits beside her.*]

RAY Water's risin'. I tells my Micheleisha when we start to see it oozing in. I want to protect her, get her to safety. Course, once she gets an idea in her head, she like that stubborn old McDonogh oak in City Park. I tells her to come to the attic, that I leave her, leave her and get in the attic alone, if she don't. Just tryin' to get her to listen to reason, ya know?

[*Beat.*]

She saw the men, boys really, taking her bike. Sixty-four year old and she ride that bike every day. Let 'em have it, I says, and the car too. No. She rush outside; I come down the ladder, almost get to the front door...

[*Sound of single gunshot.*]

I couldn't protect her.

KATHLEEN You didn't know what those boys would do, you. Couldn't know.

RAY   Maybe I'll believe that when I see her in the promised land.

[*Beat.*]

Course, she always goin' to be with me long as I stay here. Always my heart. We was together just shy o' forty years. Gawd, I miss that woman, loved her like red beans love rice.

KATHLEEN   I sorry for your loss.

RAY   I sorry for all our loss...and thank you.

[*Rises, offers a hand to help* KATHLEEN *up.*]

I best be gettin' on back to my trailer. I can't leave you here, chére, it ain't safe. Can I take you someplace?

KATHLEEN   I told you, I got no place to go.

RAY   How'd you get here?

KATHLEEN   I ain't worked in a hound's age, but I got me a tax refund in the mail. I hide it under my mattress figuring the gov'ment gonna want it back. But when they don't, I head to the check casher quicker than a coconut fling from a Zulu float. So I got me a Greyhound ticket and then a taxi cab from U.P. Terminal right here to my li'l Alice Court, even though the driver keep sayin' he don't want to be ridin' out here and leavin' me off in the middle of nowheres. I tell him this ain't nowheres, this here be my home.

[*Looks around, bewildered.*]

My home. Me and these here steps.

[*Pats the steps.*]

They nice steps, solid, strong, they last through anything, these here steps.

RAY   We workin' on gettin' better, sure enough are, but still lots a work to be done.

[*Beat—looks around, then looks at* KATHLEEN.]

Didn't you know nothin' been done to your home yet?

KATHLEEN   How's I 'spose to know, way out in Utah? Nothin' on the TV no more. Nobody carin', people think we all right. Nobody tellin' me nothin', 'cept the gov'ment peoples and I don't trust them no way, no more. So I come find out for myself.

RAY   Trick is figuring out who you got to believe.

KATHLEEN   I believed 'em all. And now look where I is.

RAY   Chére, let me takes you on over to my church. We good peoples there, all together like family. Miss Sally, the min'sters wife, can fix you up some gumbo and we find you a place to stay tonight, someplace safe and dry.

KATHLEEN   No place safe and dry. I gonna stay right here for when they start to build me my house back. I want 'em to know this is my place, my home, my steps.

RAY   You just says you don't trust the gov'ment to fix this. Trust *me*. Please. We need to be on our way. What's your name, chére? I'm Ray.

KATHLEEN   You don't need to be knowin' me that much, you. I knows me. I says what I says. I believes what I believes. I knows what I knows. I'm staying home, not leavin' no more.

RAY   But they ain't gonna be buildin' round these parts for a long time, if ever.

KATHLEEN   Don't you say that! Don't you say that to me, you! They promise they gonna take care o' me, they promise and I's gonna hold 'em to it. I is! And I ain't leavin', again. I ain't.

[*Takes the handkerchief from her bosom and wrings it in her hands.*]

Now you just go away and leave a old woman alone right here. Why you even stop and talk to me, you? I just mindin' my own business, settin' on my steps, *my steps*, and you comes and bothers me. I ain't doin' nothing' wrong 'cept maybe waitin' for my Mojo. He might come home, ya know. And you, I don't needs you. No, I don't!

[*Pause as* RAY *ponders his decision to leave her or stay. He crosses to stepladder, folds it under his arm, crosses back to cooler.*]

RAY   You surely ain't done nothin' wrong, chére, but I don't want to be leavin' you out here all alone. It ain't right.

[*Pause as* RAY *looks at* KATHLEEN. *He picks up his cooler.*]

Chére? Please.

[KATHLEEN *rubs the steps with her old handkerchief.* RAY *begins to leave towards stage left. She lies down on the steps and starts humming "When the Saints Go Marching In." He stops. He turns back to look at her, sets the ladder and cooler down, crosses to her, takes off his jacket, and places it around her. He sits beside her and sings a verse to "When the Saints Go Marching In" in tune with* KATHLEEN's *humming.*]

We are trav'ling in the footsteps
Of those who've gone before,
And we'll all be reunited
On a new and sunlit shore

[RAY *and* KATHLEEN *hum. As the thunder grows louder, lights fade.*]

• • •

Ella

Dano Madden

Dano Madden

Dano Madden grew up in Boise, Idaho. His play *Beautiful American Soldier* was a finalist for the National New Play Network's 2010 Smith Prize. His plays have been produced by Actors Theatre of Louisville, The Source Festival, Mile Square Theatre, Burnt Studio Productions, Northwest Playwrights Alliance, Idaho Theatre for Youth, Kitchen Theatre Company, Rutgers University, the University of Tulsa, and the Samuel French Off-Off Broadway Festival, among others. Dano's plays have received readings and/or development at Seattle Repertory Theatre, Lark Play Development Center, Seven Devils Playwrights Conference, Boise Contemporary Theater, Boston Theatre Works, and the Last Frontier Theatre Conference. He is a two-time Heideman Award finalist. Dano's Kennedy Center awards include: the 2007 National Student Playwriting Award for *In the Sawtooths*, the 2008 Quest for Peace Playwriting Award for *Beautiful American Soldier*, and the 1997 National Short Play Award for *Drop*. Published works include: *In the Sawtooths* and *Drop* (Samuel French, Inc.), *Beautiful American Soldier* (*Best American Short Plays 2005–2006*), *Ella* (*Best American Short Plays 2009–2010*), *The Save* (Playscripts, Inc.), *The Soft Sand* (Northwest Playwrights Alliance), *Survival* (Northwest Playwrights Alliance) and several monologues (Smith and Kraus, *The Best Men's Stage Monologues and Scenes 2010*). He was the recipient of the 2001 Idaho Commission on the Arts Fellowship in Playwriting. In 2007, Dano was named one of "50 Playwrights to Watch" by *The Dramatist* magazine. He received his BA from Boise State University and his MFA from Rutgers University. Dano was the 2008–2009 National New Play Network playwright-in-residence at Interact Theatre Company. He is an adjunct professor of playwriting at Stockton College and at the Playwrights Horizons Theatre School/NYU. Dano lives in Hoboken, New Jersey, with his favorite person in the world, Lauren.

···production note···

Ella was originally produced by the Rutgers Theater Company in the Jameson Studio Theatre. It was directed by Chris O'Connor; the setting was designed by Kina Park; the costumes were designed by Ellen Pittman Stockbridge; the lighting was designed by Laura L. Cornish; the stage manager was Alison M. Roberts. The cast was as follows:

ELLA   Kianné Muschett
MATTY   Mark Hairston
VANESSA   Tai Bosmond
CUTTER   Josh Clayton
CHARLES   Will Schmincke

Acknowledgments: Lee Blessing, Eric Brooks, Chris Connors, Tiffany Connors, Sharon Farrell, Stephen Gnojewski, Peter Hanrahan, Gerald Hensley, John Madden, Jerry Madden, Alice Madden, Kianné Muschett, Justin Ness, Dawn Nicholas, Sarah Kate O'Haver, Isaac Perelson, Katie Pietrzak, Jason Pietrzak, Nicholas Pietrzak, Allie Pietrzak, Joe Novak, Sheri Novak, Nick Garcia, Amy Saltz, Lauren Singerman, Lane Smith, Addie Walsh, Samuel Brett Williams, and Bryan Willis.

characters

ELLA, an African American woman, 29

MATTY, an African American man, Ella's ex-husband, 30

VANESSA, Ella's sister and a student at the University of Washington, 22

CUTTER, a white Florida farm boy, 19

CHARLES, a student at the University of Washington, 22

place

An apartment in Seattle, Washington

time

Close to the loneliest holidays

A note about the text: The longer monologues in the play are laid out on the page in a way that is contrary to the traditional "block" format. This is in an attempt to indicate changes in idea, rhythm, or to emphasize a specific word or phrase. The space in between lines is not specifically there to indicate a beat or a pause.

For performance of copyrighted songs, arrangements, or recordings mentioned in this play, the permission of the copyright owner(s) must be obtained.

• • •

[*Lights up on a bedroom. There are stacks of empty boxes. There is also a table with a large lump of clay on it.* ELLA, *a 29-year-old African American woman, stares at the clay. She occasionally moves around the lump for a different point of view.*]

[*Beat.*]

ELLA   Step one: A brilliant idea. Simple. Nothing huge. Just a simple, brilliant idea.

[*Pause.* ELLA *stares at the clay.*]

Fine. Just an idea. A stupid idea. I'll take a stupid idea. My ideas are never brilliant anyway. Maybe on occasion for a brief, rare moment, my ideas are brilliant. At the moment of conception.

But not now. Nothing.

Okay. Okay.

I know I can still do this.

I hope I can still do this.

New step one: Just start. That's worked before. Ready, and . . .

Begin. Clay. Fingers. Shape. Find a rhythm.

Fingers to clay and shape. Anything. A donut. A snake. Just something to regain a feel. It doesn't matter. It doesn't matter.

Why is this clay so cold?

Come on . . . fingertips and shape. Oh, please. Just one idea.

I've forgotten how.

Something, something, something.

You are something. Anything.

[ELLA *sits and stares at the clay. Ella Fitzgerald music begins to quietly play.* MATTY, *a handsome 30-year-old African American man, enters. He wears a tuxedo and a classic black top hat.* ELLA *closes her eyes as* MATTY *stares at her.*]

[*There is a knock at the door.*]

VANESSA Hello? Hello, hello?

[*At the sound of* VANESSA's *voice,* MATTY *begins to slowly disappear.*]

VANESSA Hello?

ELLA Yes? Hello?

[ELLA *continues to stare at the clay.*]

VANESSA Can I come in?

[VANESSA *pokes her head in. She is 22 and bouncy.*]

VANESSA Hi.

ELLA Hi.

VANESSA Oh, wow. You're pretty much unpacked. That was fast. We can, if you need some shelves for some of this stuff, these books, I know some good places we can go. So many books!

ELLA Yeah.

VANESSA   I, umm... I'm going to have a few people over tonight. From the biology department. We finished finals yesterday and I thought it might be nice to have a little Christmas get-together.

My friend Jannie is already here. She's helping me set up. She is so smart. Maybe the smartest person I've ever met. She saved me on my advanced biology final. Saved me. We had to basically label all the parts of these sea creatures. Anything you can imagine. Sharks. Shrimp. Clams. And it wasn't just, just labeling parts. We had to write short essays about how the parts functioned as well. Four hours of testing. Jannie saved me. Her notes were so good. She remembered everything. That girl is a sponge.

[VANESSA *laughs*.]

Sponge. Get it?

[*Beat.*]

So you should come down. You should. A small gathering, but really fun, upbeat people.

[*Beat.*]

What's this gonna be?

[VANESSA points at the clay.]

ELLA   I... I don't know yet.

VANESSA   I remember that bowl on the mantle, the one you made in high school.

ELLA   I've made a lot more since then. Lots. Better than bowls.

VANESSA   Sure, sure. I remember Mom telling me about it.

ELLA   I'm going to try and work tonight.

VANESSA   Work? Your room seems almost done. What are you
       going to work on?

[ELLA *points to the clay.*]

VANESSA   Oh. Clay. Wow. Okay. Right.

       [*Beat.*]

       Do you like Seattle so far?

ELLA   It's—

VANESSA   People say it rains too much. It's depressing. I don't know,
       though. I stay pretty upbeat. What about you?

ELLA   I just got here.

VANESSA   Of course. The gray is nice. I think you'll like the gray
       sky. It hardly ever gets to be too cold here.

ELLA   I was just getting started.

VANESSA   Oh, I'm sorry. I don't mean to bother you.

       [*Beat.*]

       Ummmm... Mom called again. She... she and Dad are just
       wondering what's going on. So I just said, I told her you're
       fine. But... I think you should call.

ELLA   I will.

VANESSA   Okay. Yeah. Because they think you're just visiting. For a
       few weeks.

ELLA   Yeah.

VANESSA   So. I don't want to... I mean, it's none of my business. If
       you want, I can just tell them about how you're planning to
       stay.

ELLA   No. I'll take care of it.

VANESSA   Okay. I really don't mean to bother you about it.

[*Beat.*]

ELLA   I'd, I'd sort of like to get to work . . . if that's okay.

VANESSA   Yes, yes, of course. Do you have a deadline or something?

ELLA   No. Just—I just need to work.

VANESSA   Sorry.

> [VANESSA *begins to exit.*]
> Oh, Ella?

ELLA   Yes?

VANESSA   There's going to be a lot of single guys downstairs. Cute guys. Yes, science majors, but no, no, not nerds. I swear. It might be fun for you, good for you. A little flirting.

ELLA   How old are these guys?

VANESSA   Ummm . . . pretty good ages. Normal ages. The same age as other people.

ELLA   Twenty-one? Twenty-two?

VANESSA   Mostly. But no one has to know your age, not that your age is bad, and I haven't told anyone what's going on with you. Well, I told Jannie, but that's it.

ELLA   No thank you.

VANESSA   Cool. Okay. But if you change your mind, we have cider and eggnog and Secret Santa gifts—I wrapped a few extra, just in case. I can even make sure you get something you like. Do you like products? Facial cleanser or glittery lip balm or pineapple-peach body lotion?

ELLA Not so much.

VANESSA Sorry. Sorry. I'll go.

ELLA Thank you.

VANESSA Okay. See you downstairs. Maybe.

[VANESSA *exits. She pokes her head back in.*]

Bye. I'm really glad you're here.

[ELLA *is alone. She walks to the clay. She stares at it for a moment. She begins to poke at the clay as Ella Fitzgerald music gently rises. MATTY enters, doing a little jig to the music. ELLA begins to pound the clay. First lightly and then very hard in an attempt to ignore MATTY.*]

[*A knock at the door.*]

VANESSA Ella?

[MATTY *smiles and disappears.*]

VANESSA [*Singing.*] Ell-a.

ELLA Yes.

[VANESSA *pokes her head in.*]

VANESSA Our first guest has just arrived! I thought you might like to meet him.

ELLA Oh, Vanessa, I'd rather—

VANESSA This is Charles.

[CHARLES *enters. He is a nerd. Please pardon the stereotype, but he is 22 and he came directly from the lab.*]

CHARLES   Uh, hello.

[*Beat.*]

VANESSA   This is Ella.

ELLA   Vanessa—

CHARLES   Uh, Ella, so, uh, is that after—

ELLA   Yes, yes.

VANESSA   Ella Fitzgerald! Exactly!

CHARLES   Wow! Do you, uh, sing?

ELLA   No. No, I don't. I wish I did, but I don't. I've tried.

CHARLES   Oh, wow. I, uh, love music. Ella Fitzgerald is amazing. I teach a couple of, uh, calculus courses, introductory stuff, and I have a technique. A unique technique. I, well, when we, uh, tackle really difficult material, I, uh, sort of sneak some Ella Fitzgerald music on, or something classical, and if the students react or try to say something about the music, I say no, no. Focus on the problem. Let the music move you to solve. Solve, and I sort of whisper it. Solve, solve, solve.

ELLA   Vanessa.

CHARLES   I think math is musical.

ELLA   I hate math. And music.
        Vanessa.

[VANESSA *pushes* CHARLES *from the room.*]

CHARLES   Oh. Alright, see you later then.

[*She pokes her head back in.*]

VANESSA   Sorry. Sorry. He is a little odd. Sweet, but odd.

[VANESSA *exits.* ELLA *closes the door behind her.*]

ELLA   I'm okay—I'm okay—I'm okay—I'm okay—I'm okay.

> [ELLA *turns and* MATTY *is sitting on the bed. He smiles.* ELLA *looks at him for a moment and then returns to the clay, pounding.* MATTY *glides across the room until he is standing in front of* ELLA. *He poses as a model. Ella Fitzgerald music begins to play.*]
>
> Augh! Fuck Ella Fitzgerald! I'm okay—I'm okay—I'm okay— I'm okay—I'm okay.
>
> [*The bedroom door suddenly opens and* CUTTER *walks in. He is a 19-year-old Florida farm boy. His head is shaved in the traditional Marine style.*]
>
> I'm sorry. I'd rather not meet anyone else right now.
>
> [CUTTER *remains.*]
>
> Can I help you?

CUTTER   Where's the bathroom?

ELLA   Oh, there's one downstairs.

CUTTER   Someone's in there. They told me I could find one up here.

ELLA   Oh. Okay. Fine. There's one in here. Right over there.

> [CUTTER *crosses the room and enters the adjoining bathroom. The sound of urinating can be heard in the bathroom.*]
>
> I'm okay. I am okay.
>
> And you are something. You are something. Something else. You are something else.

Please, something else.

[ELLA *begins to dance around, attempting to cast a spell on the clay.*]

Something, something, something—

[CUTTER *comes out of the bathroom. He stares at* ELLA. *Her ritual continues for a moment before she notices him.*]

All finished?

CUTTER   Yeah.

ELLA   Okay.

[*Pause.*]

Look, can you just tell Vanessa . . . just tell her I want to be alone.

CUTTER   I'm Cutter.

ELLA   Fine. Can you just tell Vanessa I don't want to meet anyone else.

CUTTER   She told me there was party here tonight. You from down South too?

ELLA   Yes.

CUTTER   Where?

ELLA   North Carolina.

CUTTER   Florida.

ELLA   You're from Florida?

CUTTER   Yeah. Okeechobee.

ELLA   Aha. Okay. So the party's downstairs.

CUTTER   You Vanessa's sister?

ELLA   Yes.

CUTTER   What's yer name?

ELLA   Listen, I was just trying to explain to Vanessa—

CUTTER   Nice girl. Talks too much, but nice girl.

ELLA   Yes. I suppose. I was just telling her that I want to be alone—

CUTTER   What's yer name?

[*Beat.*]

ELLA   Ella.

CUTTER   Ella?

ELLA   Yes. After Ella Fitzgerald.

CUTTER   Who?

ELLA   Ella Fitzgerald. You know, famous singer?

CUTTER   Don't never heard of her.

ELLA   Oh? Interesting. So, the party is downstairs—

CUTTER   Shot me a gator.

ELLA   Excuse me?

CUTTER   Shot me a big gator. Out on Lake Okeechobee. My daddy takes all his sons, when they the right age. We in a boat movin' along, near the shore. Real late at night. We move real slow. I up front in the boat aimin' my gun. Night's black, gators is black. Then, all a sudden, I hear movement in the water. Bang! I shoot. Lots a splashin', water in the boat, I's soaked to the bone. Then nothin'. First try and I got him. We shined a light in the water. There he is, a real big boy. He got a fourteen-inch nose so we knows he a fourteen-footer. Nose size tells ya the whole size. Daddy slap me on the back, "Atta boy, Cutter! You a natural. Your brothers ain't got nothin' for aim. Atta boy!"

[*Beat.*]

ELLA   I'm sorry. Where did you come from?

CUTTER   Okeechobee.

ELLA   You were at the party?

CUTTER   Yes, ma'am.

ELLA   And you're a student? At UW?

CUTTER   No, ma'am.

ELLA   You're not?

CUTTER   Was. Waste a my time. Quit. Joined the military.
Daddy proud a me when I shot that gator. Straight 'tween his eyes.

ELLA   That's nice. Cutter, was it?

CUTTER   Yeah. Cutter.

ELLA   I actually have some work to do tonight.

CUTTER   That party's weird. No beer. No chips.

ELLA   Yes. Well, Vanessa apparently prefers wine and brie.

CUTTER   Nice enough girl, though.

ELLA   Yes, she seems to be.

CUTTER   You don't know?

ELLA   Not so much.

CUTTER   Isn't she your sister? I thought she was—

ELLA   She is my sister. But I haven't seen her in a long time.

CUTTER   Still yer sister.

ELLA   How do you know her?

CUTTER   Live next door. Or, I did. Leavin' tomorrow. Like I said, joined the military. Figure I got good aim. Make my daddy proud. I can shoot a gator tween the eyes. Same as shootin' a raghead.

ELLA   Great. Listen, I have work to do.

CUTTER   What sorta work you gotta do?

ELLA   That's none of your business.

[ELLA *is trying to steer* CUTTER *towards the door.*]

CUTTER   What the hell work you do on a Saturday night?

ELLA   I'm sure I'll see you around.

CUTTER   That party's boring as hell.

ELLA   I'm sure my sister only had the kindest intentions in inviting you. Holiday spirit. Reaching out to those in need.

CUTTER   All they does is talk about this experiment or that class or this degree or that. Don't mean nothin'.

ELLA   And shooting people does?

CUTTER   What the hell's that supposed to mean? Some people need to be shot. Like gators. Gators is a nuisance. Better to get rid of 'em before they have a chance to bite you in half. Protectin' you.

ELLA   Cutter, I have work to do.

CUTTER   What? You gotta problem with me protectin' you?

ELLA   No. Listen, if I want to talk, I'll come downstairs, okay?

CUTTER   I don't like that party.

[*Knocking.* VANESSA *enters.*]

VANESSA   Ella, I was just going to tell you that—

Oh. Hey, Cutter. You came.

CUTTER   Yeah.

VANESSA   I thought you said you were going to have company this weekend. Isn't your father in town?

CUTTER   Yes, ma'am, he is.

VANESSA   Shouldn't you be with him?

CUTTER   Aw, I wanted to stop by the party.

VANESSA   Okay. There's a lot of food downstairs if you want anything. What's your father doing? Does he want to stop by?

CUTTER   Oh, no, ma'am. He went out.

VANESSA   Ella, I was just going to tell you that Bill just arrived. We call him the lab master at school. He's really funny.

ELLA   The lab master?

VANESSA   Yes. Or master of the laboratory.

ELLA I . . . probably not.

VANESSA Okay. Well. Does either of you need anything to eat or drink? Hot cider?

ELLA Cutter might. I think he was just heading downstairs.

CUTTER Well—

VANESSA Okay. Cutter, we have a wide range of drinks and appetizers. Come on. Oh, and you can meet the lab master.

[VANESSA *and* CUTTER *exit.*]

ELLA Whew.

[ELLA *sits.*]

Okay. Okay. Okay.

[*Ella Fitzgerald music begins play.* MATTY *enters with the top hat in his hands. He moves to* ELLA *and sits down.*]

Come on. Come on, Ella.

[*Knocking.*]

Oh, for fuck's sake.

[ELLA *moves to the door.* MATTY *exits, leaving the top hat behind.*]

I'm working. I need to work.

Sorry.

[*Pause.* ELLA *moves cautiously to the door. She listens to see if anyone is outside. She opens it.* CUTTER *is standing outside holding a glass of wine and a mug of cider.*]

Oh, Cutter, what're you doing?

CUTTER Brought you cider. Vanessa said you like cider with caramel in it.

ELLA   How did she know that?

CUTTER   She's yer sister.

ELLA   Who's the wine for?

CUTTER   Figure I'd give it a shot.

ELLA   Thank you. This is very nice. I just need to be alone, to work. Thank you for the cider, though. I may come downstairs in a bit.

CUTTER   You sculpt?

[*Beat.*]

ELLA   Yes.

CUTTER   Wow. I never met someone who sculpted.

ELLA   Well. I do.

CUTTER   I seen books. Mostly about really old sculpture. Michelangelo, that sorta thing. You the first modernized sculptor I ever met.

Is it hard work?

ELLA   Sometimes.

[*Pause.* ELLA *moves into the room.* CUTTER *remains in the doorway. Beat.* ELLA *waves* CUTTER *into the room.*]

Just long enough for a drink. Okay?

CUTTER   [*Nods.*] You have work to do.

[*Pause.*]

[*Picking up the top hat.*]

Who's hat?

ELLA No one's.

CUTTER No one's?

ELLA It doesn't matter.

[ELLA *takes the hat and places it out of the way.*]

[*Pause.*]

CUTTER I'm my momma's favorite.

ELLA What?

CUTTER My momma. I'm her favorite.

ELLA Oh.

CUTTER Course I'm her only son. The others is stepsons.

ELLA How many? Brothers?

CUTTER Three. All older'n me.

ELLA Half-brothers then?

CUTTER Yeah. So. I 'spose it's likely I would be my momma's favorite. But even if my brothers were her real sons, I still be her favorite.

ELLA That's nice. And what about your father. He's visiting?

CUTTER Yeah. He's in town.

ELLA Where is he?

CUTTER He went out to get some food. Something to drink.

ELLA Shouldn't you be with him if he's visiting?

CUTTER   Aw. Your sister invited me to the party.

>   [*Beat.*]

>   You gotta boyfriend?

>   [ELLA *laughs.*]

>   Well? Do ya?

ELLA   How old are you?

CUTTER   Nineteen. Almost twenty.

[ELLA *laughs.*]

CUTTER   What the hell you laughing at?

ELLA   Cutter, you're so young.

CUTTER   How old are you?

ELLA   Older.

CUTTER   How old?

ELLA   Not nineteen.

CUTTER   I figured as much. But how old?

ELLA   You should never ask a woman her age. Didn't your momma teach you that?

CUTTER   No, ma'am.

ELLA   Well, you shouldn't.

CUTTER   Why not?

ELLA   Cutter—

CUTTER   Something wrong with it? Can't control it, can ya?

ELLA   I don't have a boyfriend. I'm divorced.

CUTTER   What? You leave your husband?

ELLA   I'd rather not. Okay? I'm divorced. And I'm definitely not twenty. Okay?

CUTTER   That his hat?

ELLA   It's my hat. Can we not? Please.

[*Pause.*]

You're not drinking your wine.

CUTTER   Bitter.

ELLA   Do you want my cider?

CUTTER   Naw. I brought it for you.

ELLA   Please. I could use the wine. I'll trade you.

CUTTER   You sure?

ELLA   Yeah.

CUTTER   I drink beer.

ELLA   I'm sure you do.

[ELLA *sips the wine.* CUTTER *sips the cider.*]

CUTTER   That's good.

ELLA   So is this.

CUTTER   Wow. That's real good. I like that. Mmmm.

ELLA   I'm glad you like it.

[ELLA *goes to the clay. She pounds a bit.*]

CUTTER   What are you sculptin'?

ELLA   Nothing yet.

[*Beat.*]

I haven't. Uh, I haven't figured out what it is yet. Does that make sense?

CUTTER   No. How long you been sculptin'?

ELLA   As long as I can remember. I mean, since I was very young.

CUTTER   What kind of stuff you make?

ELLA   Oh. All kinds.

CUTTER   Yeah?

ELLA   Yeah. But for some reason, I'm having a lot of problems starting this new one. I only have one idea over and over and over.

CUTTER   Oh.

[*Beat.*]

ELLA   So, why are you your momma's favorite?

CUTTER   'Cause I do anything for her. Anything.

ELLA   Like?

CUTTER   Like I wanted to stay in Okeechobee. I had my eye on a little piece of my daddy's property. I planned to build a house out there. Nothing huge, but nice. Hardwood floors. Two story high. Big windows. Wanted a little room upstairs to work in. Figure out someway to make some money. Nice thing about building on my daddy's farm, I could still be near my momma.

ELLA   What's the room upstairs? You said a room upstairs to work in. What sort of work?

CUTTER   Ah, I'd rather not say.

ELLA   Come on. I'm curious.

CUTTER   Naw.

ELLA   Looks like you're almost finished with that cider.

[*Beat.*]

CUTTER   Writin'.

ELLA   Really? You write?

CUTTER   Sort of. Not much time with all the work my daddy had me doin' on the farm. Sometimes at night I do some writin'.

But I planned to stay in Okeechobee, on the farm, and my momma, one day, when my daddy was gone to Miami on business, my momma sits me down and says, "Cutter, you go. Okay? I want you to leave Florida."

I didn't want to. But I did. I applied to a few colleges. And my momma chose here. West Coast. As far away as possible she says. I said okay. Never question my momma.

ELLA   So you didn't want to come here?

CUTTER   No, ma'am.

ELLA   Then why did you?

CUTTER   I said 'cause my momma asked me to.

ELLA   But if your momma loves you so much, if you're her favorite, why would she want you to leave?

CUTTER   To go to college, I suppose.

ELLA   I can understand that. I'm just surprised she sent you so far away.

[*Pause.*]

CUTTER   Yeah. It's different out here.

I think you'd like Okeechobee.

ELLA   Yeah?

CUTTER   My favorite thing to do is just take the boat out on the lake at night and drift. Millions of stars to look at. I like to lay in the bottom of the boat and just look up.

ELLA   That sounds pretty nice. But is this the same lake where you and your father shoot gators?

CUTTER   Yeah. Lake Okeechobee. But I only shot a gator that one time. Most a the time my daddy do the shootin'. He likes to go out and hunt gators at night.

ELLA   It seems so cruel. I couldn't handle watching your father shoot gators.

CUTTER   Oh, if I took ya on the boat, he wouldn't be there.

ELLA   Oh?

CUTTER   Yeah, we'd hafta sneak out.

ELLA   Why?

CUTTER   It don't matter.

ELLA   Because I'm a woman? Because I think it's cruel to shoot innocent animals? Why wouldn't your daddy want me to go?

CUTTER   Oh, he, uh, he don't much like your kind.

[*Pause.*]

ELLA   My kind?

CUTTER   Yes, ma'am.

   [*Pause.*]

   He probably kill me if he knew I was sittin' here with you. He'd shoot me square 'tween the eyes.

ELLA   Your father would shoot you for sitting here with me?

CUTTER   Yes, ma'am.

ELLA   You need to leave.

CUTTER   What?

ELLA   You need to leave. Now.

CUTTER   No, please—

ELLA   Cutter, you need to leave. I'd rather not be around *your* kind.

CUTTER   No, no. Please. I said my daddy. Didn't you listen?

ELLA   I was listening. I think you should go have dinner with your father. He sounds like a lovely man.

CUTTER   No. You don't understand. I ain't got no problem with no one.

ELLA   Oh? How's that? Didn't your father raise you?

CUTTER Yes, ma'am.

ELLA So you don't believe the same things as your daddy?

CUTTER No. Not anymore. Not the bad things.

ELLA Not the bad things?

CUTTER My, well, my daddy ain't all bad.

ELLA Time to go.

CUTTER Naw—you just, I don't know what you want me to say.

ELLA Good-bye, Cutter.

[*Knock on the door.*]

CHARLES Hello?

ELLA Yes? Come in.

[CHARLES *enters.*]

CHARLES Hey. Ella. Named after the amazing Ella Fitzgerald. I'm Charles. Remember me?

[*Beat.*]

Charles.

ELLA You look familiar.

CHARLES I'm Charles.

[CHARLES *sees* CUTTER.]

Oh, hey, uh, I'm Charles.

CUTTER Cutter.

CHARLES Cutter. Yeah. Nice. What's your real name, Cutter?

CUTTER Cutter.

ELLA Do you…did you need something?

CHARLES I need lovin'. Sweet, sweet lovin'. Aw, just kidding.

Tough crowd. Actually, uh, Vanessa wants to know if you guys want to come down and join us for a game of Sci-Fi Trivial Pursuit. The board is set. The pieces are in the starting blocks and we need one more person. Or two, I suppose. We could make room for two, if you wanna play, Cutter.

ELLA No thanks. Nice of you to ask. Maybe later on, though.

CHARLES Aw. Are you sure?

ELLA Yes.

CHARLES Cutter?

[*Pause.* CUTTER *looks at* ELLA. ELLA *looks away. She goes to the clay and pokes at it.*]

CUTTER Um, thanks, I think I'm gonna pass. Appreciate the offer, though. Not much for games.

CHARLES Aw. It's gonna get crazy down there. If you change your mind, I'm sure we'll need a substitute or two, just so the rest of us can catch our breath.

[*Pause.*]

Okay. Cool. Catch you guys later.

[CHARLES *exits.*]

[*Silence.*]

CUTTER Please don't make me go.

[*Beat.*]

Please.

[*Pause.*]

ELLA What's good about your father?

CUTTER Ma'am, I'd rather not—

ELLA You said your father was, what did you say?

CUTTER Ma'am—

ELLA "Not all bad"?

CUTTER I'd rather not, ma'am.

ELLA How is it that he's "not all bad"?

CUTTER I just sayin' there're good parts. But I'd rather not talk about it.

ELLA Well, I'd rather not be in the same room with you. You come in here and interrupt my work and you have the nerve to tell me your father doesn't like my kind. And then you tell me your daddy ain't all bad. You need to leave, Cutter! I'm not kidding. I think it's best if you go home now.

[*Beat.*]

CUTTER I know why my momma wanted me to move.

ELLA What?

CUTTER She wanted me to get away from my daddy.

ELLA Why?

CUTTER My daddy. I seen the way he lookin' at the ladies. My momma's his third wife. I seen him. Lookin' at the ladies.

Speakin' to the ladies like he a real nice man. Lots a things bad in what my daddy does, but that's the one that bother me the most.

That's why my momma tells me to leave. She seen me lookin' at him. She knows the look. The way I stared at my daddy sometimes.

[*Beat.*]

Like I wanna put a bullet tween his eyes.

[*Beat.*]

My momma saw the look in my eyes.

And, one time, my daddy, he saw it too. He saw me lookin' at him, at him speakin' to my momma's sister. The way he's laughin' and treatin' her so nice.

My daddy saw me. Didn't say nothin'. I knowed he saw me. He looked right at me.

Middle of the night, he kickin' me to wake me up. He and my brothers. They all kickin' me.

"Get up, Cutter, get up." And they cursin', ma'am. Things I'd rather not say to you.

No one in the world awake at this hour of the night. So I get up and they shove me outside. And we in the truck, drivin'. Humid night. Hotter than usual. I asked where we goin' and Daddy says we goin' out gator huntin'. We drive and we drive out to Lake Okeechobee. It's a real big lake.

Daddy park the truck and my brothers throw me in the boat. They real strong, my brothers. Muscles from farmin'.

My daddy steers us out, real near where he like to hunt gators. And he stops the boat. The night is so quiet. I never heard a night this quiet.

My brothers pick me up and hold me over the water. And daddy says,

Pardon me, ma'am, but,

"Who the f— do you think you are? You gotta a problem with your daddy gettin' a little action? Your brothers don't mind."

And they still holdin' me out over the lake.

"No woman gonna tell me what to do. Not your momma. No one. You look at me like you think you so good. You look at me like I'm a, he used the "n" word, ma'am. He use that word a lot.

I'm sorry for that, ma'am.

He told me I looking at him like he were a "n."

And my brothers throw me in the water. In the lake. I can't see nothin'. I started cryin' like a girl. I thinkin' about what's in the water with me. I try to swim to the boat, and my brothers push me away, kick at me.

My daddy says to me, yells,

"You gonna look at me like a 'n' again?"

And I yell, "No, Daddy! Please let me back in the boat."

And I out in the water, feels like a long, long time. Forever.

Finally, my brothers, they grab me up out the water and throw me back in the boat.

My daddy says, "You look at me like that again and I leave you out here." And that's the end a that.

[*Pause.*]

ELLA   I can't believe anyone would do that.

CUTTER   Oh, he done it. That's why my momma told me to leave. She knew I could see who he was. And she knew that was bad.

But now my money ran out. Too expensive out here. School and rent.

ELLA   I thought you said school was a waste of time?

CUTTER   Oh, I suppose I lied a little. I enjoy school quite a bit. Like all the readin'. Never had much time to read before.

ELLA   Then why would you join the military?

CUTTER   Like I was sayin', my money ran out. My daddy mad when he found out I come here in the first place. When my money was gone, daddy says I gotta come home. I said no.

He said if I don't come home, then he come to get me.

So I joined up. Put the law tween me and my daddy. This a month ago.

My daddy showed up yesterday. On my doorstep. Come to get me.

Military flyin' me down to basic training at 4 a.m. Fine by me. Long as I far from him.

ELLA   Cutter, if you're nineteen, you can do whatever you want. You don't have to go back home.

CUTTER   You don't know my daddy.

ELLA   What did he say when you told him?

[*Beat.*]

CUTTER   I didn't. He thinks we're goin' back to Florida tomorrow.

ELLA   Where is he?

CUTTER   Out drinkin'. He'll probably be back soon. Come lookin' for me if I ain't there.

[*Pause.* ELLA *hands* CUTTER *a lump of clay.*]

What am I 'spose to do with this?

ELLA Mold it.

CUTTER Into what?

ELLA Here...

[ELLA *takes the clay from* CUTTER. *She quickly forms gator-like jaws.*]

There. I started a gator for you. You just need, you need to put teeth in. They have teeth, don't they?

CUTTER Sound like you makin' fun of me.

ELLA I am.

[*Beat.*]

Cutter, you don't have to do this.

CUTTER It's okay. I already signed up. Only a few years. I wanna save some money, go back to school. Study literature, I 'spose.

ELLA My sister must have connections. I know she could get you a job.

CUTTER Already signed the documents.

ELLA Your father could be arrested for what he did to you.

CUTTER Naw. What my daddy did is considered discipline where I's from. Sheriff and Daddy are good friends.

ELLA That still doesn't make it okay.

[*Pause.*]

CUTTER   Do you have any examples?

ELLA   Examples?

CUTTER   Yeah. I wanna see what kind of art you've done.

ELLA   I don't have any here.

CUTTER   Why not?

ELLA   I gave a few to my grandmother. The rest are in galleries.

CUTTER   Galleries? That sounds like a big deal.

ELLA   Not really. Small galleries in North Carolina. Really small. Places that like local artists.

CUTTER   Do you have any pictures?

[*Beat.*]

ELLA   Yes.

CUTTER   Can I see 'em? Please? I really wanna see what you've done.

[*Beat.*]

Please.

[ELLA *goes to a drawer and pulls out a photograph flip book. She hands* CUTTER *the book. He begins to slowly look through. He stops and stares at one photo for a long moment. Pause.*]

Ma'am . . . I don't know how . . . I, uh, I've never seen anything like these before.

ELLA   Is that bad?

CUTTER   No. No, ma'am. It's. I don't . . . I'm a little embarrassed to say.

[*Beat.*]

This one. This one with the woman under the umbrella.

ELLA   Oh, I know. That's not my best work.

CUTTER   No, no, I mean, uh...something about her face...it looks...normal...but how do you...It's hard for me to stop lookin' at her face...it...

[CUTTER *slowly touches his chest. He is having difficulty speaking.*]

[*Pause.*]

ELLA   Alabama.

Louisiana, Texas, Kansas, Indiana.

CUTTER   What?

ELLA   Arizona, California, Nevada—

CUTTER   What're you talking about?

ELLA   I'm trying to list all of the states I drove through to get here.

CUTTER   You drove?

ELLA   About two weeks ago, I just left. I climbed into my little Honda and drove away.

CUTTER   You drove through all those states?

ELLA   Yes. And Wyoming, Montana, Michigan—

CUTTER   Not much of a straight line. Sounds like you drove all over the place.

ELLA   Well, it's hard follow road signs when you're crying.

I called my parents from Austin, Texas. I told them I was going to visit Vanessa.

CUTTER   You all over the damn map.

ELLA   My parents, they don't even know I've really left.

CUTTER   Why'd you leave?

ELLA   Because.

CUTTER   I'm sorry. Ain't none of my business.

ELLA   Because there's a memory of him on every corner. Sometimes six or ten memories on a single corner in my hometown.

CUTTER   Your ex-husband?

ELLA   Yes.

CUTTER   What's his name?

ELLA   Matthew. Matt.

   [*Beat.*]

   Matty.

CUTTER   Stupid.

ELLA   What?

CUTTER   Man that let you get away not a very smart man.

ELLA   Easy for you to say. You hardly know me. And you're nineteen.

CUTTER   What? Are ya' pretendin' to be this amazin' woman? You smart and you an artist. I like that. I like your clay.

   [*Beat.*]

   And you're pretty. Pardon me for sayin'.

ELLA   I have plenty of flaws, Cutter. I'm stubborn and self-centered and reclusive and jealous.

CUTTER   So.

ELLA   But our relationship was good. It was. We loved each other so much. We could talk about anything. And we could sit in a room together saying nothing for hours. We were happy.

CUTTER   Then what the hell you drivin' like you drunk across the map for?

ELLA   Our relationship was it. The one everyone is looking for. Until.

CUTTER   Until what?

ELLA   Matty went back to school. He wanted to study law and I worked—I wanted to work to support us. He was wonderful and generous to me and I wanted to help him with his dream. And I'd make him dinner and he'd tell me everything about the other students and his days and laws and the judicial system and I learned it all with him.

Until—

CUTTER   Until what? Ma'am, you keep sayin' until, leave me hangin' out here.

ELLA   Until he stopped telling me everything. Until he didn't tell me anything. He still smiled and kissed me and was kind to me—but—

He was telling everything to someone else.

CUTTER   What?

ELLA   He had an affair with another law student.

CUTTER   Knew it was him that blew it! I knew it! I'd a shot him tween the eyes.

ELLA   Her name was Alicia and she was beautiful and they were
seeing each other for three months before he told me.

The funny thing is, I wasn't so upset by the fact that he was
sleeping with her. What devastated me was the way he said he
talked to her. He told me that they truly talked to each other
like two unique individuals. He felt like he could be his own
person with her.

CUTTER   He'll be sorry. I know he'll be sorry.

ELLA   Oh, he was. We separated. He kept seeing Alicia, who was a
lot younger. It didn't take him long to miss me.

CUTTER   Fool.

ELLA   I sent the divorce papers and he called to beg. He begged and
cried and pleaded. He wanted another chance.

Even my momma said it was one time. It is not part of the
marriage vows to give up. She knew what he had done, she
knew about Alicia, and she still told me to go back.

But I didn't listen. I divorced him.

And he still called. It was so hard for me to say no, but every
time I thought of him and Alicia . . .

I couldn't.

[*Beat.*]

And I guess I was, I was, too selfish to realize how much he
was hurting.

CUTTER   Whaddya mean?

ELLA   I mean, I think he really did love me. I think he regretted
what he did so much. He left me messages. He. And he . . .

CUTTER   What?

ELLA He's gone.

CUTTER Gone? Like he...

ELLA Yes.

[*Beat.*]

Cutter, I'm not doing so well. It's been two months and...I'm sorry, I don't mean to burden you with all of this.

CUTTER Ain't no burden to me.

[*Pause.*]

ELLA Every time I'm alone or when I close my eyes I see us. Matty and me. The same memory over and over and over. Our wedding. It was an outdoor wedding, near the mountains, and he insisted on wearing a top hat. I thought it was so silly, but Matty had to have that hat. It was such a beautiful night, a perfect summer night. All of our friends and family were there. And what I always imagine is us, dancing, Matty dancing with that top hat on. And I, he was so beautiful, Cutter. That night was so perfect.

Perfect.

I still love him.

How could I give up on him? If I would've forgiven him, if I didn't file for divorce, he'd still be here.

I see him dancing in his top hat and I know it's my fault that he's gone.

CUTTER It's not, though.

ELLA It's wrong to not forgive.

CUTTER Getting divorced don't mean you weren't forgiving him.

ELLA If I stayed with him, he'd still be here, Cutter.

[*Beat.*]

CUTTER   Ma'am. I, when I's leavin' like my momma asked me to, I, well, ma'am, I begged her to do the same. I begged her to leave, 'cause no matter how many good parts there is in my daddy, the bad is so much more.

And my momma said no. She told me she couldn't leave.

And, ma'am, I realized I can't make my momma leave. And I can't make my daddy treat her right.

I's only in control of what I do.

[*Beat.*]

Ma'am, your ex-husband, I'm tryin' to be respectful here, ma'am, but Matty, he hurt you. So much. You didn't have no control over him. Whether he was romancin' another lady or...well...doin' what he ended up doin'.

You only in control of what you do. Takin' care of yourself. You did what you had to, ma'am.

ELLA   I just, this wasn't supposed to be my life. When you're a kid, you never imagine that your life will be the one that gets all screwed up. I'm not such a good person, Cutter.

[*Pause.*]

CUTTER   Can I tell you something?

ELLA   Yes.

[*Beat.*]

CUTTER   I saw you. When you came to town. Tuesday.

It was really foggy outside and I was lookin' out my window. My momma called to warn me that my daddy was comin'. So I just, I just starin' down at the street.

Waitin'.

So foggy I couldn't see nothin'. Then I saw somethin' move. I jumped. Thought it was him.

But then ... I saw ... you. Comin' out of the fog. One minute nothing and then, you. It look like you just appeared. Just there.

Most beautiful thing I ever seen. You just good. I knowed it without even meetin' you.

I saw you go into Vanessa's apartment, here. And I knew, I might not have normally, but I knew I had to come over and meet you.

ELLA   That's very kind. You're very kind. But I'm, just because you think I'm good doesn't make it true.

CUTTER   I see it even if you don't.

[*Pause.*]

I should get going. Wanna finish packin' before my daddy gets back.

[*Beat.*]

ELLA   I think I know what this is going to be.

CUTTER   Oh.

ELLA   I have a new idea.

[*Pause.*]

You wanna hear it?

CUTTER   Yes. Please.

ELLA   Okay.

Ummm ...

[*Beat.*]

Well. I, I once heard a song. About a weeping willow. The song is about a man who lays under a weeping willow, sleeps under it. And, in the song, the tree cries all night. And in the morning, he wakes and is happy again.

I recently heard that song.

So I was thinking I would make a sculpture, of a weeping willow, about the size of a person. And underneath, there will be a tiny man. Sleeping.

I think it'll be you, Cutter, the man underneath the willow.

CUTTER   Me?

ELLA   Yes.

CUTTER   Why not you?

ELLA   Oh, I don't know—

CUTTER   I think you should be there too.

ELLA   Oh. Okay. So underneath the willow will be a tiny little Cutter and a tiny little Ella. Sleeping.

Waiting to wake up again.

[*Pause.*]

CUTTER   Never had me a girlfriend.

ELLA   It's overrated. I think loneliness might be better than heartbreak.

CUTTER   I hope not.

[*Pause. Knocking on the door.* VANESSA *and* CHARLES *enter.*]

CHARLES [*Sings.*] Dancing queen, young and sweet only
seventeen...

VANESSA Hello again. I just wanted to tell you we're making
Christmas cookies.

CUTTER Thank you, ma'am. I have to go. Leavin' early.

CHARLES Aw! Cutter! The party is just getting heated up!

VANESSA Are you sure? Just a cookie or two?

CUTTER Thank you, but no, ma'am. I have a little more packin' to
do.

VANESSA Ella?

ELLA Maybe in a minute.

VANESSA Please come down. Everyone would love to meet my
older sister.

CHARLES Yes! We would all love to meet Vanessa's older sister!

ELLA Okay. In a few minutes.

CHARLES Promise?

ELLA Okay.

[VANESSA *and* CHARLES *exit.* CHARLES *resumes his ABBA rendition.*]

[*Pause.*]

CUTTER I'd like to see some of your artwork someday. Especially
the weeping willow. Or the one I looked at earlier. The one
with the woman under the umbrella...

ELLA Why did you like that one so much?

CUTTER   That woman's face. It...she looked like she was in a lot of pain...I...it reminded me of my momma's face.

ELLA   Oh.

[*Beat.*]

Well, I hope you will see some of my work someday.

CUTTER   Me too.

[*Beat.*]

ELLA   Cutter, you really don't have to do this. There must be some legal way to get you out of that military contract.

CUTTER   Wouldn't a signed up if I didn't want to. Ain't the easiest thing, but that's okay.

[*Pause.*]

Been nice meetin' you, ma'am.

ELLA   Ella.

CUTTER   Alright. Ella.

[CUTTER *extends his hand for a handshake.* ELLA *hugs him.*]

Alright then.

[CUTTER *begins to leave.*]

Ummm, ma'am...Ella.

ELLA   Yes?

CUTTER   Two things I want you to remember.

One: I am not my daddy. I will never be like my daddy.

And two: Well, if I'm not lucky enough to marry you someday, then I know, I can promise ya' there's a man that'll treat ya right.

My momma would call a lady like you an angel.

[*Pause.*]

[CUTTER *exits.*]

[*Knock.* VANESSA *enters.*]

VANESSA   Hi. I'm so sorry. I didn't mean for you get caught hanging out with that guy. He is so weird.

ELLA   It's okay.

VANESSA   It's just, he was living in the apartment next door and I invited him. I didn't think he'd actually come.

ELLA   He's nice.

[*Pause.*]

VANESSA   Please come downstairs and decorate a few cookies?

ELLA   I'd like that. I'll come down in a few minutes.

VANESSA   Okay. I'm so glad you're here.

ELLA   Me too.

[VANESSA *exits.* ELLA *crosses the room and stares at the clay. Music begins to play, something other than Ella Fitzgerald, possibly the song "Underneath the Weeping Willow" by Grandaddy.* ELLA *begins to sculpt. At first slowly and then with great passion. The lights fade to black.*]

• • •

This Is Your Lifetime

Jill Elaine Hughes

Jill Elaine Hughes

Jill Elaine Hughes's plays have received productions and staged readings in New York City, Los Angeles, Chicago, Seattle, Atlanta, Boston, Phoenix, Ohio, Toronto, the United Kingdom, and elsewhere. She also founded the nationally renowned Stockyards Theatre Project, Chicago's only theater company dedicated exclusively to women's theater and performance art, in 1999, and served as its artistic director/producer for five years. She served three years as president of Chicago Women's Theatre Alliance (2000–2003) and formerly served as treasurer on the executive board of the International Centre for Women Playwrights (ICWP). Her plays and monologues have been excerpted and anthologized by Smith & Kraus, Applause Books, and Meriwether Publishing, and she has written plays for the high school drama market, which are published and licensed by Brooklyn Play Publishers. In addition to her theatrical endeavors, Jill Elaine is a fiction writer, essayist, and humorist, and has contributed to many newspapers and national magazines, including the *Chicago Tribune*, *Chicago Reader*, *Missouri Review*, *New Art Examiner*, *Dialogue*, *Cat Fancy*, *Black Gate*, and many others. She is also a published novelist under her pseudonym "Jamaica Layne." She is represented by Lori Perkins of the L. Perkins Agency.

Ms. Hughes resides in Arlington Heights, Illinois, with her husband and son.

characters

MARISSA, a single woman in her mid-30s

LIFETIME TELEVISION ANNOUNCER

LIFETIME WOMAN #1, rich-voiced inhabitant of TV Femme Heaven, athletic, any age/ethnicity (can double as LIFETIME TELEVISION ANNOUNCER)

LIFETIME WOMAN #2, inhabitant of TV Femme Heaven, athletic, any age/ethnicity

LIFETIME MOTHER GODDESS, mature regal woman who rules over TV Femme Heaven

• • •

[MARISSA *is at home alone in her apartment late one Saturday evening, recuperating from a recent auto accident. Her upper leg is in a large femur cast up to the waist. Her leg is propped up on a pillow. MARISSA is eating Ben & Jerry's Chunky Monkey ice cream while absently flipping channels looking for something more interesting to watch.*]

MARISSA   [*Flipping channels.*] This is bad. Oh, this is very bad. Nine days cooped up in this apartment with nothing but the TV to keep me company and I've gotta watch *this* crap. How many clones of *Who Wants to Marry a Millionaire?* do we need? Jesus. And I've still got at least forty more days to go before they take this lovely contraption off. Funny, I'm almost growing attached to it. And I don't mean attached like you get attached to a kitten or something—I mean literally *attached*. It's becoming, like, a part of my skin. I guess that's what happens when you can't take a bath. Oh well. They'll just have to cut my leg off at the groin to get it off.

[MARISSA *flips more channels. A mixture of static and sound blips are heard from the television.*]

Infomercial . . . Infomercia . . . Jay Leno rerun . . . Infomercial . . . Televangelist . . . Rerun of *The Jeffersons* . . . Lifetime Network movie. God, there is nothing on. But I can't sleep, and my good friends Ben and Jerry need devouring. Ben and Jerry, I really have to tell you guys—at four bucks a pint, it would be a real shame to waste you just because nothing's on but the Lifetime Network movie, which probably has the same old crappy plotline as all the other Lifetime Network movies I've been watching for the past *nine days*. That's it. I'm never breaking my leg again. Well, maybe when I have someone to take care of me I will. Nope—not even then.

[MARISSA *settles on a channel, tosses the remote aside, and settles back to watch.*]

LIFETIME TELEVISION ANNOUNCER [*Offstage.*] Lifetime: Television for Women. You are watching *Love and Sexy Men Conquer All, Even When She's in a Coma*, the Lifetime Late-Late Saturday Movie.

MARISSA Somebody's always in a coma on this network.

[*Cheesy romance music floats from the television.* MARISSA *is transfixed for a moment, then rolls her eyes.*]

Oh, come on. Nobody looks *that* good in a coma. Yeah, and I can see your roots, lady. Time to go get a touch-up, Miss Bottle Blonde—but you can't, 'cause you're in a coma. Ha!

[*Beat.*]

Oh, *that's* compelling. Yeah, just bring in some impossibly blue-eyed guy with eighteen-inch biceps to fawn over the coma lady and weep at her bedside. Like that's really gonna happen in real life. Hey, buddy, so ya think stripping down's gonna wake her up? Yeah right.

[*Beat;* MARISSA's *jaw drops.*]

Holy shit! With *those* abs, you could wake up *anybody.* Yowza. Baby, you can bring me out of a coma anytime.

LIFETIME TELEVISION ANNOUNCER/LIFETIME WOMAN #1
[*Offstage.*] You are watching Lifetime. We'll be right back after these messages.

MARISSA   No—wait. Wait! Go back to the sexy ab guy.

LIFETIME WOMAN #1   [*Offstage.*] Do you ever have days where you just don't feel fresh? I do, too!

MARISSA   Oh no. No, no, no. If you just cut away from the sexy abs guy to do a fucking douche commercial, I swear I am never watching the Lifetime Network again.

[*Indicating ice cream carton.*]

Right, guys? See, Ben and Jerry agree with me. Bring back the abs.

LIFETIME WOMAN #1   [*Offstage.*] To restore that feminine freshness, use Springtime Vinegar and Water Disposable Douche—

MARISSA   I want some abs, baby! I don't want no stinkin' douche!

[MARISSA *clicks off the television.*]

That's it, Lifetime Network. You're fired. I should probably get some sleep anyway.

[MARISSA *stretches out to sleep. Lights shift to indicate a dream state.*]

[*Enter* LIFETIME WOMAN #1. *Music accompanies her entrance. She is wearing long, flowing robes decorated with leaves and flowers, carries a magic wand, and she should "sparkle."* LIFETIME WOMAN #1 *dances up to* MARISSA *and taps her with her magic wand.*]

MARISSA [*Asleep.*] Oh yeah, baby. Bring that washboard stomach over here...

> [LIFETIME WOMAN *shows irritation at this, and taps* MARISSA *harder with her magic wand.* MARISSA *jerks awake.*]

I'm awake now, baby—wait. Who the hell are you? Where's Sexy Abs Guy?

LIFETIME WOMAN #1 My child, you don't need a man to achieve true satisfaction.

MARISSA Um, yes, I do. And until you showed up I was very close to achieving true satisfaction with Sexy Abs Guy. Godammit—

LIFETIME WOMAN #1 There are other ways to love your body, Marissa, and have it love you back. *Without* a man.

MARISSA How do you know my name?

LIFETIME WOMAN #1 I know *every* woman's name. Every woman that watches Lifetime, anyway, and in this country, that's pretty much *every* woman.

MARISSA [*Embarrassed.*] Uhhhh—I don't watch Lifetime. I mean—I *used* to watch Lifetime, but I really don't anymore—

LIFETIME WOMAN #1 Oh yes, you do, Marissa. We *know* you do. You were just watching *Love and Sexy Men Conquer All, Even When She's in a Coma* and stuffing your face full of Chunky Monkey.

MARISSA I—

LIFETIME WOMAN #1 It's okay. Lots of women watch Lifetime. It's nothing to be ashamed of. In fact, we know that you watch Lifetime on a regular basis. In fact, you've been watching it for the past nine days straight, with brief breaks for *The Bachelor* and *Who Wants to Marry My Dad?*

MARISSA   How do you know that? Do you work for the Nielsen ratings people? Or the government?

LIFETIME WOMAN #1   You know, the Lifetime Women's Auxiliary of TV Femme Heaven used to work for the Nielsens, but we've gone freelance. The Nielsens were a little too white-male-corporate for us. We're now an independent contractor of Lifetime.

MARISSA   Uh-huh. So, uh, Miss Independent Contractor Lady, why are you in that weird getup?

LIFETIME WOMAN #1   We prefer to be called Sisters of TV Femme Heaven. And my getup is not weird. My getup is beautiful. What makes you think it's weird?

MARISSA   Well, if you work for Lifetime, shouldn't you dress like Melissa Gilbert does in all those Harlequin Romance movies or something? Frilly blouses, spike heels—

LIFETIME WOMAN #1   As a Sister of Lifetime's TV Femme Heaven, my purpose is to represent Life. Women's Life. Why do you think I'm covered in flowers? Flowers are plants' women. They are the way plants reproduce. And flowers are *fresh*. Lifetime was just trying to give you, Miss Marissa Chunky-Monkey Eater, important information on how you can feel fresh each and every day before you so rudely turned off your television set. That's why I'm here, *personally*, to tell you all about Springtime Fresh Vinegar and Water—

MARISSA   Hold it. Hold it. What are you, some kind of subliminal commercial? I already said I want Sexy Abs Guy! I don't want no stinkin' douches! I don't need to—to—you know—use that stuff. I'm . . . clean!

LIFETIME WOMAN #1   Every woman has days where she doesn't feel—fresh. And I think today is one of those days, Marissa.

MARISSA   I am perfectly fresh. Okay?

LIFETIME WOMAN #1   Oh, I don't know about that. How long has it been since you had a bath?

MARISSA   Well, um—I've been taking sponge baths. See, I can't get my cast wet—

[LIFETIME WOMAN #1 *leans toward* MARISSA *and sniffs—then winces.*]

LIFETIME WOMAN #1   Uh, I think you're getting pretty ripe down here. You'll definitely be needing some Springtime Fresh.

MARISSA   Hey. Hey! Stop sniffing—that. Get out of here, Flower Freak Show Woman, or whatever the hell you are. I'm going back to my Sexy Abs Guy dream.

LIFETIME WOMAN #1   [*Calling offstage.*] BACKUP! I need backup!

[*No response.*]

LIFETIME WOMAN #1   Backup! WHERE ARE YOU, BACKUP? I'm WAITING! BACKUP!

[*Enter* LIFETIME WOMAN #2, *in a stumbling hurry. She is dressed to resemble the Tampax "Pearl" brand of tampons and is carrying a wineglass and a rhinestone-studded evening purse.*]

LIFETIME WOMAN #2   I'm here! I'm here!

LIFETIME WOMAN #1   Where have you been?

LIFETIME WOMAN #2   [*Gulping her wine.*] I'm sorry. I was at the premiere.

MARISSA   Premiere?

LIFETIME WOMAN #2   You know, the premiere? The *commercial* premiere? Tampax Pearl? It was a gala.

MARISSA   They have gala premieres for tampon commercials?

LIFETIME WOMAN #2   All feminine products commercials have gala premieres. It's what separates them from the ordinary male-dominant commercials.

LIFETIME WOMAN #1   That's right. All feminine products commercials are celebrated in the advertising world for their beauty and gentility with glorious gala premieres. And *you* turned one off in the middle like it was just another Budweiser commercial.

LIFETIME WOMAN #2   [*Shocked.*] It wasn't one of mine, was it? Anybody who turns off Tampax Pearl's gotta answer to me.

LIFETIME WOMAN #1   Nope. It was mine. Springtime Fresh Vinegar and Water.

LIFETIME WOMAN #2   No! Girl—

MARISSA   My name's Marissa.

LIFETIME WOMAN #2   I knew that. Marissa, girl, you are in big trouble.

MARISSA   But—what—no, I'm not! This is a free country! I can turn my TV off whenever the hell I want!

LIFETIME WOMAN #2   Whatever you gotta tell yourself.

MARISSA   What is going on? This is not right. Am I dreaming this?

LIFETIME WOMAN #1   Do *you* think you're dreaming this?

MARISSA I don't know.

LIFETIME WOMAN #2 You *definitely* are in big trouble.

MARISSA Will the both of you—hygiene ladies just go away? I want Sexy Abs Guy back.

LIFETIME WOMAN #1 Oh, you can have Sexy Abs Guy back. You can have him back all night long and into next week if you want.

LIFETIME WOMAN #2 Mmm-hmmm. And I'll take him when you're done with him. Mmm-mmm-mmm.

LIFETIME WOMAN #1 But there are some things you have to do first. *Then* you can have him back.

MARISSA What do I have to do to get Sexy Abs Guy back?

LIFETIME WOMAN #1 You gotta get in touch with yourself. You gotta get in touch with the parts of you that you wanna show to Sexy Abs Guy. Make 'em clean and fresh and rosy.

MARISSA But I'm already in touch with—with that. I don't need you to—you know.

LIFETIME WOMAN #2 Oh, I could tell right when I walked in the room that's not true. You definitely have got some major freshness problems down there.

MARISSA No, I don't!

LIFETIME WOMAN #2 Oh, you got some problems all right. Phew-ee! Stinky, stinky, stinky!

MARISSA Look. I'm a little bit limited in the amount of bathing I can do right now, but I assure you, my—area is perfectly hygienic.

LIFETIME WOMAN #1 Hygienic? Ha! If that's hygienic, then they must have started making perfume outta tuna fish.

LIFETIME WOMAN #2 I know that's right!

MARISSA I *do not* smell like tuna fish. Okay? Maybe I don't exactly smell like daffodils right now—I'll give you that—but you do not have to play the tuna fish card, okay?

LIFETIME WOMAN #1 Hey. Sometimes the truth hurts, babe. I think we're gonna have to bring out the big guns on this one.

LIFETIME WOMAN #2 Most definitely. Here, Marissa. Why don't you try a Tampax Deodorant Pearl Tampon. Delicate, comfortable, and nicely scented to control odor.

MARISSA No thanks. I'm allergic to perfumed tampons.

LIFETIME WOMAN #1 If I had known before I came out here tonight that you have some more *elevated* freshness problems, I would never have targeted you for our Springtime Fresh Vinegar and Water product.

MARISSA Well, that's good, because you see, I really don't—

LIFETIME WOMAN #1 You need Springtime Fresh's Super-Acidic Lysol-Based Feminine Wash. Designed for female prison guards, Springtime Fresh's Super-Acidic Lysol-Based Feminine Wash is *guaranteed* to knock out even the worst feminine odor problems. Be tuna-fishy no more with Springtime Fresh! (May cause irritation, lesions, and cancer.)

MARISSA Look. It's just me here. I'm single. I live alone. My goddamn leg is in a hundred-pound plaster cast. I can't take a shower, or a bath, or—anything. And who the hell cares? I'm just trying to watch my movies and let my leg heal in peace!

What does it matter that I might smell a little—earthy for a while? Single men sit around stinking in their own filth all the time, you don't see douche and tampon freaks showing up in their dreams!

LIFETIME WOMAN #1   I can see you're going to be a tough sell. Sister, a conference please.

[LIFETIME WOMAN #1 *and* LIFETIME WOMAN #2 *huddle and whisper, while* MARISSA *looks on, mystified.*]

MARISSA   Can both of you just go away? Hey! Hello?

[LIFETIME WOMEN *ignore her.*]

Okay, so I seem to be stuck in some parallel douche and tampon universe. Um, is there somebody else in charge here? Hello? Anybody?

LIFETIME WOMAN #2   Uh—I'd be quiet if I were you.

MARISSA   Will whoever is in charge of this crazy fucking douche and tampon world please show up and get rid of these feminine wash flower freaks for me?

LIFETIME WOMAN #1   [*Worried.*] Please stop talking.

MARISSA   I really need to get back to my Sexy Abs Guy dream! Please? Anybody?

[*A fanfare of music and a puff of smoke.*]

LIFETIME WOMAN #1   Oh shit.

[LIFETIME MOTHER GODDESS *appears, in regal robes and carrying a scepter.*]

LIFETIME MOTHER GODDESS   Did someone call for me?

LIFETIME WOMAN #1   We're in trouble.

LIFETIME WOMAN #2   You said she was dead. You said she wouldn't interfere with our commercial work anymore!

LIFETIME WOMAN #1   I—that is, I—

LIFETIME MOTHER GODDESS   [*Laughing.*] You told somebody I was *dead*?

LIFETIME WOMAN #1   Well, I really thought you were when you disappeared after the Danielle Steele Weekend Marathon last year—

LIFETIME MOTHER GODDESS   HAHAHAHAHAHA! You disappoint me, my Lifetime daughter. Surely you know that the Lifetime Mother Goddess—that's me—is *immortal*.

LIFETIME WOMAN #2   I heard the network executives canned you and then you committed suicide!

LIFETIME MOTHER GODDESS   Oh, how they mislead you, my Scented Tampon Daughter. Network executives might "can" me all they want—that doesn't mean they can make me go away. You see, I am a *divine* being. I don't need advertising revenue to survive.

LIFETIME WOMAN #1   What? No advertising revenue? Then how *do* you survive?

LIFETIME WOMAN #2   Yeah, how do you stay on the air with no advertising? What do you live on?

LIFETIME MOTHER GODDESS   I live on *air*. Or more specifically, a compound that's distributed in the air. Good old-fashioned secreted estrogen. *Pure* estrogen, mind you—not any of that chemical-perfume-altering stuff you two are peddling. I'm here to put a stop to this. You both are a disgrace to TV Femme Heaven, peddling these men's-fantasy vaginal perfumes in the middle of people's dreams like this. I should fire the both of you.

LIFETIME WOMAN #2 Um, oh, Great Lifetime Mother, please forgive me, oh, Great One, um, but you can't fire us. We really don't work for you anymore.

LIFETIME MOTHER GODDESS HAHAHAHAHA! And who is it you think you work for, my Scented Tampon Daughter?

LIFETIME WOMAN #2 Uh, the Lifetime Network?

LIFETIME MOTHER GODDESS Well, maybe the network signs your paychecks, but you aren't really working for *them*.

LIFETIME WOMAN #1 Then who are we working for?

LIFETIME MOTHER GODDESS You work for me. You *all* work for me. Even the Lifetime Network executives work for me.

LIFETIME WOMAN #2 Oh, the Great Goddess has gone completely off her rocker.

MARISSA Hey, you should respect your Mother Goddess.

LIFETIME MOTHER GODDESS Ah. Here is a beautiful woman who understands. And I can see why you understand. You are emitting pure estrogen. Pure, beautiful, and *very* pungent estrogen. Why else was I drawn here so quickly when you called for me?

MARISSA [*Embarrassed.*] Oh, well, you know—

LIFETIME MOTHER GODDESS Don't be ashamed, my daughter. I see you are healing yourself.

MARISSA I'm just wearing a cast. That's why I'm stuck here—you know, not bathing.

LIFETIME MOTHER GODDESS But you are healing yourself. You are keeping yourself at rest, in a natural state, while allowing your body to do what it will to heal itself. This is a lovely thing. So you're not shampooing twice a day—big deal! You are a powerful woman. You are emitting a life force.

MARISSA Life force?

LIFETIME MOTHER GODDESS A man has been here recently, yes?

MARISSA Well, sort of. I think I was just having an erotic dream.

LIFETIME MOTHER GODDESS [*Testing the air.*] Hmm. I'm sensing—I'm sensing that this was a very handsome, very masculine, very *muscular* man. Ah, of course! The leading man of tonight's Late-Late Saturday Movie.

MARISSA Sexy Abs Guy.

LIFETIME MOTHER GODDESS Yes, he does have very nice abdominal muscles. I'm also sensing from the air that you had a liaison with this individual? A very *stimulating* liaison? His name is Abner, by the way.

MARISSA Well, we did sort of have a liaison, but—

LIFETIME MOTHER GODDESS You were interrupted? You were left unsatisfied? Isn't that so?

MARISSA Yes. How did you know?

LIFETIME MOTHER GODDESS My child, I *am* the Lifetime Mother Goddess.

LIFETIME WOMAN #1 Well, you used to be, until they canned you—

LIFETIME MOTHER GODDESS Silence!

[*The* LIFETIME WOMEN *cower.*]

LIFETIME MOTHER GODDESS I can also tell from your estrogen scent. You are emitting the aroma of a natural, earthy woman left unsatisfied. It's very distinct. And very unfortunate.

MARISSA [*Indicating the* LIFETIME WOMEN.] Well, it's their fault.

LIFETIME MOTHER GODDESS And why is that, my child? Although I can well imagine.

MARISSA I was just dreaming along, having a very nice time with Sexy Abs Guy—I mean, Abner—and then this Springtime Fresh Douche Lady showed up and shut down my dream, telling me that I needed to wash with vinegar and water—

LIFETIME MOTHER GODDESS Just like the commercial that interrupted your movie watching.

MARISSA Right.

[LIFETIME MOTHER GODDESS *walks over to the cowering* LIFETIME WOMEN.]

LIFETIME MOTHER GODDESS Daughters, arise.

[LIFETIME WOMEN *get up, shakily.*]

LIFETIME MOTHER GODDESS Moonlighting, are we? Taking a little cash on the side, are we?

LIFETIME WOMAN #1 We didn't do anything wrong—

LIFETIME WOMAN #2   We get really good money for subconscious advertising now.

LIFETIME WOMAN #1   And that woman needs it. She stinks.

LIFETIME MOTHER GODDESS   She does not stink. And I don't care how much money those Lifetime suits bought you off with. What you did here was wrong. Sacrilegious.

LIFETIME WOMAN #2   But—

LIFETIME MOTHER GODDESS   SILENCE! I never approved much of selling out our network to those suits just so they can sell advertising that brainwashes women into thinking their vaginas stink, but I know the network was short of cash and in danger of going under, so I allowed it just to keep women's programming on the air. But now, my daughters, you have gone too far. Not only that, you and those network suits are stupid. Short-sighted. If those suits are telling you to hawk products that wipes out estrogen in the middle of women's estrogen-producing dreams—and you're dumb enough to do it just for a little money—well, by the end of it all you're putting yourselves out of business permanently. If there's no estrogen, my daughters, there is no Lifetime. Women won't watch your network anymore because they'd have become too much like men. And then where would you be? You'd be in the Big Land of Canceled Programming in the Sky, that's where.

LIFETIME WOMAN #1   But, Great Mother—

LIFETIME MOTHER GODDESS   Don't you "but" me. Have you forgotten that I'm omniscient? I see and know all. As Lifetime members of the TV Femme Heaven, you know that invading erotic dreams for profit is tantamount to blasphemy. And you know what the punishment for blasphemy is, daughters.

[LIFETIME WOMEN *exchange looks and shrug.*]

LIFETIME WOMAN #2   Actually, we don't know what the punishment is, exactly.

LIFETIME MOTHER GODDESS   Oh. Well. I'll tell you then. The punishment for blasphemy against the Lifetime Mother Goddess is that you must live the rest of your lives as men.

[MARISSA *laughs.*]

LIFETIME WOMAN #1   What? Oh no—

LIFETIME WOMAN #2   Oh, please, Great Mother Goddess, spare us, show us mercy—

LIFETIME WOMAN #1   We were wrong. We were *so* wrong—

LIFETIME WOMAN #2   *Please* don't turn us into men! Please? *Anything* but that!

LIFETIME MOTHER GODDESS   Well, daughters, there is one alternative.

LIFETIME WOMAN #1   What is it?

LIFETIME MOTHER GODDESS   Death.

LIFETIME WOMAN#2   Death?

MARISSA   It's either that or become a man, right, Great Mother?

LIFETIME MOTHER GODDESS   That's right. Death, or become a man. Which punishment do you choose, my daughters?

LIFETIME WOMAN #1   Um, I choose death.

LIFETIME WOMAN #2   Yeah. Death works for me.

LIFETIME MOTHER GODDESS An excellent choice. By the power of Hera, Mistress of the Hearth and Protector of All Women, I hereby send you to the Other World!

[LIFETIME MOTHER GODDESS *sweeps her arms and taps her scepter; the* LIFETIME WOMEN *both drop dead.*]

MARISSA Wow. Did you really have to kill them?

LIFETIME MOTHER GODDESS I'm afraid so. We can't have TV Femme Heaven Sisters going around at night mucking up women's erotic dreams, stealing estrogen all over the place. Then where would women be? But don't worry, my Chunky Monkey Daughter. They're in a better place now.

MARISSA Am I still dreaming?

LIFETIME MOTHER GODDESS No, daughter. But you will be again in a moment. And I think a certain sexy someone will be waiting for you there. But first, know this. You'll be here alone, healing yourself, for many more days to come. Enjoy it. Enjoy it while you can. You might feel lonely now, but there will come a time in your life when you'll look back on these days and relish the privacy you had, the freedom to let your body do what it will, the quiet mornings, the lighthearted romance movies on TV until the small hours. As the seasons of our lives change, our lives become more difficult, more challenging, less carefree. This is not a bad thing, my daughter. The challenges of love, children, family are wonderful. But when others depend on us, we cannot relish the simple pleasures of the single life—eating ice cream in bed, meeting our fantasy lovers whenever our mind conjures them up, not changing our underwear for a few days—you know what I mean. It's fine to indulge in that for a time, but when the time comes to move into the next season, be sure you let the leaves turn.

But for now, whatever you might think of those silly made-for-TV movies and douche commercials, the next time you turn on that television, I want you to remember something.

MARISSA   What?

LIFETIME MOTHER GODDESS   This is *your* Lifetime. It is what *you* make it. The Goddess's blessings unto you, daughter.

MARISSA   Thank you.

LIFETIME MOTHER GODDESS   I must go now. There's a woman in Detroit having premature labor who needs my assistance. Go with the Goddess, my child.

[LIFETIME MOTHER GODDESS *exits with a puff of smoke and fanfare. Lights dim as* MARISSA *goes back to sleep.*]

MARISSA   [*Asleep.*] Oh, there you are, Abner! Sorry—I just got a little tied up for a while, but I'm back now! Bring that washboard of yours over here, baby! Oh, and bring that big tub of Chunky Monkey with you.

• • •

Pair and a Spare

Avi Glickstein

Avi Glickstein

Avi Glickstein is a New York–based writer and actor. He frequently collaborates with Object Collection (www.objectcollection.us), an experimental theater and music performance group, and is a company member of Polybe + Seats (www.polybeandseats.org). For P + S, he has contributed writing to *The Charlotte Salomon Project* (which was the recipient of a National Foundation for Jewish Culture new play commission, a Mabou Mines/Suite residency and grant, and a sponsored residency at the University of Michigan) and was commissioned to write *Granada*, which P + S produced at the Access Theater in November 2009. He also produced and performed in their week of plays for Suzan-Lori Parks's *365 Days/365 Plays* at various venues in Brooklyn and at the Public Theater. His ten-minute play, *Generator City*, was produced at NYU/Tisch's 2008 Ten-Minute Play Festival, selected for the KCACTF, Region II Festival in Philadelphia, and produced as part of Adelphi University's Ten-Minute Play Festival. Full-lengths include *A Small Tight Voice* (semi-finalist for *wordBRIDGE* Playwrights Lab), *In-Patient*, and *Alter Idem*, which received a reading at the Public Theater in May 2009, was part of Naked Angels' First Mondays Series in October 2009, and was selected as a semi-finalist for the 2010 Eugene O'Neill Theatre Conference. A graduate of Columbia University and the William Esper Studio's Meisner training program, he received his MFA in dramatic writing at NYU/Tisch, where he was the recipient of the Dalio Family Foundation Scholarship.

characters

ONE, M, young adult, crisply dressed

TWO, M, slightly older, slightly less crisp

setting

Outdoors, indoors, and generally around

time

Now

Recognize:
1: to acknowledge formally: as **a:** to admit as being lord or sovereign **b:** to admit as being of a particular status **c:** to admit as being one entitled to be heard: give the floor to **d:** to acknowledge the de facto existence or the independence of **2: to acknowledge or take notice of in some definite way:** as **a:** to acknowledge with a show of appreciation <*recognize* an act of bravery with the award of a medal> **b:** to acknowledge acquaintance with <*recognize* a neighbor with a nod> **3a: to perceive to be something or someone previously known** <*recognized* the word> **b: to perceive clearly:** REALIZE

Merriam Webster's Collegiate Dictionary, 11th Edition

• • •

··· scene 1···

[ONE *sits eating a sandwich outside. He munches quietly and reads a newspaper.* TWO *walks by. He notices* ONE.]

TWO   Hi.

[ONE *looks up.*]

ONE   Hello.

TWO Wait. Are you—

ONE What?

TWO Oh. Um. I think—

ONE You thought I was someone else.

TWO Yeah.

ONE That happens to me a lot.

TWO I'm really sorry.

ONE No problem.

TWO You just look exactly like this guy I know.

ONE Yeah?

TWO Well. I'll . . . I'll let you eat.

ONE Thanks.

TWO Take it easy.

ONE Yeah. Sure, you too.

[TWO *exits.* ONE *eats. Blackout.*]

· · · scene 2 · · ·

[*A bathroom.* ONE *at the urinal.* TWO *walks in.*]

TWO Hey!

[ONE *is startled.*]

ONE Uh. Hey.

[*Another beat. Another look between the two.*]

TWO Oh no.

ONE Yeah.

TWO I did it again, didn't I?

ONE You did.

TWO This is so funny. I mean, what are the odds?

ONE Well, I live around here.

TWO Me too.

ONE I guess that accounts for—

TWO Probably. He lives around here too. In my building, in fact.

ONE Who?

TWO The guy you—

ONE Oh, right.

TWO And you really do. Exact same—

ONE Not exact.

TWO Yes! And everything. It's really strange. The whole thing tickles me a little.

ONE I'm not ticklish.

[*Awkward.*]

TWO So what's your—

ONE I'd kind of, uh ...

TWO   No, no. Go ahead.

ONE   I . . . was just saying that . . . I'd like to continue . . . you know—

TWO   Oh my god. God, right. I'm so sorry. I didn't even notice you were—

ONE   No big deal. It's just hard—I have trouble while someone's— while you're—trying to have a conversation—

TWO   Course, course. I'm out.

ONE   You don't have to leave. I mean, you can still . . . do whatever you came in to do . . . it's just hard to talk while I'm finishing—

TWO   That's okay. I didn't have to go anyway.

ONE   You didn't have to . . . so why'd you—

TWO   All right then. I'll just leave you to it.

ONE   Thanks.

TWO   Take it easy.

[TWO *exits and* ONE *continues his business at the urinal.*]

··· scene 3 ···

[*A bus stop.* ONE *waits.* TWO *appears.* ONE *notices, sighs, and nods at him.* TWO *beams.*]

TWO   You nodded.

ONE   I was being polite.

TWO   You wouldn't believe me if I told you, but there's someone else walking around who has your exact—

ONE   It's me again. The "someone else."

[*Sound of a bus pulling up.*]

TWO   Oh.

ONE   I'm going to get on my bus and you're going to stop following me.

TWO   I'm not—

ONE   STOP FOLLOWING ME!

[*As* ONE *turns to step onto the bus,* TWO's *face falls and lights bump out.*]

···scene 4···

[TWO *stands waiting.* ONE *walks by quickly without acknowledging* TWO.]

[*Flash!*]

[TWO *stands waiting.* ONE *walks by quickly, circling behind* TWO.]

[*Flash!*]

[TWO *stands waiting.* ONE *walks in, sees* TWO, *turns around, and walks out.*]

[*Flash!*]

[TWO *stands waiting. And waiting. And waiting. Blackout.*]

···scene 5···

[*Church.* ONE *crosses himself and kneels.* TWO *enters, crosses himself, and kneels next to* ONE. *They speak in whispered tones.*]

TWO   I'm sorry.

ONE   You've got to be kidding.

TWO   I'm not sure what's happening.

ONE   You're stalking me.

TWO   No.

ONE   Maybe you don't think so, but that's what this is.

TWO   Whatever you think I'm doing, I'm not doing it on purpose, but I know that I'm bothering you and I wanted to say—came over to say—I'm sorry. I thought this would be a good place. I won't bother you again.

[TWO *crosses himself, gets up, and leaves.* ONE *looks back.*]

···scene 6···

[TWO *sits eating a sandwich.* ONE *enters behind him, walking and reading a newspaper. He sees* TWO *and, after considering moving on, taps him on the shoulder.*]

ONE   Did you find whoever you were looking for?

TWO   I had to stop trying. It was always you.

ONE   It just seems hard to believe that two people look so alike that you can't tell them apart at all.

TWO   It does, doesn't it? And all I really wanted was a conversation with him. Just a simple conversation. I'm sure it's just me, though. I have such a hard time recognizing people out of context. Like a student bumping into his teacher in the middle of a public pool. Doesn't compute.

ONE   What context do you know him in?

TWO   We've traveled together. In the vicinity of each other.

ONE   I don't know what that means. Vicinity of...you *do* know this person, don't you?

TWO   I have knowledge of him.

ONE   Uh-huh. But you *have* met him.

TWO   Define *met*.

ONE   You know his name.

TWO   No. But I don't know yours either and we've met.

ONE   We've interacted. I wouldn't call this *met*.

TWO   We've spoken. I've spoken to him.

ONE   And he's spoken back.

TWO   Not really. He just presses the button when I ask him.

ONE   Riding the elevator? That's not what you mean by traveling together.

TWO   We are moving from one place to another. I call that traveling.

[ONE *is stupefied.*]

I don't ride with him on purpose. We just happen to be in there together every day. I'm on first and he gets on at seven and we ride down. He never turns around but I know he knows I'm there. Sometimes we ride up together too. That's when I've asked him to push the button for me.

ONE   The seventh floor of this building right here?

TWO   Yes.

ONE   That's where you both live. You and this...other me.

TWO   Yes.

ONE   Huh.

TWO   Is there something—

ONE   And he was there, in the elevator, this morning?

TWO   Yes. Always.

ONE   You could have your conversation there, then, in the elevator, when you know it's him. Say whatever you want to say and be done.

TWO   It's not a matter of simply speaking to him once. I want our speaking to each other to maybe be the start of something.

ONE   You mean a friendship.

TWO   I wouldn't want to assign it a label.

ONE   Still. Start it there.

TWO   I can't. I don't want to disturb what we have in there.

ONE   If *he* spoke to *you*, though—

TWO   First you mean?

ONE   Yes. You'd—

TWO   Be unprepared. Taken aback. Make an idiot of myself. He wouldn't, but if he did, I couldn't . . . that wouldn't happen.

ONE   It may.

TWO   I hope not. I think I'd completely implode.

ONE   All right. Let's try to figure this out. Look at me closely. Pick something small and specific that'll tell us apart.

TWO Me and you?

ONE Me from him. Him. Take a look.

[ONE *stands still, facing* TWO, *while* TWO *looks him over carefully. It is taking longer than it should.*]

Just pick something.

TWO Nothing.

ONE The shape of my nose. The turn of my eyebrows. The curve of my hairline. Anything. It's bound to be a little different.

TWO Those are all the same as him.

ONE You can't possibly know that.

TWO We've been in close proximity for an extended period of time. I know what he looks like.

ONE Clearly you don't or we wouldn't be in this situation!

TWO Fine! Fine! I'll choose . . . your ear. The spot where it connects to the side of your head. How the negative space between the lobe and the cheek creates a serif, like on top of the letter *n* or *w*. I'll pick that and look and come back here and tell you whether it's the same.

ONE Tomorrow?

TWO Sure.

[*They are standing opposite each other. Lights down.*]

[*An elevator door dings.*]

[*Lights up. They've reversed positions.*]

It was the same. I told you it would be the same and it was the same. Everything on you's the same and I'm not sure how that is.

ONE   I thought it might be.

TWO   You said it was impossible.

ONE   It is. I wanted to be sure.
       [*Beat.* ONE *knows this will be hard for* TWO *to swallow.*]
       You didn't make a mistake.

TWO   How do you mean?

ONE   I *am* him. You've been right. This whole time.

TWO   But...? No.

ONE   Why not?

TWO   It can't.

ONE   Why not?

TWO   You didn't recognize me. Not even a little. I've ridden the
       elevator with him—

ONE   Me.

TWO   No. Him. We haven't established that as definite. Him. I've
       ridden the elevator with him every day for the last year. He
       doesn't say much, it's true. Barely looks up—

ONE   From his newspaper?

TWO   —But still. Something about me would be familiar—smell,
       voice—something.

ONE   I stood in the elevator this morning, realizing for the first time
       there was someone behind me. That it was you behind me. I
       didn't turn around, though. Like always. Kept reading so that
       you could get a good look at my...serif space. Let you

investigate. I carry a briefcase. Coach Connor Brief, doe-brown, strapped, with silver buckles. I wear it—

TWO —On his right shoulder, crossing his chest, and resting on his left hip.

ONE I'm him.

TWO But... no... not even vague recognition? Nothing? It couldn't—

ONE I stand in the middle of the car. Like this.

[ONE *stands in front of* TWO.]

TWO Oh my god.

ONE It's me.

TWO Middle of the car. Isn't awkward or uncomfortable, leaning against a wall or corner. Completely at ease, not swaying or rocking, just firmly planted. Waiting to land in the lobby.

ONE Yes.

TWO Oh my god.

ONE Look, I'm sorry if I didn't recognize you. I just...

TWO Really? You? I was right? And... nothing.

ONE I guess... I—I guess I just didn't notice you.

[TWO *is destroyed.*]

TWO Didn't...?

ONE But today... I knew your voice today. Even though all you did was cough. I knew it today.

[*It's not enough.*]

So, now, we ... what?

[TWO *is silent.*]

Are you okay? I don't know what to say truthfully. I guess
you ... may have ... I suppose ... strong feelings for ... I really
appreciate the ...

[*Not knowing what else to do,* ONE *sticks his hand out.*]

Look, why don't we shake? We can shake, put it behind us,
and really say hi to each other from now on. C'mon.

[TWO *doesn't do anything.*]

C'mon. Shake.

[TWO *doesn't know what to do. He is completely lost.*]

ONE   Shake?

[TWO *looks at* ONE's *outstretched hand, wanting to take it, wanting to not take
it. His hand may twitch. His feet may make the slightest shift forward and back.
He thinks. And thinks. And thinks ...*]

[*Blackout.*]

• • •

The Trash Bag Tourist

Samuel Brett Williams

Samuel Brett Williams

Samuel Brett Williams hails from Hot Springs, Arkansas, where he was raised in a Southern Baptist environment. He received his BA in English and political science from Ouachita Baptist University in Arkadelphia, Arkansas, and his MFA in playwriting from Rutgers University, where he studied under Lee Blessing. Brett's plays have been developed at the O'Neill, the Kennedy Center, the Lark, Naked Angel, New York Theatre Workshop, Yale University, the Flea, WordBRIDGE, and P73 Productions. Brett's plays have been produced at Cherry Lane Theatre, Ars Nova, Project Y Theatre Company, XIII Pocket, Mutineer Theatre Company, and New Orleans Theatre Experiment. Brett is published by Playscripts, Northwestern Press, and Applause Books (*Best American Plays 2004–2005* and *Best American Plays 2006–2007*). He has received commissions from the National New Play Network and Playwrights Theatre of New Jersey (where he was the resident playwright in 2008). Brett is a past winner of the Helen Merrill Emerging Playwright Award (other winners include: Sarah Ruhl, Adam Rapp, and Annie Baker). Recently Brett's play *The Revival* was optioned by Naked Faith Entertainment, and he was hired to write the screenplay.

• • •

characters (in order of speaking)

DOROTHY, female, sixty, moves with a walker

MOLLY, female, thirty

CHUCK, African American, male, forty

time

October 2005

place

Arkadelphia, Arkansas. A dilapidated trailer.

··· scene one ···

[*Night. Lights rise on* DOROTHY *in an oversized floral muumuu, sitting on the sofa, watching television.*]

NED PERMY [*From the television.*] The count is six down, the amount two hundred and twenty dollars. I'm Ned Permy, and it's time to go *Dialing for Dollars!*

[DOROTHY *removes a telephone from her muumuu. Sits it down beside her. Claps excitedly.*]

[*From the television.*]

I am now dialing the number of one lucky Arkansan.

[*Beat.*]

And there's the first ring.

DOROTHY Dang it to heck.

[DOROTHY *huffs. Puts the telephone back in her muumuu, removes a remote control from her muumuu, turns the television off, puts the remote control back in her muumuu, begins eating Sam's Choice double-mint-fudge ice cream with a spork. A few seconds pass. Noises offstage. MOLLY—wearing a clown outfit and carrying a Wal-Mart bag—enters through the front door. Exhausted, she drops the bag to the ground and plops down in a lawn chair.*]

Tired?

MOLLY I'm a fuckin' rodeo clown. What do you think?

DOROTHY [*Concerned.*] Ya' ain't hurt, is ya'? Didn't break your legs or nothin'?

MOLLY [*Agitated.*] Lemme check, Mamma.

[*Raises left leg.*]

One.

[*Raises right leg.*]

Motherfuckin' two.

[*Beat.*]

Na', I didn't break my legs or nothin'. Thanks for askin', though.

DOROTHY You can quit if ya' want, Molly. Go back to cuttin' meat at the Piggly Wiggly.

MOLLY I ain't never goin' back there. Too many people from high school. Used to call me a pilla' head.

DOROTHY Those people wuz just jealous.

MOLLY [*Looking around the trailer.*] Of what?

[DOROTHY *has no answer for this, so she eats more ice cream.*]

DOROTHY [*Beat.*] Ya' wanna order a cheesy-crust pizza?

MOLLY   You haven't even finished your Goddamn ice cream, and you sure as shit know I gotta keep my weight down for my tryout. Why ya' gotta tempt me like that, Mamma?

DOROTHY   Stop your dreamin', baby girl. You're too old. You had a window of opportunity, but unfortunately your ass wuz too fat to fit through it.

[*Goes back to eating, then stops.*]

And you're a woman.

[*Goes back to eating, then stops.*]

And you know how I feel 'bout that tour. Bad enough you're workin' the local rodeo.

[MOLLY *begins taking off her shoes, slowly, laboriously.*]

[*Looking at* MOLLY's *Wal-Mart bag.*]

Did ya' get my Icy Hot?

MOLLY   No, but I did get to wait in line for over an hour, 'cuz of all them trash bag tourists. I mean, don't get me wrong. I'm sorry Katrina took all their houses, and I'm glad Brother Eric is bein' hospitable by openin' up Arkadelphia to 'em, but I don't need the hassle of maneuverin' around 'em all at Wal-Mart when I'm just tryin' to buy my Tampax after a long day of rodeo-ing, ya' know what I mean?

DOROTHY   [*Still eating ice cream, matter-of-fact.*] Tyler from next door said that all the trash bag tourists have done since they got here is steal cars and rape little boys.

MOLLY   I would expect Tyler to be nicer—what on account of him bein' gay and all.

DOROTHY   Why, I've never heard such a thing. Tyler gay? You know damn well what Brother Eric would do if he thought there were homosexuals livin' in this town.

[DOROTHY *finishes her ice cream and throws the container on the floor.* MOLLY *looks up.*]

MOLLY   You best be pickin' that up, Mamma. 'Fore I rip your wrinkled titties off.

DOROTHY   It's not mine.

MOLLY   If you ain't been eatin' that Sam's Choice double mint fudge—then why you got a spork in your hand?

DOROTHY   [*Throwing the spork down.*] I don't remember.

MOLLY   Good, that means you have the Alzheimer's, so now I can finally call the hospice to come and kill ya'. Put *me* outta *my* misery.

DOROTHY   [*Beat.*] Maybe it wuz mine.

[MOLLY *stares at* DOROTHY. DOROTHY *gets the picture. Moaning, she rises and hobbles over to the ice cream container. Picks it up, then hobbles back to the couch and places the container on the table.* MOLLY *removes a bottle of malt liquor from the Wal-Mart bag. She opens it and begins taking swigs straight from the bottle for the rest of the scene.*]

I used to be a debutante, ya' know.

MOLLY   Ya' done told me that a thousand times too many, Mamma.

DOROTHY   Pilla' head.

MOLLY   You know what that means? I used to ask people at Piggly Wiggly, but they would just roll their eyes and laugh at me. The day we broke up Davy told me what it meant. A pillow head is a girl who's so ugly that when you fuck her you have to put a pillowcase over her head.

DOROTHY   [*Beat.*] I always hated Davy.

MOLLY He wuz at the rodeo tonight. With some girl from Burger King. She wuz wearin' a paper crown.

DOROTHY Whore.

MOLLY Definitely.

DOROTHY Pay him no 'tention, Molly. You're so much better than him it hurts. Goin' 'round cheatin' on you—just like I said he would. I hate him. Hate him so bad I wanna cut his ding-a-ling off.

MOLLY [*Touched.*] You'd do that for me, Mamma?

DOROTHY I'd do anythin' to protect my baby girl.

[MOLLY *reopens her Wal-Mart bag. Removes a container of Icy Hot. Throws it to* DOROTHY.]

My Icy Hot.

[DOROTHY *opens the container and immediately begins rubbing Icy Hot all over her body.*]

MOLLY Ya' know, Mamma, I wuz thinkin' at Wal-Mart today— when I wuz waitin' in line—what if . . . well . . . I tried to help one of them trash bag tourists?

DOROTHY Have you done lost your mind, baby girl? I told ya' 'bout the little boys, and I didn't even mention how smelly they are.

MOLLY Your Icy Hot don't smell like roses and I still haven't thrown you out yet.

DOROTHY Couldn't collect my Social then. I know why you keep me around. It ain't got nothin' to do with love and everythin' to do with five hundred dollars a month.

MOLLY   Once I join the tour I ain't gonna need none of your Social.

DOROTHY   Wind up just like your daddy. If he'd a gone to work at the Piggly Wiggly, then—

MOLLY   Daddy ain't got nothin' to do with this, and you don't know shit bout the Piggly Wiggly, so shut the fuck up.

DOROTHY   I know it paid better than—

MOLLY   I'd go in there in my white apron and cut meat for hours, Mamma. Never glancin' up to look at no one—never so much as sayin' a word. The mind drifts when you're slicin' pig intestines—it drifts to places far away from Arkansas—it drifts to places where no one knows me—where I can just…be… without people starin' or talkin' or hatin'. I wuz the best butcher they had, 'cuz I detached myself from my meat—I detached myself from…you.

   [*Beat.*]

   I'm gonna get outta here. You mark my words, Mamma. I'm gonna join the tour, and I'm gonna get out.

[*Blackout.*]

···scene two···

[*The next day. Lights rise on the empty living room.* CHUCK *enters. He is carrying a trash bag.* MOLLY *enters behind him. She has another Wal-Mart bag and is once again dressed like a clown.*]

CHUCK   Accusin' me of takin' that knife. You hadn't stopped us—we would'a come to blows. I ain't gonna take a step back for that man—he can't treat me like trash.

DOROTHY   [*From her bedroom.*] Molly! Molly, is that you?

MOLLY [*Yelling back to* DOROTHY.] No, it ain't me.

CHUCK Who's that?

MOLLY Dorothy, my mamma. Don't mind her none. She's old and crazy. You can put your trash bag down now. Make yourself comfortable.

CHUCK Four days I been holdin' this—all through my eatin', sleepin', and movin'. If I had been with a woman at the gymnasium, then I would've had one hand on a boobie and the other on this here trash bag.

MOLLY I ain't gonna steal nothin'.

CHUCK Don't suppose ya' will, but . . . I wanna keep it just the same. It's all I got left. I lose this and there ain't nothin' to prove I exist.

DOROTHY [*From her bedroom.*] Who's there?

MOLLY [*Yelling back to* DOROTHY.] A burglar—now go back to bed, ya' old hag!

[*To* CHUCK.]

Wanna sit?

[CHUCK *nods; sits on the couch with his trash bag.* MOLLY, *still holding her brown paper bag, sits beside him.*]

Why'd Mr. Mack think you stole his knife?

CHUCK I went in that man's store lookin' for a job. He said he wuzn't hirin', so I decided to glance around. 'Fore I leave he stops me and says he wants to look in my trash bag. I tell him, "Let me go to your house and look in your underwear drawer." He wuz none too kin to that idea, Miss . . . uh . . . what'd she say your name wuz again?

MOLLY   Molly.

CHUCK   Chuck.

[*They shake hands awkwardly.*]

DOROTHY   [*From her bedroom.*] Molly, I need my Icy Hot.

MOLLY   [*Yelling back to* DOROTHY.] I got you some last night! Use that!

[*To* CHUCK.]

What she needs is my boot up her ass.

CHUCK   No need to be talkin' 'bout your mother that way. Mothers are the only people who can truly love. No one should put a boot—or anythin' really—in a mother's ass.

MOLLY   Your mother must not be alive no more.

CHUCK   Never met my mamma. She died birthin' me.

[MOLLY *produces a bottle of malt liquor from the Wal-Mart bag. Opens it. Swigs. Passes to* CHUCK.]

Mighty hospitable of ya'.

MOLLY   Church looked crazy when I drove by it today.

CHUCK   Crowded. Not much food. Hot like July. Smelled of sport. Reminded me of a locker room. Wuz a high school janitor once. That's what it smelled like—a giant football locker room.

MOLLY   Brother Eric seems to be doin' a lot.

CHUCK   I ain't never seen a man so excited 'bout tragedy in my whole life. Tellin' people to go here—tellin' people to go there. He don't care 'bout Katrina victims—he cares 'bout news cameras. Told me to wash his truck for three dollars—like I'm a bum or somethin'.

DOROTHY [*From her bedroom.*] I'm all out of the Icy Hot, Molly. I used it today.

MOLLY If you used an entire container of Icy Hot in one day, then you don't deserve no more, ya' smelly bitch!

[CHUCK *gives her a look.* MOLLY *feels bad.*]

[*Yelling at* DOROTHY.]

Ya' ain't that smelly, Mamma.

[CHUCK *nods in approval.* MOLLY *opens her Wal-Mart bag and removes a box of cookies. She tosses them to* CHUCK.]

CHUCK Really?

[MOLLY *nods.* CHUCK *devours the cookies.*]

[*Eating.*]

Can I ask you a personal question, Molly?

MOLLY I suppose.

CHUCK Why're you dressed like that?

MOLLY Ya' ain't never been to a rodeo?

CHUCK There's a lotta places I ain't never been.

MOLLY [*Proud.*] I'm a rodeo clown.

CHUCK Meanin'?

MOLLY Meanin' I distract the bulls. Keep 'em from sitting on riders and stuff.

CHUCK Ever been hurt?

MOLLY Everyone works a rodeo is always hurt—ya' just don't wanna get injured—that means you can't do it no more. Bull got his horns in my barrel once and cracked my nose. Iced it 'tween rides. Next day—I didn't have ta wear no clown paint. My eyes wuz as black as a farmer's mornin' coffee.

CHUCK Ya' like the rodeo that much, huh?

MOLLY When I'm out there, and the rider's been bucked—I can feel everyone's eyes—in a good way. They're watchin' with hope— hope that I'm gonna keep the bull from getting' the rider— hope that I'm gonna keep the bull from gettin' me. That bull—he's death—and I'm dancin' with him. I can smell his sweat, and he can smell mine. We respect each other.

[*Beat.*]

[*Pointing to the bookshelf.*]

That belt—it's got real gold in it. Most valuable thing I own. Arkadelphia Rodeo Association gave it to me for my "heroism in the line of fire."

[MOLLY *gets up, grabs the belt, and shows it to* CHUCK.]

It actually has Brandon Smith's name on it, but a bull tore off his face 'fore they could give it to him, so they gave it to me instead.

CHUCK Congratulations?

MOLLY Tomorrow I got a tryout for the PRCA Tour. It goes all across the South. If they pick me up as a professional rodeo clown, then I'll be rich. We're talkin' like four hundred dollars a week. Plus vacation.

[*Beat.*]

Mamma wants me to quit the rodeo and go back to the Piggly Wiggly, though. She thinks it's too dangerous, 'cuz . . .

[*Beat.*]

She just don't wanna be alone.

CHUCK If you go back to Piggly Wiggly, then how ya' gonna be a famous rodeo star?

[MOLLY *smiles. Silence. They share a moment.* CHUCK *removes brochures from his trash bag. Hands them to* MOLLY.]

That's the Merv Moore School of Wrestlin'. I've always wanted to go there. It costs fifteen hundred dollars. That's where The Rock wuz trained. Once I get my government check and my FEMA trailer—I'm gonna go.

MOLLY Ya' think you're too old?

CHUCK Nope. Not even close. As soon as you let your dreams expire, that's when ya' die. I know. I've seen it happen.

MOLLY Well, why haven't ya' gone to school sooner then?

CHUCK I wuz barely makin' 'nough for food and shelter 'fore the storm hit.

MOLLY What wuz it like? The storm that is.

CHUCK Water pushed the walls outta shotgun shacks. Dropped roofs. Took everythin' away. Nobody made it. People survived. But they ain't the same people.

[*Beat.*]

Don't wanna talk 'bout it really.

DOROTHY [*Screaming from her bedroom.*] I'm calling the police if you don't tell me who's in my house!

MOLLY I'll be right back.

[MOLLY *gets up and heads for* DOROTHY's *bedroom.*]

CHUCK   Be nice now.

MOLLY   Oh, I will. I promise.

> [*As she exits.*]

> Mamma, if you don't go to sleep right now, then I'm gonna take off my boot and use it to beat ya' brain-dead!

> [MOLLY *exits.* CHUCK *stays seated for a nervous second or two. Finally, he gets up and looks around (all the while still clinging to his trash bag). He touches the championship belt, looks under the sofa, and even inspects an empty pizza box. The whole time he is glancing back to the bedroom for* MOLLY. *Eventually, he returns to the malt liquor and drinks, while standing up.* MOLLY *reenters. Stares at him.*]

> [*Worried/hurt.*]

> Ya' leavin'? Where ya' going? Why ya' wanna leave me so soon?

CHUCK   Ah, I ain't goin' nowhere, Molly. Just stretchin' my legs. If I'm welcome—I'd like to stay a few days. In a week I get a FEMA trailer. I ain't goin' back to the church gymnasium—so if I could just stay a week that would be—

MOLLY   You can stay as long as you want.

CHUCK   [*Smiling.*] Mighty hospitable of ya'.

[*Silence. Another moment.*]

MOLLY   Ya' wanna see my room? I got my own refrigerator. Might have some leftover cheesy-crust pizza—that is if Mamma ain't gone snoopin' again.

CHUCK   I'd like that. I'd like that a lot.

[CHUCK *approaches* MOLLY, *slowly.*]

MOLLY [*Nervous rambling.*] Cheesy-crust pizza is my favorite kind in the whole world. I dip it in French dressin'. Most people dip it in—

[CHUCK *kisses* MOLLY. MOLLY *pulls away.*]

CHUCK I'm sorry, I thought—

MOLLY Davy. My last...did things to me...things I ain't gonna let no man do again.

CHUCK Ya' want me to stab him?

MOLLY No. I just...I gotta be able to trust you. That's all.

   [CHUCK *opens his trash bag. Removes a scarf. Hands it to* MOLLY.]
   What's this?

CHUCK I found it at the gymnasium. Wuz gonna take it to the pawn shop and ask for 'bout three dollars. But I been thinkin' maybe...well...you might be worth more than three dollars.

[MOLLY *is touched. They kiss.* CHUCK *releases his trash bag. It drops to the ground. They continue kissing.* DOROTHY *enters. Gasps.* CHUCK *and* MOLLY *turn to her, holding each other. Blackout.*]

···scene three···

[*The next day. Lights rise on* DOROTHY *sitting on the couch. She has a knife in her hand.* CHUCK'S *trash bag is on the table in front of her.* CHUCK *enters, wearing only jeans.*]

CHUCK Whadda ya' think you're doin'?

[*Startled,* DOROTHY *points the knife at* CHUCK.]

DOROTHY   Why are you still here?

CHUCK   [*Walking toward her.*] Molly said I could stay till I get my FEMA trailer. Now, put that knife down.

DOROTHY   [*Still waving the knife.*] Did ya' fuck her?

CHUCK   That's none of your business.

DOROTHY   Did ya' give it to her good? Flush her cheeks? Make her brow sweat? Touch her down there?

CHUCK   Gimme my fuckin' knife back 'fore someone gets hurt.

DOROTHY   You threatenin' me, boy?

CHUCK   I ain't no boy, and you're the one with the knife.

DOROTHY   I'm callin' the police on ya'.

CHUCK   For what?

DOROTHY   Fuckin' my daughter.

[*Beat.*]

And stealin'.

[CHUCK *grabs* DOROTHY *and wrestles the knife away from her. He puts it to her throat. Pulls it back.*]

CHUCK   Don't feel too pleasin'—does it?

DOROTHY   You stole that. I know you did.

CHUCK   Don't go thinkin' you know my business—cuz you don't know nothin' near my business.

DOROTHY   I know I can hear everythin' from my room and I heard ya' tell Molly you didn't steal a knife from Mr. Mack—but now ya' got a nice big one in your trash bag—a nice big one with a price tag on it—a price tag from Mr. Mack's store.

CHUCK [*Looking around.*] Ya' got my sheath too?

> [DOROTHY *holds the sheath out for* CHUCK. CHUCK *reaches for it.* DOROTHY *slaps him.*]
>
> What the—
>
> [DOROTHY *slaps* CHUCK *again.*]
>
> Listen here, you—
>
> [DOROTHY *slaps* CHUCK *again.* CHUCK *grabs the sheath. Puts it on his knife. Puts the knife in his trash bag.*]
>
> Don't ever fuckin' touch me again. Ya' stupid bitch. You're outta your Goddamn mind.

[DOROTHY *huffs.*]

DOROTHY Molly's gonna be none too pleased 'bout that knife—I can tell ya' that right now, mister...but...maybe...I could be inclined not to say anythin'.

[*Still angry, but now somewhat interested*—CHUCK *looks at* DOROTHY. DOROTHY *smiles seductively.* CHUCK *almost vomits.*]

CHUCK Oh, hell no.

DOROTHY You best not be gettin' comfy then, 'cuz Molly don't like liars. She's been down that road and back. A couple times. When she finds out what you done, then she's gonna throw your black ass outta here.

CHUCK [*Serious.*] No need to be gettin' racial, Dorothy.

[DOROTHY *huffs. A long, awkward silence.*]

DOROTHY [*Finally.*] Molly has AIDS.

CHUCK No she don't.

DOROTHY How do you know? I'm her mamma. I should know, and I do know. She's got a lot of AIDS—all over her.

CHUCK I don't believe you.

DOROTHY Shut up. It's true. Now, I reckon it's time you left. I'm tired of your face.

[CHUCK *stares at her. He is not happy.* DOROTHY *removes a remote control from her muumuu. Turns on the television.*]

NED PERMY [*From the television.*] What's up, Arkansas? The count is four down, the amount two hundred and sixty dollars. I'm Ned Permy, and it's time to go *Dialing for Dollars*!

[DOROTHY *can't help but clap excitedly.*]

CHUCK Ned Permy ain't never gonna call Arkadelphia—he only calls big Arkansas cities, like Lonoke or—

DOROTHY They got *Dialing for Dollars* in Louisiana?

NED PERMY [*From the television.*] I am now dialing the number of one lucky Arkansan.

DOROTHY I wuzn't joshin' 'bout the police. I'm gonna call 'em and tell 'em 'bout that knife. You're a Bayou bum—so you don't know 'bout Arkadelphia jails—but they ain't too hospitable ta people like you.

CHUCK What do you mean—people like me?

NED PERMY [*From the television.*] And there's the first ring.

DOROTHY Dang it to heck.

[DOROTHY *turns the television off.* CHUCK *reaches for the remote control.* DOROTHY *puts it back in her muumuu.*]

You best be leavin' without sayin' good-bye to Molly. I heard ya' fillin' her head fulla lies last night—'bout her being a rodeo star and what not. She ain't never gonna make the tour 'cuz she's too old and too fat. She needs to know that. 'Sides, rodeo . . . it . . . takes people. Now the food industry on the other hand—

CHUCK   She don't wanna go back to the Piggly Wiggly—she told me—

DOROTHY   I don't care what she told you. This is my trailer and it's my Social that feeds us every month. And Molly ain't never gonna leave me—ya' hear?

[CHUCK *says nothing.*]

I said—did ya' hear?

[CHUCK *remains silent.*]

Did ya' hear, Negro?

CHUCK   [*Serious.*] Twice. You've been warned twice now.

[DOROTHY *removes a container of Icy Hot. Puts some on her finger. Reaches for her mouth.*]

I don't think you should put Icy Hot—

[DOROTHY *puts it in her mouth.*]

Jesus, woman. That's disgustin'.

DOROTHY   Whadda you know 'bout Icy Hot? Whadda you know 'bout anythin'? I wuz a debutante. What wuz you?

CHUCK   I've been alotta things—a farmer, a janitor, a burger flipper, a—

DOROTHY   My granddaddy wuz a farmer.

CHUCK   My daddy wuz till some fellas came and destroyed his crops.

DOROTHY   Why would somebody come and destroy your crops?

CHUCK   Nobody wants to see a black man succeed.

DOROTHY   That ain't true.

CHUCK   When I wuz nine some white men came in the middle of the night. Killed our cows, put herbicides in our crops, and set our barn on fire. I came out in my pajamas and watched it burn. Smoke filled the air like death, and Daddy didn't say nothin'. We moved to another city and the only job my daddy could get wuz flippin' burgers. Daddy and I didn't talk much after that—my mamma wuz dead, so we had a real quiet house. I dropped outta school at fourteen to flip burgers alongside my daddy. He passed away a few years later. If we hadn't lost that farm—he'd still be alive today. I know it. White people trampled his soul. Killed it. They ain't gonna get mine.

[*Long silence.*]

DOROTHY   Where'd ya' flip burgers?

CHUCK   Burger Barn.

DOROTHY   I like the Burger Barn a great deal.

CHUCK   Yeah, it's purty—

DOROTHY   The double-decker bacon cheeseburger. That's what I get.

CHUCK   I'm more partial to the crispy chicken deluxe. Sometimes they put too much mayonnaise on it, though. When I worked there—'fore they shut my store down—I never put too much mayonnaise on sandwiches. I wuz sensitive to that.

DOROTHY   Too much mayonnaise will ruin a sandwich.

CHUCK   [*Beat.*] Dorothy?

DOROTHY   Yeah.

CHUCK   Are ya' still gonna call the police on me?

DOROTHY   You bet your black ass I am.

[*Angry—CHUCK gets up, grabs his trash bag, and goes to the bedroom. DOROTHY smiles. CHUCK reenters and takes DOROTHY's Icy Hot. He then runs back to the bedroom.*]

Hey! Hey, get back here you—

[MOLLY (*wearing the scarf CHUCK gave her and once again dressed like a clown*) *enters, excited.*]

[DOROTHY *immediately.*]

Molly! Molly, your colored boy is worse than Davy!

MOLLY   What?

[CHUCK (*now fully dressed*) *enters with his trash bag in hand. Silence. Awkward.*]

Where ya' goin'?

CHUCK   Don't feel welcome no more.

MOLLY   [*Hurt.*] Just like that?

CHUCK   Just like that.

DOROTHY   Good-bye.

CHUCK   Don't know where I'm gonna go. Still got a week till my FEMA trailer comes. Might sleep in a tent display at Wal-Mart. One thing's for sure—I ain't goin' back to the church.

[CHUCK *goes to the front door. Opens it.*]

MOLLY   Chuck, wait!

[CHUCK *stops. Turns around. Looks at* MOLLY.]

DOROTHY   Ask him where your championship belt is.

CHUCK   What're you talkin' about?

DOROTHY   That means he stole it.

CHUCK   [*To* MOLLY.] You know how I told you to love your mamma? Well, I wuz wrong. She's a crazy, old bitch.

DOROTHY   You stole Mr. Mack's knife!

CHUCK   I needed that knife for protection. I got in a fight with Brother Eric 'bout washin' his truck. He kicked me outta the church gymnasium. I didn't know where I wuz gonna have to stay till my FEMA trailer came. I wuz scared and depressed and ... well, then, I met you, Molly, and I knew that if I could just lay down beside ya' then nothin' would be too troublin' no more.

MOLLY   [*Hurt.*] So you really did lie to me?

CHUCK   I'm sorry. I didn't know if I could trust you.

MOLLY   Now *I* can't trust *you.*

[*Silence.*]

DOROTHY   He's a thief and a liar, and he don't love you.

MOLLY   [*Not angry, just sad.*] Why ya' do this to me, Mamma? It's like ya' enjoy givin' me hurt. Mammas shouldn't do that— Mammas should just love.

[*Silence.* DOROTHY *says nothing.* CHUCK *puts his head down, and goes to leave once more.*]

CHUCK   I guess I'm goin' to Wal-Mart now. It's okay. Last time I wuz there they had a real nice family-sized tent with a sleepin' bag and bug zapper and everythin'.

MOLLY   Wait.

[CHUCK *turns around.*]

DOROTHY   No, don't wait. Keep goin', ya' fuck face.

MOLLY   Show me everythin' that's in your trash bag and ya' can stay.

[CHUCK *looks at his trash bag. Thinks.*]

CHUCK   I can't do that. It's all I got left that's ... that's mine.

MOLLY   Wal-Mart'll kick you out so fast. They might not even let you shop in there.

[*Silence.* CHUCK *thinks about this.*]

CHUCK   [*Sadly/almost to himself.*] I don't got nowhere else to go.

DOROTHY   He won't do it 'cuz he's got your belt in there. Let him go, Molly. 'Fore he tries to rape us both.

CHUCK   [*To* DOROTHY.] Woman, are you insane? A blind, backwards boy with no teeth wouldn't touch you out of loneliness and you're sayin' rape?

[DOROTHY *huffs.* CHUCK *turns back to* MOLLY.]

Molly, I ain't got nothin' of yours. I swear.

MOLLY   Prove it.

CHUCK   You don't trust me?

MOLLY   That belt...it's important. It's a sign that I got some talent at somethin'. It's about the only thing in Arkadelphia that don't make me sad.

[*Silence. CHUCK takes his trash bag over to the table. Opens it. Slowly. This is embarrassing, hard, emotional. He removes some shirts, underwear, socks, and a small card. He places the card in his pocket.*]

CHUCK   That's my Pizza Hut discount card. I got a free pizza comin'. We can share it.

MOLLY   Keep goin'.

[CHUCK *looks to* MOLLY. MOLLY *nods.* CHUCK *glares at* DOROTHY. *Removes the knife. Drops it on the table. Silence. He holds his trash bag upside down, showing that it is empty. Tosses it aside.*]

CHUCK   [*To* MOLLY.] You've seen all of me now.

[CHUCK *looks down.*]

MOLLY   Is there anythin' else you wanna tell me?

    [CHUCK *goes to say something, stops.*]

    I can't take no more lyin'. I've done told ya' how I feel 'bout that.

CHUCK   There is one more thing.

    [DOROTHY *huffs.* CHUCK *stares at her.*]

    I don't love cheesy-crust pizza as much as I said I did. I think it's okay. I like thin and crispy crust more.

MOLLY   Did you mean what you said—last night—when we wuz in bed?

CHUCK   Every single word.

MOLLY   You really don't think I'm too ugly?

CHUCK   I don't think you're very ugly at all, Molly.

[CHUCK *and* MOLLY *walk toward each other.*]

DOROTHY   I think I'm gonna throw up all over myself.

[CHUCK *and* MOLLY *kiss.*]

And I'll have you know a blind, backwards boy with no teeth would touch me out of loneliness. He'd do it, and he wouldn't hate it none at all. I wuz a debutante.

[DOROTHY, *disgusted, rises and begins to leave the room. The championship belt falls out of her muumuu. It crashes on the floor.* CHUCK *and* MOLLY *look at it. Silence.*]

MOLLY   [*Finally.*] Guess what, Mamma. I had my tryout today and the PRCA Tour picked me up as a professional rodeo clown. I'm joinin' it in Houston next month, and if Chuck wants— he's comin' with me. But you ain't. You're stayin' here. To die. Alone.

[DOROTHY *is speechless. Blackout.*]

···scene four···

[*A week later. Lights rise on* CHUCK, *wearing Fruit of the Loom underwear and sitting on the couch with his legs propped up on the table. He has a bottle of malt liquor in one hand and the remote control in the other. He is watching wrestling.* DOROTHY *hobbles into the room. She makes her way to a chair, sits down arduously, and removes an empty container of Icy Hot. She begins trying to rub some out.* CHUCK *puts the remote control in his underwear.*]

CHUCK   I ain't never seen a woman loves Icy Hot more than you. Ya' been scrapin' that container dry for a week now. There ain't no more left.

DOROTHY   I hurt.

CHUCK   We all do, Dorothy. Get over it.

DOROTHY   Could ya'...maybe get me some more at Wal-Mart? Please?

CHUCK   We don't got no more money left for the month. Your Social can barely support two people—much less three. And Molly don't make shit. Don't worry, though—as soon as my FEMA trailer gets here—

DOROTHY   My FEMA trailer this, my FEMA trailer that—it wuz supposed to be here last week—where is it, Chuck?

CHUCK   Church said there's some complications.

DOROTHY   The only complications are you and all the other trash bag tourists. Tyler from next door said you people have made the grocery store too crowded, slowed down our school system, and pissed all over everythin' we've given ya'. Everyone wants Arkadelphia back the way it wuz. I heard that Brother Eric's even 'bout to lose his temper.

CHUCK   Brother Eric's the reason the trailers ain't here yet. If that asshole were in charge of a two-car parade, then one car would disappear and the other would explode into flames. Then he'd say it wuz all God's will.

DOROTHY   At least he's not a thief.

CHUCK   Ya' know damn well I took that knife back and humbled myself to Mr. Mack.

DOROTHY   'Cuz you wuz scared I wuz gonna call the cops.

CHUCK   [*Threatening.*] Look, Dorothy, I don't wanna fight no more, alright? I'm just gonna watch my wrestlin' videos, and you're gonna be quiet for once in your stupid fuckin' life.

DOROTHY   My life ain't stupid. Yours is.

CHUCK   I'm watchin' wrestlin', woman!

DOROTHY   That's all you ever do!

CHUCK   I done told ya' already—I'm goin' ta wrestlin' school. Molly inspired me. Supports me even. So if you don't mind—I'm studyin' right now.

DOROTHY   You don't have to study for wrestlin' school—ya just hit people.

CHUCK   That's like sayin' Michael Jordan just put a ball in a hoop, or Beethoven just put paint on a canvas.

[*Silence.*]

DOROTHY   *Dialin' for Dollars* is comin' on in a minute.

CHUCK   That's nice to know.

[CHUCK *continues watching wrestling.* DOROTHY, *frustrated, throws her Icy Hot container on the floor. Huffs.*]

DOROTHY   [*Almost in tears.*] Look at me. I used to be a—

CHUCK   I know, I know—a debutante—ya used to be a fuckin' debutante. Congratulations, Dorothy.

DOROTHY   I wuz my mamma's only child. She cleaned houses for rich folks all her life. Only thing she wanted wuz for me to be a debutante.

CHUCK   [*Pointing to the television.*] Shaun Michaels is tuning up the band—he's 'bout to give Bret "The Hitman" Hart some sweet chin music.

DOROTHY   She cleaned houses for a month and didn't charge nothin'—just to get the committee to let me go to one dance. I wuz thirty-two.

CHUCK   [*Still with the television.*] Here comes the sharpshooter!

DOROTHY   My mamma made my dress by hand. I felt like a princess. None of the other girls would talk to me, but I didn't care—'cuz that wuz the only time I've ever looked in a mirror and not been sad at all. Nate wuz waitin' tables that night. He came up to me and said I wuz his. He wuz right. I ain't never seen a man more handsome. We married and moved into this trailer twenty-nine years ago.

[DOROTHY *breaks down crying.*]

CHUCK   [*Looking at the television.*] He wuz Molly's father?

DOROTHY   He wuz till he left us both for the rodeo. Drew a bull one day that...that couldn't be ridden.

[*Silence.* CHUCK *looks at* DOROTHY. *He picks up a fast-food napkin off the floor. Tries to hand it to* DOROTHY. *She reaches out and...grabs the remote control out of* CHUCK's *underwear. Turns on* Dialing for Dollars.]

CHUCK   Hey! What the fuck you think you're doing?

DOROTHY   It's my television and my remote control!

[CHUCK *grabs the remote control back.*]

CHUCK   Not no more it ain't!

NED PERMY   [*From the television.*] Hello, Arkansans! The count is seven down and three hundred dollars. I'm Ned Permy, and it's time to go *Dialing for Dollars*!

CHUCK   Three hundred dollars?

DOROTHY   It's been a long time since anyone's won anythin' in Arkansas.

CHUCK   Well, now three hundred dollars is kind of exciting.

DOROTHY   I always think I'm gonna win.

NED PERMY   [*From the television.*] I have one lucky telephone number in my hand and I am now dialing . . .

CHUCK   Well, that's a shame—maybe tomorrow.

[CHUCK *turns off the television.*]

DOROTHY   It takes a second to ring!

CHUCK   Listen, Dorothy, I done told ya' Ned Permy don't call small—

[*The telephone rings.* CHUCK *and* DOROTHY *look to the bookshelf, speechless.*]

DOROTHY   Oh my God! Oh my God! Oh my God! We're rich! We're rich!

CHUCK   Hot damn!

[CHUCK *dashes to the bookshelf and answers the telephone.*]

DOROTHY   Tell Ned Permy I love him! I watch him every day!

[*Looking up to the Heavens.*]

Thank you, God! I never thought you wuz listenin', but now I—

CHUCK   [*Into the telephone quickly.*] Four up, and three hundred dollars!

[*Beat.*]

What? Yeah, she lives here. This is—it don't matter who this is.

DOROTHY   Don't be rude to Ned Permy.

CHUCK   [*To* DOROTHY.] Shut up, bitch.

[*Into the telephone.*]

Calm down, calm down. Not you. The other bitch.

[*Beat.*]

What? Huh? How? When? Is she—yeah, I can get there. I mean, I gotta get my shoes, but—is . . . is she gonna . . . gonna make it? I understand. Okay. Alright. I'm comin' right now.

[CHUCK *hangs up the telephone.*]

DOROTHY   What happened? What's going on?

CHUCK   A bull sat on Molly. I gotta go.

[CHUCK *rushes to the bedroom.*]

DOROTHY   [*Yelling to the bedroom.*] Is she gonna be okay? Take me with you. Please.

[CHUCK *enters with shoes on, but still no pants.*]

DOROTHY   Tell her . . . tell her . . .

[CHUCK *exits.*]

I love her.

[*Silence.* DOROTHY *sits alone in the trailer, worried about her daughter, trying not to cry. The telephone rings. She makes her way to the bookshelf as fast as possible.*]

[*Out of breath.*]

Molly? Ned Permy? Hello?

[*Beat.*]

Oh. Hello, Brother Eric. Did ya' hear? Molly broke her legs. A bull sat on her.

[*Beat.*]

Well, prayers don't mean much in my trailer, but that's a nice gesture.

[*Beat.*]

I got a question for ya', Brother Eric. Do you think God has a ding-a-ling? 'Cuz, ya' know, I think I'd be more inclined to believe in Him if He didn't. Have a ding-a-ling that is.

[*Beat.*]

Hello? Brother Eric? Are ya' still there?

[*Beat.*]

Yeah, we got one staying here. Yeah, Chuck—ya' know him? I don't know his last name. He's been here two weeks—waitin' on his FEMA trailer. He can't talk right now 'cuz he just ran to the hospital in his underwear.

[*Beat.*]

Oh, really? You don't say. That's interesting, Brother Eric. That's very interestin'. No, no . . . keep going. I wanna hear all of this . . .

[*As* DOROTHY *listens to* BROTHER ERIC *a huge smile comes across her face. Blackout.*]

··· scene five ···

[*Later that night. Lights rise on* DOROTHY, *sitting in a lawn chair.* MOLLY *enters in a wheelchair with two broken legs.* CHUCK *is pushing her. He still doesn't have pants.*]

DOROTHY   How's my, baby girl?

[MOLLY *is silent. Deeply depressed.*]

CHUCK   She ain't said nothin' since I picked her up.

       [CHUCK *rolls* MOLLY *over to the couch.*]

       [*To* MOLLY.]

       I got some liquor left.

       [CHUCK *picks the liquor up off the table and holds it out.* MOLLY *grabs the bottle and begins chugging it.*]

       Don't you worry none, Molly. I'll turn us on some wrestlin' and then order a cheesy-crust pizza. How 'bout that?

DOROTHY   [*To* CHUCK.] I know somethin' bout you, mister.

CHUCK   Pipe down, bitch. I don't got no time for your nonsense.

       [CHUCK *sits on the couch. Turns on wrestling.*]

       [*To* MOLLY.]

       I think you're takin' this too hard, Molly. Your legs'll heal.

MOLLY   That bull didn't just sit on my legs. He sat on my dreams too.

CHUCK   Listen, you can rejoin the tour just as soon as—

MOLLY   When that bull sat on me—nobody rushed to help. I wuz stuck. Couldn't move. I could see, though. I saw a daddy nudge his little boy. They pointed and laughed.

       [*Beat.*]

       I wuz wrong. Rodeo don't respect me. It just laughs like everyone else.

[*Long silence.* CHUCK *gets the Pizza Hut discount card out of his blue jeans— which are now hanging over the edge of the sofa.*]

CHUCK   [*Finally.*] What do you want on your cheesy-crust pizza? I'll get ya' anythin' you want. Up to three toppings. Or a specialty. That's what my card says.

MOLLY   Stuck under that bull . . . in front of all those people I know from school and Piggly Wiggly and church . . . it wuz . . . it wuz worse than the time Davy . . . gave me to his friends.

[*Another long silence.* CHUCK *puts the card on the table.*]

CHUCK   [*Finally.*] Molly, listen to me, baby—when I get my FEMA trailer and my money, then we're gonna get outta here—just you and me. I'm gonna go to wrestlin' school and take care of you for a change. You won't have to do nothin' that brings ya' hurt or sadness no more. Your mamma won't be around to hassle us, so we can just . . . be . . . together . . . forever . . . livin' the American Dream.

DOROTHY   Chuck ain't a flood victim.

[*Silence.*]

MOLLY   What?

[CHUCK *says nothing.*]

DOROTHY   His name ain't Chuck either—accordin' to his Pizza Hut discount card—it's Marvin Jones. Brother Eric said some people been fakin', so the church checked Social Security numbers and Chuck—or rather Marvin—ain't legit. Brother Eric took it upon himself to call everyone and warn 'em 'bout the scam.

MOLLY   [*Beat.*] Did ya' lie to me . . . again . . . Marvin?

DOROTHY   [*To* CHUCK.] I think ya' best be goin' now.

[CHUCK *looks to* MOLLY. *She says nothing.*]

CHUCK   I didn't mean ta deceive ya' much, Molly—I really didn't. I wuz livin' in Lonoke—in a dump smaller than a shotgun shack—I wuz workin' at the Burger Barn and they got shut down, and no place else'd hire a forty-year-old black man with no education—I lost my house, and—

DOROTHY   Don't believe anythin' he says—he's a liar.

CHUCK   It's true—it all is—on my mother's grave it is. I wuz usin' the Best Buy bathroom to clean up one day, and I saw Katrina on the news, and heard Arkadelphia wuz helpin'—givin' food and shelter—and no one ain't never helped me 'fore, so I came here, and I...I'm sorry, Molly—I am. I wanted ta tell ya', but...but I wuz scared...I just couldn't get nothin' to work out...till you come into my life.

[*Silence.* MOLLY *looks away from* CHUCK.]

DOROTHY   Here, I already packed your luggage. Don't say I never did nothin' for ya'.

[DOROTHY *throws the trash bag on the floor.*]

CHUCK   Molly...Molly...I believed in ya'.

[*Silence.*]

DOROTHY   *Dialing for Dollars* is comin' on, Molly. Turn that wrestling shit off.

CHUCK   [*To* MOLLY.] I meant it when I said I didn't think you wuz too ugly, and you're worth three dollars, and—

DOROTHY   Listen up, Negro. She don't want you here no more. Nobody in this town does. The time for bein' hospitable is over. So get the fuck outta my trailer. Now.

[CHUCK *rises and puts his pants on, slowly. He then gets his trash bag and begins to leave.* DOROTHY *grabs the remote control off the table. Turns on* Dialing for Dollars.]

NED PERMY   [*From the television.*] Hello, Arkansas. The count is six down, and the amount is three hundred and twenty dollars!

CHUCK   I don't got nowhere else to go. Can I just stay one more night? Look, if I wuz ta find a job...somewhere close... maybe...to where I could make some money...could I then...maybe...just...please...maybe...

NED PERMY   I have the number of one lucky Arkansan in my hand, and I am now dialing!

CHUCK   Dorothy, what if I wuz to get you some Icy Hot? I could go down to the Wal-Mart and pick some up real quick. If I did, could I—

NED PERMY   And there's the first ring!

[*The telephone rings.* MOLLY, DOROTHY, *and* CHUCK *are all shocked. They look to the table.* DOROTHY *picks the telephone up and answers it.*]

DOROTHY   Hello?

NED PERMY   [*From the television.*] This is Ned Permy and I'm *Dialing for Dollars.* Do you know the count and the amount?

DOROTHY   Six up, three hundred and twenty dollars!

NED PERMY   No, I'm sorry, ma'am. It's six *down.* But don't worry, there are no losers in *Dialing for Dollars*—I will make sure we send you a twelve-pack of Diet Mr. Pibb—thanks for playing, and better luck next time!

[DOROTHY *hangs up the telephone. No one knows what to say. Finally,* DOROTHY *turns to* CHUCK.]

DOROTHY   That wuz your fault, you Goddamn piece of trash. I couldn't concentrate 'cuz of all your jabberin'. If you don't leave right now, I'm callin' the motherfuckin' police—and we both know you don't want that, 'cuz Arkadelphia's kindness has been all used up, and there ain't no tellin' what they might do.

[*Silence.*]

CHUCK   Thank ya' for lettin' me stay these last two weeks, Molly... I appreciate it... it wuz real nice... I ain't never been treated so nice.

[CHUCK *opens the front door. Looks to* MOLLY *one last time. Walks out.* MOLLY *then looks to the empty doorway. A few seconds pass.*]

DOROTHY   I warned ya' 'bout pickin' up bums. But you don't listen to your poor old, grey-headed mother, now do ya'? What do I know? I wuz just a debutante.

[MOLLY *looks to* DOROTHY *and then back to the open door.*]

MOLLY   CHUCK! I MEAN, MARVIN! WHATEVER, JUST WAIT! DON'T GO! PLEASE, DON'T LEAVE ME! NOT HERE! NOT WITH HER! NOT LIKE THIS! I FORGIVE YOU! I LOVE YOU! I'M SORRY! I'M SO SORRY! PLEASE COME BACK! PLEASE! PLEASE! PLEASE!

[*Silence.* MOLLY *stares at the empty doorway.*]

DOROTHY   He's gone, and he ain't never comin' back.

[DOROTHY *gets up. Walks to the front door. Slams it. Locks it. Goes back to the couch and sits down.*]

Still wanna order a cheesy-crust pizza?

[MOLLY *says nothing.*]

We got a little money left. Could maybe even get buffalo wings. 'Fore long you'll be healthy enough to go back to the Piggly Wiggly anyway. And if not, we can just sell your belt.

[DOROTHY *picks up the Pizza Hut discount card. Looks at it.*]

DOROTHY   That figures. His Pizza Hut discount card is expired.

[DOROTHY *wads the discount card up and throws it on the ground.* MOLLY *stares at it.*]

MOLLY   Someone'll help him ... don't ya' think?

DOROTHY   Don't nobody care 'bout that nigger. At least not no more. His time's done come and gone.

[DOROTHY *removes the Icy Hot from her muumuu. Lights slowly fade to black with* MOLLY *staring at the discount card and* DOROTHY *trying to rub a little more out of the empty container.*]

• • •

The Date

Joan Lipkin

Joan Lipkin

Joan Lipkin is the artistic director of That Uppity Theatre Company, specializing in facilitating civic dialogue and creating work with marginalized populations. A playwright, director, activist, educator, and social critic, her work has been featured on network television, National Public Radio, the BBC, and in the Associated Press, as well as academic journals and mainstream publications. Her plays have been published and produced throughout the United States, Canada, the United Kingdom, and Australia. Honors include a Visionary Award, a Arts for Life Lifetime Achievement Award, the James F. Hornback Ethical Humanist of the Year Award, a Healthcare Hero Award, and the Missouri Arts Award, among others. Her work is published in *Upstaging Big Daddy: Directing Theater as if Race and Gender Matter*, *Amazon All Stars*, *Nice Jewish Girls: Growing Up in America*, *Mythic Women/Real Women: New Plays and Performance Pieces*, *One on One: The Best Women's Monologues for the 21st Century*, and *Radical Acts*, among other publications. For more info, visit www.uppityco.com.

characters

PUN, a gay man in his late thirties or forties

ZAK, a gay man in his late thirties or forties

setting

The present. It is late. Somewhere in urban America. The entire scene takes place in front of PUN's door.

• • •

[PUN *and* ZAK, *two gay men, are at* PUN*'s door. They've just had their first date.*]

PUN So now what?

ZAK Now I kiss you good night...

PUN Yes?

ZAK I kiss you good night, and you thank me for a lovely evening...

PUN Yes?

ZAK And I say, I'll call.

[*Beat.*]

PUN Oh. And will you?

ZAK Will I what?

PUN Call. Will you call?

ZAK Sure.

PUN When?

ZAK   I don't know. When I do?

PUN   Right.

       [*Beat.*]

       You won't call.

ZAK   I won't?

PUN   No. No, you won't. But the thing is, you know, you really
       should get it right. What you really should say is, I'll call
       tomorrow.

ZAK   Oh?

PUN   Yeah. See, that's better than saying, I'll call. Because if you say
       I'll call you tomorrow, then I only have to feel like shit until,
       say, the day after tomorrow. The day after tomorrow when
       you don't. But if you say I'll call…whenever…it's purgatory,
       see? And purgatory stretches on. As purgatory will.

       [*Beat.*]

       I'm Catholic.

ZAK   I gathered.

PUN   It doesn't work too well with the gay thing but I'm managing.
       They have their version, and I have mine. And I still think
       God loves me, although lately he must be pissed because I
       haven't had a date like this in so long. Hell, I haven't had a
       date…And then you come along and you're cute and funny
       and smart. And then you say, "I'll call." You say, "I'll call."

ZAK   Well, maybe I will.

PUN   Uh-huh. See? See, that's what I mean.

ZAK   Maybe I just wanted to think about it.

PUN Right.

ZAK Right.

PUN I can't believe I'm saying all this, but what the hell. I'm tired of being, you know, polite and going through the motions because this is our lives. Right? There's an epidemic. It's hard.

ZAK I know.

PUN So I just decided, I decided after Jamie died that I wouldn't put up with the games anymore. No more games. No more bullshit. I may be a big queer, but at least I can be an honest one.

[*Beat.*]

ZAK I'm sorry.

PUN Uh-huh.

ZAK Really, I'm sorry.

PUN Forget it. It's late. I don't know what I'm doing.

ZAK I'm sorry I hurt your feelings.

PUN Right. Look, I'll see you around. Okay?

ZAK Will you?

PUN Sure.

ZAK When?

PUN When I do.

[*Beat.*]

ZAK   You're going to drive me nuts. You know that?

PUN   Ohh, careful now. You're speaking in future tense.

ZAK   I know. I said it, didn't I?

PUN   So say it again.

ZAK   What? You're driving me nuts?

PUN   No. No, not past tense or present tense but future. Say it in the future tense.

ZAK   How can there be a future if you can't keep your pants on long enough to see? You see, I was going to call.

PUN   Were you?

ZAK   Yeah. How does it go? Soon enough to seem interested but not too soon to look pushy.

PUN   So not tomorrow then?

ZAK   No, probably the day after, the day after tomorrow.

PUN   Oh.

ZAK   Not that I didn't want to call you tomorrow.

PUN   You didn't?

ZAK   No, I didn't. I didn't. No, I mean, I did.

PUN   You did?
[*He looks at his watch.*]
It is tomorrow.

ZAK   So it is. Hell, it's the day after tomorrow somewhere.

[*Beat.*]

PUN   Right. So call me.

ZAK   What?

PUN   Call me now.

ZAK   I don't have your number and this is really...

PUN   [*Overlapping.*] You wrote it down on the...

ZAK   You want me to call you?

PUN   Yeah, I really do.

ZAK   Now? You want me to call you now.

       [*Beat.*]

       [ZAK *pulls out a cell phone from his pocket and dials. The phone rings in* PUN's *pocket.*]

       [*Into phone.*]

       Hello?

PUN   [*Into phone.*] Hello.

ZAK   Um, is Pun there?

PUN   Speaking.

ZAK   Pun, this is Zak.

[*Beat.*]

PUN   Oh. Hi.

ZAK   Hi.

PUN   How are you?

ZAK   Fine. And you?

PUN   Good, I'm good. So what's up?

ZAK   I had a really nice time with you last night.

PUN   Me too.
[*Beat.*]
Go on.

ZAK   Um, I liked the restaurant? I always wanted to try that place?

PUN   Uh-huh. Go on.

ZAK   This is silly.

PUN   Is it? Well, silly is okay. Don't you think? I mean, sometimes.

ZAK   It's just that you're making me do all the work.

PUN   Am I? I think I just did a ton.

ZAK   You did?

PUN   Well, what do you think? So go on.

[*Beat.*]

ZAK   I, um . . .

PUN   It's okay. Go on.

ZAK   I, um, I think you're really funny and sexy and I want to see you again.

PUN   Good, that was very good. So when do you want to see me?

ZAK   Now.

[*Beat.*]

[*They slowly kiss and hang up the phones.*]

[*Beat.*]

PUN   Hi.

ZAK   Hi.

PUN   God, I hate being a fag sometimes. You know? How are you supposed to date someone when you meet them at the Club Baths?

ZAK   Date. An interesting question. Is that what we're doing?

PUN   I don't know. We're talking. We had dinner, and we're talking.

ZAK   We're talking alright. We're talking so much, I feel like a Goddamned lesbian.

PUN   Careful, you.

[*He kisses ZAK.*]

ZAK   What? Was it the Goddamned? Or the lesbian thing?

PUN   Shhhh.

[*They kiss again.*]

ZAK   God, it's late. I really need to get going.

PUN   It's beyond late.

ZAK   Yeah.

PUN   Yeah. So stay.

ZAK   What?

PUN   Zak.

ZAK   I don't know.

PUN   Really. It's okay.

ZAK   It's just that I really like you.

PUN   And I like you. And this is a bad thing?

ZAK   Are you sure?

PUN   About staying? Sure.

ZAK   No. I mean, sure that you like me.

PUN   I'm positive. You big nut.

        [*Singing.*]

        Sometimes you feel like a nut, sometimes you don't . . .

ZAK   Pun. Pun?

PUN   Oh, sorry. Am I tired or what? So you gonna stay?

ZAK   I don't know.

PUN   Aw, come on. I thought we had it settled. I want you to stay. Really. I'm positive.

ZAK   No.

        [*Beat.*]

        I'm positive.

[*Beat.*]

PUN   Oh.

ZAK   Yes. Oh.

[*Long beat.* PUN *opens his arms and embraces* ZAK.]

PUN   So now we begin.

ZAK   We begin?

PUN   Yes. Really. Now.

[*He embraces* ZAK.]

• • •

Death Comes
for a Wedding

Joe Tracz

Joe Tracz

Joe Tracz is playwright living in New York. His plays include: *Boy Wonders*, In the *Woods Where Wolves Are*, *Song for a Future Generation*, *Man Up and Away*, and *Phenomenon of Decline*, which won the American College Theatre Festival Reg. III Award for Best Short Play. His work has been performed around the country, from Aspen to Los Angeles, including productions at Ars Nova, Long Wharf Theater, Kalamazoo College, and 59E59. He has developed work with the Roundabout Theatre, Chicago Dramatists, Partial Comfort Productions, Performance Network, and the Playwrights Realm.

Death Comes for a Wedding had its world premiere in 2009 as a workshop production at the Williamstown Theatre Festival. In 2010, Joe was an inaugural writing fellow at the Playwrights Realm, and his play *Song for a Future Generation* premiered in Chicago (Lights Out Theatre Company) and Off-Off-Broadway (The Management). Joe has contributed a teleplay for the FX boxing drama *Lights Out* and is a member of the Ars Nova Play Group, which commissioned his short play *Mario & Sonic at the Olympic Winter Games*. Tracz has a BA in English from Kalamazoo College and an MFA in dramatic writing from NYU-Tisch.

characters

> **BETH**, a young woman of about twenty
>
> **OLD WOMAN**, one hundred and seventy-seven years old
>
> **EDDIE**, aka Death, looks like he works in advertising
>
> **GIRLS**, let's say three of them

time

Not as long ago as you might think

setting

The porch of a house on the edge of a small farming town. In the distance, a great mountain.

• • •

[*Morning. An* OLD WOMAN *sits on the porch, mending an extremely long bridal veil. Nearby, a trio of* GIRLS *jump rope and chant.*]

GIRLS   The bride of Death-Death-Death
Her name was Beth-Beth-Beth
She took her vows one day
He took her breath away

He took her home-home-home
Her soul to own-own-own
He took her skin-skin-skin
He left the bone-bone-bone

And that is why-why-why
Before you die-die-die
You listen close-close-close
You hear her—

[BETH *enters from the house.*]

BETH   Stop that! Go home! Don't you have anything better to do than rhyme about other people's misfortunes?

OLD WOMAN   Good morning, Beth.

BETH   Since when did every little thing that happens in this town get its own jump-rope chant?

OLD WOMAN   I don't mind. I haven't had to read a single newspaper since they put that playground next door.

[*The* OLD WOMAN *holds up the veil.*]

OLD WOMAN   How do you like it?

BETH   Is it a funeral shroud or a bridal veil?

OLD WOMAN   I wasn't sure which would be more appropriate. So I combined the two.

BETH   You can stop sewing. I won't be needing it.

OLD WOMAN   But your wedding is tonight! What else would you wear?

BETH   I won't be wearing anything.

OLD WOMAN   Scandalous!

BETH   I mean, because there won't be a wedding!
[*In a whisper.*]
I'm leaving.

OLD WOMAN   Eh? What was that?

BETH   [*A little louder.*] I'm leaving.

OLD WOMAN   I'm sorry, dear, my hearing is going. You'll have to speak up.

BETH   [*A little louder.*] I'm leaving!

OLD WOMAN   YOU'RE LEAVING?!?

[*The* GIRLS *look up, startled.*]

BETH   Not so loud. I don't want the whole town knowing.

OLD WOMAN   They'll know soon enough, when they show up for the wedding and there isn't any bride!

BETH   I had a dream last night. I'm running through a field of tall stalks of greens, but as I brush past them, they rot and turn to a curdled gray. But it's not me who's the cause of it, it's the man behind me. I can't see him because he's invisible, but because of the rotting greens I know he's there. And I realize that the greens are all the village has to eat, and the more I try to run, the more will be ruined. But I can't imagine stopping because I know that as soon as I stop he will grab me, and when he touches me I will see his face and it is *putrid*. It is *putrefying*. I look at it and I will be like the greens, my flesh and color will shrivel away and I will be dead. I will look like the dead. I will be the bride of Death. Then I woke up and thought, thank goodness that was only a dream.

And then I remembered.

I have no choice. I have to leave.

[BETH *reveals a suitcase.*]

OLD WOMAN   I wouldn't do that.

BETH   What would you do?

OLD WOMAN It's an honor to be chosen. I was never chosen for anything. Thirty years I played the lottery, my numbers never came up. Forty years of bingo. I've given memorable turns in fifty years' worth of spring musicals, but when they hand out the trophy for best actress, it's never my mantel it rests on. Sixty years ago, I went on the auction block at a date auction. No one bid. Not on me. I say it's an honor.

BETH Then you marry him.

OLD WOMAN I wasn't chosen. He'll find you, you know. He is Death. No escaping him.

BETH He's just one guy.

OLD WOMAN He's got friends in low places.

BETH Good-bye.

> [BETH *exits with the suitcase. A moment later, she comes running back.*]

You didn't see me.

[BETH *runs into the house as* EDDIE *enters. He's cute, maybe too cute. He has trendy black framed glasses, even though he doesn't actually need them. He wears an expensive Armani ensemble. He looks like he would probably work in advertising, though he is, in fact, Death. Oh, and his face is false.*]

EDDIE Good morning!

OLD WOMAN She's not here.

EDDIE Look, do you really want to lie to me?

> [*Beat. The* OLD WOMAN *points to the front door.*]

Beth? Are you in there? . . . Beth? . . . Beth, if you don't come out this instant, I'll rip the old lady's soul right out of her chest cavity and send it straight to hell and *it—will—hurt!*

[*The* OLD WOMAN *drops the veil.* BETH *slowly emerges.*]

BETH Some way to start a marriage.

EDDIE I just needed to see you. I wouldn't actually do it. Not before her time anyway.

[*To the* OLD WOMAN, *suddenly scary.*]

Unless she *really deserved it!*

BETH You're not supposed to see the bride the day of the wedding.

EDDIE You're not supposed to kill the bride either, but this isn't a traditional ceremony.

BETH Your face is falling off.

EDDIE Is it?

[*It is. He readjusts it.*]

I thought this would be a good time to go over the schedule. In ten minutes, I pick you up at your front door and lead you to the town square. There's black lace over all the gazebos and the high school orchestra is playing. We exchange vows and I lay you on the sacrificial marriage bed and there's a knife, which I plunge into your breast, and then I kiss you . . . or maybe I kiss you and then I stab you . . .

[*He pulls out a notepad and scribbles in it.*]

There. I'm reminding myself to check. Anyway, after that, your flesh will fall away and your bones will turn to dust and I'll take your soul to the Shadowlands and we can read poetry by the fire together for all eternity. How does that sound?

[BETH *is trying not to cry.*]

Do you want me to look over your vows?

BETH   Please go away. Please go away and leave me alone. I don't want to die. I love life. I'll never love you. I don't even know if I want to get married ever, but definitely not to you.

EDDIE   You don't even know me.

BETH   Two dates was all it took. And you lied to me!

EDDIE   How did I lie?

BETH   "Hi, I'm Eddie, I'm not from around here. I work in advertising."

OLD WOMAN   That's true, he's not from around here.

[*Beat.*]

And the rest is close enough.

BETH   I trusted you. I read you my poems.

EDDIE   Which I loved!

BETH   I don't read my poems to *anyone*.

EDDIE   I'm not anyone. I'm Death.

BETH   Funny how you never mentioned that.

[*They stare each other down. Suddenly,* BETH *grabs* EDDIE*'s false face and pulls it off, leaving his real, awful visage exposed. The audience can't see it, but* BETH *gasps in horror at the sight. The* OLD WOMAN *is fascinated. Finally,* EDDIE *takes the face from her hands and puts it back on.*]

EDDIE   I thought you said looks weren't important.

[*To the* OLD WOMAN.]

As long as the wedding is on, my agreement with the town still stands. If Beth says her vows, I won't touch a single crop for one whole year. If she doesn't . . . it's going to be a bitter harvest. Make sure she understands that.

[*To* BETH.]

They offered me my choice: any woman in town. And I chose you. Remember that: I chose you.

[EDDIE *exits.*]

OLD WOMAN   He's cute.

BETH   I hate him.

OLD WOMAN   You say that now, but once you're dead, you might feel differently.

BETH   *I . . . don't . . . want . . . to . . . die!*

OLD WOMAN   Who does?

[*The* GIRLS *start to jump rope again.*]

GIRLS   They're closing up the farmyards
They're boarding up the shops
Cause Death is gonna visit
And he's gonna take our crops

Will no one come to save us?
Can no one hear our plea?
'Cause when he takes our crops away
He might take *me*

OLD WOMAN   You realize I can't let you leave. There are consequences to consider. The greater good.

BETH   I can't go though with this.

OLD WOMAN   Being afraid of dying isn't much of a reason to live.

BETH   It's more than that. It's—can you keep a secret?

OLD WOMAN   That's confidential.

BETH   I'm—pregnant.

OLD WOMAN   And the father?

BETH   See over there? The mountain. And beyond it, the forest, and beyond that, the sea. At the edge of that, the shore, and on the other side, the city. On the other side of that, the desert, and above it all, the sky.

OLD WOMAN   Don't you get around.

[*She puts a hand on* BETH's *belly.*]

You carry it well.

BETH   That's because it's not here.

[*She moves the* OLD WOMAN's *hand to her forehead.*]

It's here.

OLD WOMAN   What kind of child . . . ?

BETH   Not a child. A poem. I'm pregnant with a poem. It's going to be the best I've ever written, maybe the best anyone's ever written, because it's a poem about life. But if they lay me on the marriage bed tonight and they stick that dagger through me, then it will never be written. Because life is so many things but the one thing it can't be is death. That's why I can't marry him. And . . .

OLD WOMAN   And?

BETH   . . . I'm afraid.

OLD WOMAN   I wrote a poem once.

BETH   You did?

OLD WOMAN   I climbed the mountain once too.

BETH   You mean in a dream.

OLD WOMAN   It wasn't a dream.

BETH   You've never left the town borders, everyone knows that.

OLD WOMAN   I'm one hundred and seventy-seven years old. I've done a lot of things people don't know. *You've* never left the town borders.

BETH   In my dreams I have. And I want to. I want to see all those things. I want to climb to the top of the mountain.

OLD WOMAN   I was twenty when I did it. It took six years, and for three of them all I had to eat was snow and cabbage. It was cold at the top—but the view? Made it worth it.

BETH   And I want to explore every corner of the forest.

OLD WOMAN   Well, that's wrong, there are no corners, just places where it ceases to be. They have animals like you never imagined. Terrible, terrifying, always hungry, never sated. I spent eight years there. I think they were scared of me.

BETH   And the sea? It's so deep, you couldn't possibly...

OLD WOMAN   No. I've never seen the bottom. But it wasn't for lack of trying. I spent four years going down, and it took another four to come back up. It's so deep I don't think there really is a bottom. I think it goes down forever.

BETH   But you've never been to the city.

OLD WOMAN   At fifty, I packed my bags and took the train. I shared a one-room apartment with three other women of different ages and life experiences, and one man who liked other men. We stayed up late and worked all sorts of jobs and had sex in every possible combination. Our lives became the basis of a popular television sitcom.

BETH   Which one?

OLD WOMAN   It was before your time. But they were the best eleven years of them all, because that part I didn't do alone. I've been alone a lot.

BETH   And then you came here?

OLD WOMAN   And then I came here. And I wrote my poem.

BETH   That's it! That's what I want! You've done everything.

OLD WOMAN   Not everything.

BETH   What...?

OLD WOMAN   I've never married. And I've never died. All my friends have done both. Not me.

BETH   Why not?

OLD WOMAN   I was waiting to be chosen.

[*She stares off towards the town square.*]

He is cute.

BETH   His face is false.

OLD WOMAN   And if he doesn't leave here with a bride, he'll leave with our crops. He took too many last year, and the year before that. We won't likely survive another bad harvest, and then he'll come for all of us.

BETH   I know. I know.

OLD WOMAN   And he's cute.

BETH   I met him at the bookstore. In the poetry section. When I first saw him, I thought—you look familiar. I thought—I know you. And I did. He came for my mother when I was a baby. Later, my older brother, and not long after that, my father. We reached for the same anthology and our hands accidentally brushed. His was cold. I should've paid more attention. When he said, "You know what I love? I love that our names rhyme," I should have said, "Wait a minute, Eddie doesn't rhyme with Beth."

OLD WOMAN   I wouldn't be surprised if that's the basis of the attraction. I've seen men fall in love over less.

BETH   On our second date, we were walking to the theater when he told me: "I've been watching you. I've had my eye on you since you were just a little girl." We sat through the play in silence. The next morning, he announced his intentions to the town.

OLD WOMAN   The men were too happy to meet his bargain.

BETH   They gave me no choice.

OLD WOMAN   They had the town's future in mind.

BETH   What about my own?

[*The* GIRLS *start a hand-clapping game.*]

GIRLS   There once was a girl named Beth
Engaged to be married to Death
He made her his wife
And he ended her life
With a kiss that took all of her breath

OLD WOMAN   It seems you're getting your poem after all.

BETH   That's not poetry. They're mocking me.

OLD WOMAN   It's a child's game.

BETH   It's not a game when it's your own death they're clapping hands to.

[*To the* GIRLS.]

Don't you know any other songs?

[*The* GIRLS *stop clapping. Then they start again, at a faster tempo.*]

GIRLS   Her face is white
Her lips are red
So's her blood
'Cause she's dead-dead-dead

BETH   I meant that *aren't about me!*

[*The* GIRLS *fall quiet. A pause.*]

BETH   I'll do it.

OLD WOMAN   You'll do what?

BETH   I'll marry him. I won't let everyone down.

OLD WOMAN   Even knowing what you'll be giving up?

BETH   I'll do it. For the greater good.

[*The* GIRLS *start their game again. A slower tempo.*]

GIRLS   Way up on the mountaintop
Far away from home
Somewhere past the ocean
There you'll find a poem

In the darkness of the forest
In the brightness of the sky
But you'll never write a word
Unless you live before you die

OLD WOMAN   The greater good. Means writing your poem.

BETH   But—you said—

OLD WOMAN   I said he has to leave with a bride. I didn't say it had to be you.

BETH   I don't understand.

[*The* OLD WOMAN *holds up the veil she's been mending. It's as big and long as a body—her body. She holds it up against herself, models it.*]

OLD WOMAN   How do I look?

BETH   But—

OLD WOMAN   I'm one hundred seventy-seven. I'm not waiting to be chosen. I'm choosing for myself.

[*A noise from offstage.*]

Quick! Get inside.

[*She puts the veil in* BETH's *arms and pushes her inside the house as* EDDIE *enters. He's wearing a tux. He's not as well put together as in his last appearance. Actually, he looks a little nervous.*]

EDDIE   They're all gathered. All we need is the bride. I have the dagger.

[*He holds up a gruesome-looking knife.*]

OLD WOMAN   You look beautiful.

EDDIE You think? It's so hot and sticky up here.

[*He indicates the false face.*]

When I get home, I'm not putting this thing back on for a long time. How is she?

OLD WOMAN That would be telling.

EDDIE I know you think I'm a monster, but I didn't want it to go like this. I've known her since birth. I've watched her grow.

OLD WOMAN What do you see in her? It's not really because your names rhyme.

EDDIE Have you read her poems? They're so full of . . .

OLD WOMAN Life?

EDDIE Yes, that's what that would be. The best I've ever managed is a screenplay.

OLD WOMAN I'll get her.

EDDIE Thank you.

[*The* OLD WOMAN *exits into the house.* EDDIE *gets a few nervous puffs on a cigarette. A few moments later, a figure enters, draped in the veil that covers her whole body. It is the* OLD WOMAN. EDDIE *takes her gloved hand in his and, with the dagger in the other, leads her away. The* GIRLS *begin another clap chant.*]

GIRLS Here comes the bride
The beautiful bride
When the song stops
We'll know that she's died

[*They finish and sit. A moment later,* BETH *pokes her head out the door to make sure no one is watching. She emerges with her suitcase.*]

GIRL   Where are you going?

[BETH *is startled.*]

BETH   I—Aren't you surprised I'm not down there?

GIRL   You're a little shorter than she is. I don't think *he* noticed the difference, though.

BETH   Are you going to tell anyone?

GIRL   Naw. We don't have to chant about stuff if we don't want to.

BETH   Thank you.

[*She starts to go, then turns.*]

And, uh, keep it up with the poems.

[*In the distance, something between a funeral rite and a wedding march plays.* BETH *exits towards the mountain.*]

• • •

Seven Card Draw

Created by Daniel Gallant

Featuring:

Daniel Gallant
Clay McLeod Chapman
John Guare
Neil LaBute
Daniel Frederick Levin
Quincy Long
Laura Shaine

Seven Card Draw
Playwrights

Daniel Gallant is a theater producer, playwright, director, and actor. He is also the executive director of the Nuyorican Poets Cafe in Manhattan's East Village. He previously served as the director of theater and talk programming at the 92nd Street Y's Makor and Tribeca centers. Daniel has produced and directed plays, musicals, and other events at venues, including the DR2 Theatre, Dixon Place, Center Stage, the Abingdon Theatre, the Henry Street Settlement, Theater for the New City, and the Cornelia Street Cafe. Daniel's plays and monologues have been published in anthologies by Random House and Applause. Contact: gallant.arts@gmail.com.

Clay McLeod Chapman is the creator of the rigorous storytelling session *The Pumpkin Pie Show*. He is the author of *rest area*, a collection of short stories, and *miss corpus*, a novel. He teaches writing at the Actors Studio MFA program at Pace University.

John Guare was awarded the Gold Medal in Drama by the American Academy of Arts and Letters for his Obie, New York Drama Critics' Circle, and Tony-winning plays, which include *House of Blue Leaves*, *Six Degrees of Separation*, *Landscape of the Body*, and *A Few Stout Individuals*. His screenplay for Atlantic City received an Oscar nomination. Lincoln Center is producing his new play, *A Free Man of Color*, in 2010.

Neil LaBute received his Master of Fine Arts degree in dramatic writing from New York University and was the recipient of a literary fellowship to study at the Royal Court Theatre. His films include *In the Company of Men* (New York Critics' Circle Award for Best First Feature, Filmmakers' Trophy at the Sundance

Film Festival), *Your Friends and Neighbors*, *Nurse Betty*, *Possession*, *The Shape of Things*, *The Wicker Man*, *Lakeview Terrace*, and *Death at a Funeral*. LaBute's plays include latter-day plays, *The Shape of Things*, *The Distance from Here*, *The Mercy Seat*, *Autobahn*, *Fat Pig*, *This Is How It Goes*, *Some Girl(s)*, *Wrecks*, *In a Dark Dark House*, *Reasons to Be Pretty*, and *The Break of Noon*. An early play, *Filthy Talk for Troubled Times*—along with a series of new shorter works—was recently published by Soft Skull Press.

Daniel Frederick Levin's musical, *To Paint the Earth* (written with composer Jonathan Portera), won the 2004 Richard Rodgers Development Award and was produced in the 2008 New York Musical Theatre Festival. With Portera, Daniel also wrote the short musical *The Hungry Lion* and served as a Jonathan Larson Memorial Fellow at the Dramatists Guild. His other plays and musicals include *Campaign* (words and music), the book for *Luna Park* (commissioned by SUNY Cortland, 2008), *Hee-Haw*, *Going to Belize* (Long Wharf Theatre, NWNH, 2007), *The Waiter* (Makor/Steinhardt Center, 2006), and *The Lake Walk*. He holds an MFA from the NYU Tisch Graduate Musical Theatre Writing Program and a BA from Yale. Contact: www.danielflevin.com.

Quincy Long's recent productions include *People Be Heard*, Playwrights Horizons; *The Only Child*, South Coast Rep; *The Lively Lad*, New York Stage and Film and the Actors Theatre of Louisville; *The Joy of Going Somewhere Definite*, the Atlantic Theatre Company and the Mark Taper Forum, optioned by Icon Films. Current projects: *Loulou*, a musical, in development at the Banff Centre and commissioned by Ginger Cat Productions in Toronto; *Buried Alive*, a one-act opera adapted from an Edgar Allan Poe short story and commissioned by American Lyric Theatre in New York; and *The Gospel According to Trains*, a high-speed rail extravaganza commissioned by America-in-Play and the New York State Council on the Arts. Mr. Long is a graduate of the Yale School of Drama, and lives in New York City. He is from Warren, Ohio.

Laura Shaine is a novelist and journalist, as well as an internationally known playwright. She is widely produced throughout Russia and Eastern Europe.

Seven Card Draw

created by Daniel Gallant

written by Daniel Gallant, Clay McLeod Chapman, John Guare, Neil LaBute, Daniel Frederick Levin, Quincy Long, and Laura Shaine

··· production note ···

Seven Card Draw premiered at Dixon Place in New York City on March 16, 2010.

The cast was as follows (in order of appearance):

> Germán Rivadeneira   **CARAMELLO** (in *Beware of Waiter*)
> Molly Thomas   **LILA** (in *Beware of Waiter*)
> Natalie Bird   **SUSAN** (in *Beware of Waiter*)
> Joshua Rivedal   **TOM** (in *Beware of Waiter*)
> Clay McLeod Chapman   **NARRATOR** (in *undertow*)
> Wayne Schroder   **OLD KNAVE LINCOLN** (in *What Really Happened*)
> Devon Goffman   **YOUNG KNAVE** (in *What Really Happened*)
> David Miceli   **HOST 1** (in *What Really Happened*)
> Katie Northlich   **HOST 2** (in *What Really Happened*)
> Piper Perabo   **GIRL** (in *Totally*)
> Carlos Iberra   **DEVON** (in *The Huntsmen*)
> Grant Neale   **FATHER** (in *The Huntsmen*)
> Daniel Gallant   **NARRATOR** (in *Determined to Prove*)
> Eric Slater   **NARRATOR** (in *What It Was Like*)

Four of the short works were directed by Daniel Gallant; *Totally* was directed by Carolyn Cantor; *The Huntsmen* was directed by Kathleen Dimmick; and *What Really Happened* was directed by Daniel F. Levin. The music was composed by Michael Gallant; the stage manager was Laura Archer.

   Seven Card Draw runs approximately 90 minutes without an intermission. It consists of seven short plays and monologues, and features fourteen roles (4F,

10M). If actors are double-cast, the show could be performed with as few as five actors (2F, 3M).

The original production employed a very sparse set—chairs, tables, and a potted plant were used to evoke multiple settings.

NOTE: The plays and monologues that constitute *Seven Card Draw* may be performed collectively or individually, so long as the appropriate permission is obtained from their authors.

The running order and breakdown of roles is as follows:

Work	Author	Role(s)
1. *Beware of Waiter*	Laura Shaine	**WAITER/CARAMELLO** (M), **LILA** (F), **SUSAN** (F), **TOM** (M)
2. *undertow*	Clay McLeod Chapman	**NARRATOR** (M)
3. *What Really Happened*	Daniel F. Levin	**OLD KNAVE** (M), **YOUNG KNAVE** (M), **HOST** (M), **2ND HOST** (F)
4. *Totally*	Neil LaBute	**GIRL** (F)
5. *The Huntsmen*	Quincy Long	**DEVON** (M), **FATHER** (M)
6. *Determined to Prove*	Daniel Gallant	**NARRATOR** (M)
7. *What It Was Like*	John Guare	**NARRATOR** (M)

Beware of Waiter

by Laura Shaine

characters

> **THE WAITER/CARAMELLO**, handsome, exotic
>
> **LILA**, a young actress
>
> **TOM**, a young actor
>
> **SUSAN**, a young actress

• • •

[*Very late at night. Three diners enter trendy, ethnic restaurant, Sushi Mombo. Lighting is subdued; décor is sleek, moderne—curving banquettes. Palms, orchids on table. Low-key but exotic music of undefined ethnic origin is playing.* THE WAITER, CARAMELLO, *approaches the diners. He is very beautiful/handsome, also of undefined ethnic origin. The diners chat—they have come from performing at a theatrical event.* LILA *and* TOM *are a couple;* SUSAN *is a single woman.*]

TOM   *You two* were great! I'm not sure they "got" me. Whenever I opened my mouth, the audience went dead silent.

LILA   They were attentive. I could feel it.

SUSAN   I always wanted to eat here. I look in the window every night on my way home from rehearsal and see the candles twinkling and the people inside . . . and I always wonder what it's like. Uh-oh! I think it's almost full. Listen, why don't just you and Tom stay? I can go home and heat up a Lean Cuisine.

TOM   . . . Single orchids on the table, linen napkins . . . but in offbeat colors, tiger stripes . . . Do you know what this says to me? It says, "Get the eff out of here!" Fusion adds an extra zero to the check!

LILA This is one of those "in" places... I see famous faces I can't identify! Look over there! The names will come to me! They have a table! Oooh... The big banquette! Oh, c'mon, get in the spirit.

[*Nudging* TOM.]

It's a celebration! Ooh, ooh, I know that guy! He left Jennifer Anniston! I don't know his name but that's definitely him!

SUSAN [*Wistful.*] Everybody left Jennifer Anniston. I want a plate of what just went by... I don't know what it is but I want it! I have "plate envy."

[CARAMELLO *slinks over; he comes increasingly closer, he is inappropriately close, almost rubbing against the women.*]

CARAMELLO That was the Sushi Sambal Kecap... It's on our specials tonight... sushi with chilies.

TOM I saw a diner open across the street! They have good burgers... I'd be just as happy with a juicy cheeseburger on a good old-style bun with ketchup. *Come on*, it is not too late...

CARAMELLO Welcome to Sushi Mambo—the first Japanese-Chilean-Indonesian-Estonian fusion restaurant in the city. We now have sister restaurants in Chicago, Detroit, and Port Ewen.

TOM [*Under his breath.*] I just want to eat. I could eat a table leg. With sauce.

CARAMELLO My name is Caramello and I'm going to tell you about our specials—but first, may I show you our vodka list? I recommend the ginkgo bud blossom vodka—it has a clear chartreuse flavor...

TOM   Chartreuse is a color not a flavor...

CARAMELLO   [*Gently, almost snuggling up to* TOM.] They have now proven that flavors also have color...sometimes even thoughts have color...

TOM   Off-color.

LILA and SUSAN   We'll try it. The ginkgo bud blossom vodka!

TOM   I usually don't like soda; it is a childhood habit, but tonight I really could go for a good, old-fashioned, corrosive Classic Coke!

[CARAMELLO *looks hurt.*]

CARAMELLO   I was going to suggest a carafe of the ginkgo bud blossom vodka for the table.

LILA   We'll take it!

[*Hissing to* TOM.]

You can have a can of Coke at home.

CARAMELLO   And the entrée specials are fresh soft-shell crab Sushi Sambal Kecap and tortoise roe Pisang Goreng in green curry sauce with a hint of cumin and slivers of durian fruit, served on cones of Nasi Kunung.

LILA   The Pisang Goreng does sound good!

SUSAN   I don't know. The soft-shell crab Sushi Sambal Kecap appeals to me...

CARAMELLO   I'll let you think about it...

SUSAN   [*To* LILA.] He is *so*...

SUSAN and LILA   ...Hot!

TOM   Is it male or female?

SUSAN   . . . Genetic male . . . but I'm not sure . . . He has a fusion quality himself . . .

LILA   Maybe he's a hermaphrodite . . .

SUSAN   Like the Olympic runner they gender tested—the one who ran as a woman but had a slight beard and pecs?

LILA   . . . And she had balls! I saw them bobbling, under her shorts, as "she" crossed the finish line.

SUSAN   Maybe he honestly thought he was a genetic female?

TOM   How do you "miss" a set of balls in your track shorts? *Puh-lease!*

LILA   That is so trans-gendered sexist! You are antediluvian . . .

CARAMELLO   While you think, I'd like to tell you a little more about Sushi Mombo . . . Sushi Mombo is dedicated to saving the planet in many ways . . . We are entirely green and use no trans fat . . .

TOM   The kitchen is going to close! It's one a.m.

CARAMELLO   Sushi Mambo never closes . . . while there are guests to be served . . . I will make sure you are served.

TOM   [*Under his breath.*] Yeah, for a humongous tip.

CARAMELLO   There is no tipping at Sushi Mambo . . . an 18 percent gratuity has automatically been added to your meal so you do not have to think about it . . . And 10 percent to a charity of your choice. There are two choices . . .

TOM   Yeah, well, I like to pay my rent.

CARAMELLO I'll give you a moment more to decide on your entrée. In the meantime, I will get you a basket of krupuks and our complimentary Sushi Mambo Fusion Fingers...

[*Exit.*]

TOM [*Sotto voce to the girls.*] This is a big rip-off.

SUSAN We can all split an entrée. I'll ask for three plates.

TOM Lots of luck. I don't trust this waiter. Watch him...

LILA This is celebratory! We had a great show!

TOM We made less than the meal will cost. We could still get out of here and get the cheeseburger deluxe across the street... eleven bucks tops!

LILA It's a swill-a-ria!

TOM It's good!

SUSAN It's a swill-a-ria... He's back.

CARAMELLO Here are your Sushi Mombo Fusion Fingers... one finger for each nation we fuse. Are you ready?

TOM [*Under his breath.*] For what?

LILA To order... I'll have the... the crab thing—the sushi crab enchiladas. Actually, we're... uh... not that hungry—May we have three plates so we can split the tamales?

[CARAMELLO'*s face twitches, but he controls himself and gives a small, tight smile.*]

CARAMELLO Of course. It is my pleasure to serve you.

[*He turns and walks away.*]

TOM   Actually, I want the tortoise roe.

LILA   So have it!

TOM   No! It will drive the bill up. I can see this coming—$300 and it's all over in thirty minutes.

CARAMELLO   I can give you the appetizer-size serving. It is one roe.

[TOM *nods "okay"*; CARAMELLO *vanishes.*]

TOM   Let's run out before he comes back...It's not too late.

LILA   Yes it is!

[CARAMELLO *is instantly back with both platters.*]

CARAMELLO   Careful! Plates are hot!

LILA   May I have chopsticks...? For the table.

TOM   I want a knife and fork.

        [*Aside.*]

        I really don't trust this guy. He's going to pull something!

CARAMELLO   On my island, we don't use cutlery or chopsticks, we use the first three fingers of our right hand and the leaves of the banana trees as Handi Wipes...

[TOM *secretly gives* CARAMELLO *the finger.*]

TOM   Yeah, and what do they do with the other hand? I read about this!

LILA and SUSAN   [*Raising their hands.*] We'll try it! Our fingers, the banana leaves! Yes to everything!

TOM   Why are you two so anxious to please *him*? We're going to get soaked here!

LILA and SUSAN   [*Sighing.*] Yes.

LILA   It's exotic.

[*To* SUSAN, *regarding* TOM.]

I knew I shouldn't have let him move into my apartment.

TOM   I heard that…

LILA   You were meant to! Happy casual meals out are a primary pleasure in my life! When anything good happens, I like to celebrate! I count the experience more than every penny! Tonight was fun, it was a high; I am wound up. I want to celebrate! Our show sold out!

TOM   Our show cleared $165 dollars in donations in the cellar of a synagogue!

LILA   Always emphasize the negative!

TOM   I moved in with you because I was alone, you were alone, and everyone else was a couple…

SUSAN   I'm starting to feel uncomfortable…Maybe I should just go…home.

TOM   We could cuddle up and watch Netflix and eat Thai takeout…I thought it was working…But now you have all these elitist demands, and suddenly I am a *schmuck*!

CARAMELLO   To save time, I will give you the check now…

TOM   We haven't even eaten yet!

LILA   [*To* SUSAN.] Please stay.

[*To* TOM.]

We're very different.

[*To* SUSAN.]

I'm sorry to involve you in this . . . This is couples' insanity.

[*To* TOM.]

I'll see a counselor with you or it's over.

[*To* SUSAN.]

I'm not going to put up with this.

TOM [*To* CARAMELLO *regarding the check.*] I thought we were not going to be rushed . . .

CARAMELLO [*Testy for first time.*] That's why I am giving you the check *now*!

TOM Yeah, you are! This is a three-figure check, higher than my last pay stub! Add this up, bud.

CARAMELLO Caramello! My name is not "Bud"! That is the correct figure; it includes the 18 percent gratuity and your 10 percent contribution to our charity, Save the Komodo Dragon!

LILA Komodo dragon!

CARAMELLO [*With sacred tone.*] The Komodo dragon is the world's largest living lizard. They are considered the closest species remaining to evoke the prehistoric dinosaurs. The largest verified specimen reached a length of 10.3 feet and weighed 366 pounds. The Komodo's sense of smell is its primary food detector. The Komodo detects odors much as a snake does. It uses its long yellow forked tongue to sample the air. They use their shark-like teeth and strong claws to eviscerate their victims. The Komodo's toxic breath and venom saliva paralyzes the prey. The prey quickly bleeds to death, and the Komodo begins to feed.

[*His tone changes.*]

I'll be back with your order.

[*He spins around and hands* TOM *a plate with a single tortoise roe on it.*]

Your roe. Do you want to know more about the dragons?

TOM   No!

CARAMELLO   The muscles of the Komodo's jaws and throat allow it to swallow huge chunks of meat with astonishing rapidity. Several movable joints, such as the intramandibular hinge, open the lower jaw unusually wide. The stomach expands easily, enabling an adult to consume up to 80 percent of its own body weight in a single meal. Komodos eat much more efficiently. They eat bones, hooves, and swaths of hide. They also eat intestines, but only after swinging them vigorously to scatter their contents. This behavior removes feces from the meal. Because large Komodos cannibalize young ones, the young often roll in fecal material, thereby assuming a scent that the large dragons avoid...They survived only because of their isolated habitats in my homeland.

[*Back to the spiel.*]

Do you want to know how the Komodos reproduce?

TOM   No.

CARAMELLO   Although males tend to grow larger and bulkier than females, no obvious morphological differences mark the sexes. One subtle clue does exist: a slight difference in the arrangement of scales just in front of the cloaca: their sexual opening, their hole. Sexing Komodos remains a challenge to researchers; the dragons themselves appear to have little trouble figuring out who is who. When a group assembles around the dead prey or carrion, the opportunity for courtship arrives.

SUSAN   They make love around the . . . the corpses of their dead prey?

CARAMELLO   Dominant males can become embroiled in ritual combat in their quest for females. Using their tails for support, they wrestle in upright postures. The victorious wrestler initiates courtship by flicking his tongue on a female's snout and then over her body. Before copulation can occur, the male must evert a pair of hemipenes located within his cloaca, at the base of the tail. The male then crawls on the back of his partner and inserts one of the two hemipenes into her cloaca. Komodo dragons are an endangered species. Can you imagine the world without them? Your voluntary addition to your check will feed one Komodo dragon on his captivity diet of frozen rodents for two and a half days! If we don't support Save the Komodo Dragon, it is expected that they will be extinct by the year 2199. *We have to save them!*

TOM   I don't want to save Komodo dragons! Let them be extinct!

[*He rises in anger.*]

Exterminate them!

LILA   [*Hissing at him.*] Get down, Tom; your anger is completely inappropriate to this situation!

[*To* SUSAN.]

He was just waiting to explode! This isn't about the dragon; it's about Tom's inability to process any emotion!

TOM   [*To* LILA.] Oh, shut up with your psychobabble!

[*To* CARAMELLO.]

They are hideous, horned, blood-salivating eyesores that attack island villagers . . . I read the news! They just ate a fisherman on your beloved island! They are man-eaters!

LILA   Did you say "shut up" to me? Did he say *"shut up"*? Susan?

SUSAN   [*Hiss to* LILA.] This is getting a little tense.

[*To* CARAMELLO.]

Didn't one in a zoo bite off the toes of Sharon Stone's husband?

TOM   Well, *that* was true; I saw it on CNN. A dragon in the San Francisco Zoo bit off the toes of Sharon Stone's husband.

CARAMELLO   Sharon Stone's husband should never have been allowed in the cage with a Komodo dragon! The dragon was just following his genetic disposition . . . yes, they eat men but only when given the opportunity by idiot humans!

TOM   These are the most disgusting animals I have ever heard about! The forked yellow tongue thing really bothers me! Venom saliva! Why the eff should I save them!?

CARAMELLO   Because they are endangered! There are only 4,032 of them left and [*To* LILA.] you don't find two hemipenes interesting?

SUSAN   Two penises?

TOM   Are you coming on to her?

CARAMELLO   [*Eyeing both women seductively.*] You wouldn't recognize the hemipenes as such but yes . . . they do deeply penetrate the females. That has to mean something, even to you people!

LILA   I'm not sure about being forced to contribute to a cause in a restaurant. What was the second choice charity?

CARAMELLO   You'd rather contribute to the sphincter mutilation victims...? The sphincters of my people have been systematically enlarged for centuries by a coming-of-age ritual which involves insertion of the durian fruit that leaves them permanently itching...

SUSAN   I am losing my appetite!

[*To* LILA.]

I think maybe you and I should just go back to the way it used to be before you met Tom...we can meet for lunch or you can come over to my place...just the two of us...this just isn't working.

CARAMELLO   Oh, so you richies have your little trendy upscale meal and forget the suffering of all the dying reptiles and itching suppurating humans? Eff the rest of the world! Just eat your precious morsels that are more than my salary and eff the fact I haven't seen my lovers for a weekend in two years because I am always working at Sushi Mambo!! Just *YOU! YOU! YOU!*

SUSAN   Huh? You don't mean us! Not *us*! We have no money! We're actors!

LILA   And *I* care about the itching suppurating masses *and you* but...Can't a restaurant be...a...sanctuary? A place where you can forget the world's problems...for an hour!?

[*To* SUSAN.]

It will be okay. It's just an odd night—Tom has other issues, his job, his sexual confusion...I don't think he's ever decided which side of the fence he's on.

CARAMELLO   This *is* a sanctuary.

[*He sets down a plate.*]

Here's your tortoise roe.

TOM Screw the dragons.

CARAMELLO [*Crying a little.*] You would watch them die?

TOM Yes!

LILA Why do *you* care so much?

SUSAN Yes, *why?*

CARAMELLO Because I have one!

[*They hear an offstage roar from the kitchen.*]

TOM I knew it! I totally called it!

[*He looks at the check.*]

$287.50 with tax! I could have had a cheeseburger!

[*He is ebullient.*]

It is worth it to be proven right!

[*He pops the roe in his mouth.*]

This *is* a tasty morsel!

SUSAN [*To* LILA *and* TOM.] Next time, you two go out without me.

[*She rises to leave.*]

LILA I'm sorry, I'm sorry, I'm sorry—why is everything my fault?!

[*She rises to go. To* TOM.]

Time for you to check into your old room at the Y!

[*To* SUSAN.]

And *you* could have shown me a little support!

CARAMELLO   Shall I take your plates? It looks like you're done.

[*They hear an offstage roar from the kitchen, carnal red lights blink on and off, and the roaring increases.*]

CARAMELLO   C'mon, girl! Banquette number one!

[TOM, SUSAN, *and* LILA *begin to scream; the silhouette of a giant lizard, the Komodo dragon, is projected on the rear wall. His jaws are wide open.*]

[*Sounds of roaring, carnage.*]

[*Red-out, blackout.*]

• • •

undertow

by Clay McLeod Chapman

characters

NARRATOR, male, early 30s

• • •

NARRATOR   You got to keep up with me better than this, bartender.
With as many sorrows as I've got to drown, I'm gonna be
stuck on this stool all night. *Hey*—how long's a guy got to
wait for a refill around here? I don't want to see the bottom
of that glass for the rest of this crisp twenty-dollar bill.
We're going to let Mr. Jackson decide when I've had
enough to drink. Today was payday, so I'm showing the ol'
Andrew here a night on the town. Tell you what. Next
round's on me. How about that, everybody? *Andrew Jackson
here is up for re-election and he needs your votes.* He's hired me
to personally run his campaign. We're hitting all the bars
along the highway, mustering up the drunkards to get
behind the wheel. 'Cause on this highway—I'm the worst
vulture there is. After the police and paramedics peck
through a car wreck, I swoop down for the scraps. This road
would be lumping over with rotten automobiles if it weren't
for me towing them away—*so don't you tell me I don't know
what I'm talking about here.* This highway's *my* office. *You're*
the one's walking into *my* work the second you stumble
outside the bar. I've seen what a steering wheel can do to
your chest when you hit the brakes at eighty miles an hour.
It pushes past your abdomen—your body slams against it so
hard. Your ribs grip the wheel, trying to steer—your heart
honking the horn every time it beats. *Honk, honk. Honk,*

honk. You want to tell me I don't deserve a drink after
working around that all day? I've got two kids at home and I
can't even hug them. Feel like my fingers are going to tear
right through. My hands don't deserve to know what that
feels like. I can't trust the touch of things anymore. None of
you know how flimsy your skin really is. *Look at you.* You've
all soaked yourselves up in enough alcohol, a simple pinch
between your seat and the steering wheel could tear right
through you. But hell. I figure—*I owe you.* All of you here.
You boys keep me in business, you know that? Half the calls
I get are car wrecks coming from drunk drivers. Makes me
wish I was working on a commission. I'd stop in here every
night, personally buying each and every one of you a drink
with the money from my own pocket. I'd earn it all back
right after happy hour. Tonight, I guarantee you—I'll be
towing one of your cars out from some ditch. I just figured
I'd come down here first. Pay you a visit before the
accident. I wanted to see what you all looked like in one
piece. *Bartender* . . . Is this a self-service station here or what?
Fill her up, man! My hands are still shaking. I want to hold
my children tonight. Hug them tight. Not think about their
seat belts sawing their heads off. Can you do that for me,
please? Can you wash my day away? I bet you've had to
listen through every sad sack's story that's come in here—
haven't you? They all line up along the bar and just start
sobbing away, don't they? Bet you think you've heard it all
by now. Am I right? Well . . . I got one for you. You fill up
that glass and I'll tell you a story you've never heard before.
I towed away my wife tonight. It's true. I'm not lying. Got
the call about three hours ago. The highway patrol radioed
in and said they had a wreck down on Route 27, right where
the river starts running alongside the road. I was the nearest
truck around, so I called the dispatcher and said I'd take it.

My shift was winding down, but I was near enough to tow it
in no time. Once I pulled up, I see this wine-bibber sitting
in the road. Man was so drunk, he didn't even realize he'd
already been in an accident. He's got this whole entourage
of officers surrounding him, asking questions. You could
smell the alcohol on his answers—*No, no, officer, I only had a
little nip. Nothing to fuss over, I swear* . . . He'd lost control of
the wheel, skidding over into the oncoming traffic. There
was a station wagon heading in the other direction, both
sets of headlights staring each other down. To miss kissing
fenders, that station wagon had to take a sharp turn,
running right off the road and through the guardrail—
hitting the river at fifty, sixty miles an hour. You could see
how heavy the brakes had been laid on. Half the tires had
rubbed off over the asphalt. I was told to drive towards the
water, this officer motioning for me to back the winch up
along the shore. You can't think about the people who'd
been behind the wheel when you're on the job. You tow
those cars in and you try not to look inside, see what's still
caked onto the car. You drop them off at the junkyard and
you go home and you kiss your kids good night and you
hold on to your wife until you finally fall asleep, *thanking
God* you've got a family to come home to night after night.
And you hope that you don't have dreams about all the
people on the road, imagining what would happen if it'd
been someone *you* loved. Someone who mattered to *you*.
You pray for a smooth ride through your sleep. No
nightmares about finding your family on the highway. Took
me almost two hours to tug that station wagon out from the
water. The winch kept winding in, the car getting closer.
The numbers on the license plate are starting to look real
familiar to me, like I've seen them before. But I'm not
saying anything to anybody. I figure my nerves are just

stretched. *I'm seeing things*—that's all. I could go home and find my wife already in bed, curled up underneath the sheets and sleeping. Not right there in front of me. *Whose wife was this?* Not mine—not with her hands frozen into fists from hammering against the window, trying to punch through the glass as the river swept in. No—*my wife was at home.* She wasn't out buying ice cream for the family. It had all melted, fogging up the water. It took a police officer to wipe his finger down her arm to realize what she was covered in, the entire inside of the car coated with a gallon's worth of vanilla skin. Licking his finger, he said—*My favorite flavor.* Mine, too. Instead of towing the station wagon down to the pound, I took it home. Parked it right in front of our house. What water was still caught inside was dribbling out onto the road. And I went inside, right up to my children's room. Found them sound asleep. Let me ask you something. How would you go about telling your kids all this, if something like this happened to you? Would you wake them up, sit one on each knee? Would you wait for the police to ring your doorbell? Or would you pile what was left of your family into the station wagon and go for a little ride? Maybe head down to your local watering hole, let the kids sleep in the backseat while you stepped out for a little drink? I want to know what you boys would do. I want you all to have a drink on me with the money I made towing my own wife— and think about how happy I'm going to be when I pry your car off of some tree, yanking your fender from its trunk. Me and the kids are going to be waiting in the parking lot here, with the radio on—just waiting for the dispatcher to call in with a car wreck. 'Cause I think it's time they see what their daddy does for a living, see what I've got to deal with almost every night—so that when we hug each other, we'll all know just what it is that we're holding on to. How precious that feeling is. Tonight, I'm the designated driver. We can all car-pool down to the pound together. But first— how about another round? What do you say, everybody? *One for the road?*

• • •

What Really Happened, Starring Abraham Lincoln: A Re-Enactment of the Meeting Between Abraham Lincoln and a Certain Mephilantos, Son of the Horse Rearer

by Daniel Frederick Levin

characters

ABRAHAM LINCOLN/OLDER KNAVE, [*male, 50s or 60s*] A man who may or may not resemble our sixteenth president

YOUNGER KNAVE, [*male, 20s or 30s*] Energetic and saucy. Singer who preferably plays guitar or piano

HOST, [*male, 30s or 40s*] Wishing to please, expressive, earnest, filled with a love for "history"

2ND HOST, [*female, 30s or 40s*] Confident, scholarly, funny, reflective, unknowable

• • •

[*We're in woods on a shrouded and dungeonous eve. We hear very fake-sounding birdcalls and other noises. OLD KNAVE, in a brown cloak, is seated on a chair, snoozing. Soon YOUNGER KNAVE wanders in, carrying a bindle.*]

OLD KNAVE [*Waking from groggy daze and speaking in heavy and overly theatrical British accent.*] Halt! Who goes there on this most shrouded and dungeonous eve?

YOUNGER KNAVE [*Matching accent.*] It is I, Mephilantos, my liege, son of Halastratos, the Horse Rearer, and Mylanta of the 7th Swan.

OLD KNAVE   [*Chomping a bit.*] Mylanta of the 7th Swan. Yeeeees. Yeees. I knew her. And the Horse Rearer, you say. They got together?

YOUNGER KNAVE   [*A little annoyed.*] Yes. And with whom may I have the thistly pleasure?

OLD KNAVE   Abraham Lincoln. I've been wandering this space between light and dark lands, and have rested here for the night, pondering my next move.

[*Pause.*]

YOUNGER KNAVE   Yes, Master Lincoln. If that is all, then, I shall be proceeding forward. My boy is ill and the dark lands are still several cubits hence.

OLD KNAVE   Oh yes, by all means, proceed to the next grove ...

[YOUNGER KNAVE *begins onward.*]

If you wish to die.

[YOUNGER KNAVE *stops.*]

YOUNGER KNAVE   I'm sorry?

OLD KNAVE   I said proceed to the next grove, if you wish to die.

YOUNGER KNAVE   Why on earth would I die by proceeding into the next grove?

OLD KNAVE   Because McClellan headed into that grove. And where McClellan goes, so death doth follow.

HOST   Freeze! [*Applauds.*] Good. Good. What you have just seen is a re-imagining of the historic meeting between Mephilantos, son of the Horse Rearer, and Abraham Lincoln, two months before the latter's Emancipation Proclamation. What you may not realize, though, is that this depiction might not be anything like how the actual encounter transpired. And that's history. That's the stories we tell about ourselves.

Amazing, isn't it. I love history. Now fast-forward five thousand years, to an imagined encounter between a wondering rogue, and our 850th president, on the eve of that president's Emancipation Proclamation. Unfreeze!!

[*The two* KNAVES *hadn't really frozen in the first place. They retake their opening positions.*]

OLD KNAVE   Halt! Who goes there on this most shrouded and dungeonous eve?

YOUNGER KNAVE   It is I, Mephilantos, my liege, son of Kroton-5, the Horse Rearer, and Mylanta of the 7th Swan.

OLD KNAVE   Mylanta of the 7th Swan. Yeeeeees.

[*Sadly.*]

Yeees. I knew her...

HOST   Stop! Stop, stop, stop, stop, stop. Stop. This is very much like the first encounter.

[2ND HOST *steps out from offstage. She is wearing a cape.*]

2ND HOST   And that's history, for history repeats itself.

[*Awaits applause.*]

HOST   [*Applauding.*] Ladies and gentlemen, the esteemed Lincoln scholar Clementine Ray. This is amazing! Brava. Brava!

2ND HOST   [*To audience.*] Thank you. Hello, Roderick. It's been some time.

[*The two* HOSTS *seem to have some history.*]

HOST   It was actually the conference. Reconstruction.

[OLD *and* YOUNG KNAVE *watch the* HOSTS *talk.*]

2ND HOST   [*Not positive.*] Yes.

HOST   You were so busy.

2ND HOST   Yes. So, here we are. Let's, shall we try to show a slightly different version of the scene in question, to add context...

HOST   To...add context. Wonderful...context is very important...

2ND HOST   Now let's see. You sit in that chair, and I'll stand.

HOST   Yes. Oh, I love this.

2ND HOST   And I will say. Don't just sit there, Abraham Lincoln is coming!

HOST   And I leap to my feet!

[OLD KNAVE *begins walking slowly downstage, waving.* YOUNG KNAVE *sings British song or "Pomp and Circumstance." Applause.*]

OLD KNAVE   Bless you, my child. And bless you, my child. And hello, bless you—

HOST   [*Back on knees.*] Oh, sovereign master, please tarry your steps to hear a pitiful plea from a young man.

2ND HOST   Good, Roderick.

OLD KNAVE   Yes, my lad, what is it?

HOST   I wish to meet McClellan, for I hear he has powers to heal the—

OLD KNAVE   McClellan, the Scott? That name is heresy here!

2ND HOST   Good, and songs, songs that capture the spirit of a time.

[YOUNG KNAVE *plays and sings, apparently impromptu, on piano or guitar,* "*Touch the Hem of His Garment*" *by Sam Cooke*]

YOUNG KNAVE   [*Singing.*] Oh, there was a woman...

HOST   [*Grabbing edge of cloak.*] I know that, Your Majesty, but it's my boy, William, he's sick. Very sick. Otherwise I would never...

OLD KNAVE   Willie, you say? I should behead you, but your peasant wish somehow touches me...

2ND HOST   Yes! History is about the small interactions, the little rises and falls of a peasant father. It's not about kings! Dare to create history. A real moment, not a passed-down and licensed one. Dare to act! Dare to sing! Wooohh...woohhh, wohhh.

YOUNG KNAVE   [*Singing softly, underscoring dialogue.*] In the valley she had been sick, sick so very long, when she heard that Jesus was passing by, so she joined the gathering room, and while she was pushing her way through, someone asked her what are you trying to do, she said if I could just touch the hem of his garment, I know I'll be made whole...she cried. oh lord, oh lord, oh lord, oh lord, I know I'll be made whole.

[YOUNG KNAVE *and* 2ND HOST *continue riffing softly under dialogue.*]

OLD KNAVE   Do you really think McClellan has the power to heal the sick?

HOST   Oh yes, yes. McClellan will save William! I know he will.

[*Music out.*]

OLD KNAVE   Well, I'll do anything to save my boy, anything to save my child!

HOST   My boy, Mr. Lincoln . . . Willie, my boy.

OLD KNAVE   Our boy, Willie, then, for I am sovereign. I'll do anything to save him. I'll even praise McClellan the Scott, if only my boy could be saved. Just please let's try to save him.

[HOST *and* OLD KNAVE *embrace and hug. Pause.*]

HOST and OLD KNAVE   McClellan! McClellan! McClellan!

[*They hobble offstage.*]

2ND HOST   In February 1862, Lincoln's middle son, William, died of typhoid fever. He had been considered brilliant even at eleven, passing his bubble tests and making it into the Johns Hopkins summer program for both verbal and math. He had the soft temperament of his father.

YOUNG KNAVE   [*Still with accent, a little surprised at his new role.*] Lincoln would never recover from the loss. But it did help him empathize with the parents who were sending their young boys off to meet their possible demise on Wall Street.

[OLD KNAVE *has re-entered.*]

OLD KNAVE   In October of 1862, Abraham Lincoln may have run into a young horse trader, whom we have called Mephilantos, in Rock Creek Park, who was anxious about his sick child. According to some secondhand documents, Lincoln was startled that the only thing that could lift the man's spirits was talk of the General of the Potomac, McClellan. For at that very moment, McClellan was stalling, resting his troops just outside the beltway, while Lee's troops slipped back down the Interstate to Virginia.

YOUNG KNAVE   One month later, McClellan would be relieved from duty as commander of the central Afghan force. This fact, Lincoln's encounter with the young father, and the death of Lincoln's boy are thought to have little to do with each other. But then again, history doesn't fit into neat boxes. That's why this man loves it so much.

[YOUNG KNAVE *indicates* HOST, *who enters, rather dazed. The setting is moving into a much realer place;* HOST *and* 2ND HOST *take positions of* YOUNG KNAVE *and* OLD KNAVE *at beginning, with* 2ND HOST *in* OLD KNAVE's *position.*]

YOUNG KNAVE   Now the scene again, one more time, informed by this new information. Let's see how it changes.

2ND HOST   Halt. Who is it?

HOST   It's me.

2ND HOST   Don't I know your father?

HOST   Yes, he's on the co-op board. That's how we met.

2ND HOST   And then we had Scott?

HOST   Yes. And Scott played in the White House with Montgomery Blair's children.

2ND HOST   That was after we moved to Arlington. The white house was on North Adams Street.

HOST   Oh, you're right. Then Scott first got sick when we were living by the parkway?

[*It's agreed. Pause.*]

2ND HOST   I thought what Dr. McDowell said made sense.

HOST   So did I.

2ND HOST   No, but you said we shouldn't wait, and I thought it was okay to wait. And Doctor M told us it was okay, that things wouldn't change that quickly. But he waited too long.

YOUNG KNAVE   [*To audience.*] McClellan waited too long.

OLD HOST   [*Looking off.*] McClellan, McClellan, McClellan...

HOST   You've always said that, but...

[2ND HOST *waits, then starts walking towards the next grove.*]

HOST   So you're just going walk into that grove?

2ND HOST   [*Sternly.*] I need to keep moving!

[*They talk quietly.*]

YOUNG KNAVE   [*To audience, quietly.*] It's the tiny moments, person to person, a lost child, a lost pair of stockings, a lost baseball game, that, conglomerated to the trillionth power, make up the infinite-sided polyhedron of our experiences.

OLD KNAVE   Very nice.

HOST   Clementine.

2ND HOST   Yes, Roderick?

HOST   It wasn't really any kind of fair battle, was it?

[2ND HOST *circles around stage.*]

2ND HOST   Halt. Who is it?

HOST   It's me.

YOUNG KNAVE What you may not realize is that this depiction might not be anything like how the actual encounter transpired.

2ND HOST Don't I know your father?

HOST Yes, he's on the co-op board. That's how we met.

OLD KNAVE And that even if the encounter is accurate, the facts recalled may not be.

2ND HOST And then we had Scott?

HOST Well, first we fell in love, but yes.

2ND HOST I've been meaning to show you something.

> [*Looking out.*]

There's a point where, if you sit here. Look, Roderick.

> [HOST *goes over.*]

There's an optical illusion, and you can see us on the day we had Scott. But we're like giants, holding him, see? And he's so big. It's a trick of the water, it's like we're all as tall as skyscrapers.

OLD KNAVE And that's history. That's the stories we tell ourselves.

HOST We're like mountains.

[HOST *touches* 2ND HOST'*s shoulders, and she reacts. She frees herself and walks off.*]

HOST Where are you going?

[2ND HOST *circles around.*]

2ND HOST Halt! Who is it?

HOST   It's me.

[OLD KNAVE *and* YOUNG KNAVE *light cigarettes, gather their things, and head off together.*]

YOUNG KNAVE   You really think McClellan can help us?

2ND HOST   Don't I know you?

OLD KNAVE   [*Wistfully and ruefully.*] I don't know.

HOST   I think I saw you at the history conference downtown.

2ND HOST   Lincoln.

HOST   And we also lived together in the house by Rock Creek Parkway.

2ND HOST   It was under reconstruction.

[*They turn around.*]

2ND HOST   Halt. Who is it?

HOST   It's me.

2ND HOST   Don't I know you?

[*They turn around; lights slowly fade.*]

2ND HOST   Halt. Who is it?

HOST   It's me.

2ND HOST   Don't I know you?

HOST   Vaguely, yes.

[*They spin.*]

2ND HOST   Halt. Who is it?

HOST   It's me.

[2ND HOST *exits while* HOST *continues to spin.* HOST *continues to perform dance of the turns and facing, though* 2ND HOST *is no longer there to meet him. Lights fade to black as at the end of a dance piece; movement continues into black-out. At blackout, music plays: "Touch the Hem of His Garment" by Sam Cooke. The end.*]

• • •

Totally

by Neil LaBute

characters

GIRL

• • •

[Silence. Darkness. Lights up on a GIRL. *Lovely. Standing there. Waiting.]*

GIRL . . . Oh, hey, hi, how's it going? Really? Yeah? Really? That's awesome . . .

[Beat.]

Hmmmm? Me? Oh, you know, I've been . . . I dunno, it's been interesting. Uh-huh. Totally. Very interesting. I'm not really feeling so—I mean, I'm supposed to meet someone so I can't stand around and, but okay, lemme just . . . I'll tell you the highlights. How's that? If I just skim it for now and then maybe we'll catch up at some other, whenever. Maybe I can text you or we can Skype or, or—yeah. We can do that another time. Cool. Great.

[Beat.]

So. My birthday, right? In January—and yes, you missed it, bitch, thanks, I even sent you an e-vite for it, you never responded—well, ends up being this huge day for me but, I mean, like, starting out, when I'm waking up that morning, how could I ever even know that? You know? So yes, it's a big deal, party that I throw myself every year; it's worth it, I get to see people, and the presents—not why I do it but it doesn't suck—and just a chance to, you know, keep in touch with everybody, for us to keep it real. Nice. So, yeah, that happens and I drink too much, and Douglas, you know him, right, of course you do...everyone knows Douglas apparently, that's what I find out that night. He gets me a necklace from Tiffany's, which is lovely, it is, very whatever, lovely, and they've put the gift receipt in there so I pull it out, just to get it out of the way so I can admire the jewelry—seriously, I'm not at all studying it or anything like he starts accusing me of—and it's tucked in there, right? It's just his receipt to the present, but on it is charges for, I mean, like, two other necklaces. Two more of these things. Exact same ones. And so you know how that goes, it blows up into this whole...shit, whatever you'd expect, with all the lying about they're for his mom and, and his sister for their upcoming birthdays—yeah, right, in April and November— and then it just spills out of him. Like, plop, wham, on the table...Yeah. He's been messing around and he's seeing someone—one does turn out to be for his sister, which is whatever—why he has to buy it during a trip to get me my gift, I don't know, but still, it's his family, at least—but yes, there's this girl and "it's over," he promises, just bought her this as a good-bye thing. I'm, you can imagine, I am knocked out. Flat. I'm planning to marry this guy, make a life with him and this is going on? All this time, however long? With packages and shit, too, not just fucking her and stuff, like guys sometimes do because of all that excess energy, but really...I'm dead inside. Suddenly I feel like I went outside and ate up all the dog shit that I'm able to find out there on the street. That's how I feel.

[*Beat.*]

Because, see...I had a gift for him that night, too. I'm ready to tell him, yeah—I have something all prepared for the evening and now he's gone and, like, ruined it. You think I'm gonna tell him I'm pregnant now? Are you crazy? Huh?

That's—I mean, I dunno, and maybe some girls even would, what better time to get him back on the straight and whatever, but see, he's always so worried about that, he is, he's this Mr. Protection freak with the, like, double condoms and making sure I'm caught up on my pills and whatever. Yeah. Like, insane about it to a point where I'm already nervous that he'll deny it or won't even believe it's his, and plus there's this other part of me that I get from my dad, this sort of deep-rooted stubborn streak—one whole side of me is now thinking, "Screw you, Douglas, you don't get to know this! No, it's my secret now, bitch, and you're out in the cold!"

[*Beat.*]

Do you need to go? No? Okay, cool. Yeah, so, anyhow, that's what I'm feeling inside, up in my head . . . but see, in the moment, I get all soft. I go ahead and cry and beg him to come back and we make up and all that shit—I do really believe he's done with this girl, this "Melody" something and he even has the nerve to call her up and put us on the phone together! Wants her to say it to me, that they're done and she does, whether she believes it or not, she did say it, so— and on the surface, I mean, as far as he can tell, we're fine. We are totally good and all is well in the bell tower. But—

[*Phone rings.*]

Wait, lemme just check, see if this is . . .

[*Answers.*]

Hello? Yeah, I'm at the, no, I'm already here. Yep. I'm just standing here, so . . . okay. Yes, okay, alright, got it. I'll meet you here . . . bye.

[*Puts her phone away.*]

Sorry. I hate it when someone else does that but it really was important. I told you, I think, that I'm meeting somebody. Didn't I? Yeah, I'm pretty sure I mentioned it.

[*Beat.*]

And so that's been me, for, like, the last few months, I've just been wandering around with this, this, like...knowledge in my head and I'm wanting to, I guess, maybe, do something. To risk it all, everything I have or expect to get, my happiness, to pay it back to him. To let him have it. A taste, right? Of his own whatever...medicine and shit, or however that saying goes. What's that thing they used to say, way back when to people who were, you know, avenging loved ones or fighting those mythical animals and all that? Hmmmm? Oh, come on, you know! It's..."Payback's a bitch!" That's the one. And hey, it's so fucking true: Payback is a bad-ass bitch.

[*Beat.*]

And, so, yeah, that's what I'm doing. I mean, in life. And now. Right now, that's what I am doing here in about a few minutes...yep. See, what I did—and this is wrong, I know that, and normally, you could put your purse down right there...go off to the bathroom all day long and I would not think of touching it. Looking inside. And the same for my boyfriend. Totally true. He used to leave his computer open and on the, like, Swimsuit Edition page and I'd stroll right past, couldn't care less, my show's on. Seriously. But now—shit, now it's a war, with me slinking around and digging through his sock drawer or his wallet if he's stupid enough to leave it around and...just a bunch of crazy shit like that. Looking for names or, or, or clues or something. Somebody that I can blame all this stuff on, march up to their door and pound on it, make some big fucking scene out there on their porch for the neighbors to see. That's where my head is at because of a little Tiffany's necklace—not even any diamonds in it or anything—but that's how I'm feeling as I'm sitting there in a panic with his address book open in my lap, me trying to decipher every name or set of initials like I'm some . . . and then it strikes me. Like a bolt, blazing down from the sky above—maybe not heaven but someplace up there—and zapping me right in the fucking face. Bam! Zap! You know? Oww! Shit. Stupid ol' me. It's been right here, staring at me, the whole damn time. The solution to what I'm feeling here and needing. You know. To make things right, I mean.

[*Beat.*]

It's not her I care about. It's him. My Douglas. He's the one needs to pay for this shit, true? Not any girls I spoke to for five seconds on the phone one night—I don't care about them. Nope. It's Douglas. So I decide, Okay, so you're so worried about us using protection—not right now, though, 'cause I did tell him about the baby and, surprise, he's, like, completely excited about it. Yeah, he is. Totally. So he's treating me like a tiny little fragile thing, opening doors for me and lifting shit and whatever, I don't mind, it's new to me—but this is how I figure it's all gotta go, so that by the time the kid comes we'll be even.

[*Beat.*]

I copied all the numbers in his little book there—we have one of those faxes that also do the copies, it's nice—and I'm going down the list, guy by guy, in pretty much alphabetical order, I mean, unless I know for sure that he's an ugly person or fat or whatever, a hairy back, maybe—and I'm fucking them. Once each. Name by name. And you know what, what's really shocking to me but actually not that much because you know why? Guys are pretty much whores, they really are—women are the ones who get that word thrown at 'em but it's really guys who're mostly that way—for being his "friends" or so they say, it's amazing how many of them are totally into what I'm doing. I mean, as long as you promise there's no strings and it's just a fuck and that's all—most of 'em say "Hell yeah!" and are in my pants before I finish explaining it to 'em! It's pretty...well, I find it all kinda amusing. I do. Totally.

[*Beat.*]

And that's what I'm up to. Meeting one of my guys here in a minute. Yeah. It's only my fourth month and I'm already into the Ks. So. I mean, I've had to pick the pace up a little because it was hard in the first trimester with all the...

[*She makes a puking sound.*]

...but I've kicked it into gear and it's going really good. Fast. Not sure I'll get through the whole thing but I'm gonna go for it, trying to finish it off before the kid comes. It's a boy, we already know, so there's that.

[*Beat.*]

Oh, God, should I not've—is this something you didn't wanna know? Sorry. You okay? Because I sometimes have a real big mouth and I probably should've said something first before getting all...Oh. Oh, shit, wait. No. Sorry! I know, I get it. Don't even say anything. Your fiancé, his last name starts with...honestly and I mean totally honest here: I never, and I mean ever, even considered him. I did not. I mean, hey, it's me, I'm not gonna suddenly get all—I know who's off-limits and who's not. I promise. Pro-mise. Yeah. Totally.

[*She looks away, checking watch.*]

Anyway, I should get...right. I've still got some errands to run after this and I wanna be home to cook Douglas dinner. He puts in a long day over at the Nissan so he's—that probably seems weird, right, with what I'm doing, but it works in my head so, screw it, you know, I just keep going with it! Whatever, right? Totally. Yeah, so . . . oh, I think I see him coming now, over there, by the . . .

[*She waves.*]

I gotta go but we should do something! Little spa action or, you know, before the kid comes. And I wanna hear about you, too, I do! Here I am, going on and on and on but I am dying to know what you've been up to. Okay? So call me, we'll grab a bite or, or . . . whatever, go tanning, if you want. Wait, maybe that's bad for the baby? Shit, I'm not even sure—I've been, like, six times since I got pregnant, so . . . maybe we just do lunch for now, 'kay? Great! Perfect. I'm . . .

[*Waving.*]

I'll be right there!

[*To us again.*]

Don't tell anybody, it's Doug's cousin, Tommy, who I've always had this little thing for. I didn't even call him.

I swear! I guess he just heard from somebody: he sent me a text and here we are. Go figure. Anyway! I'm off, let's keep in touch or something—God, I love what you did to your hair. Honestly, the bangs! I mean, they look awesome. So cute. Really.

[*Smiles.*]

Alright, I'm really leaving this time but let's do it, get together and . . . you pick. And next time, it's all you, I promise. My mouth is—[*Pretends to zip her lips.*]—no, I mean that! Totally.

I do!

[*Smiles.*]

You shut up, I honestly do! Bitch.

[*Beat.*]

Okay, wish me luck, 'cause I hear he's . . . totally! What's that saying? "Men: they're hell on the forearms, tough on the knees!"

[*Laughs.*]

Maybe it's not a saying, I dunno, maybe that was just my mom going on about—anyway, who knows? We shall see, right?

[*Beat.*]

What? This?

[*She points to her neck.*]

Yeah, it's nice, huh? Pretty. No, you're right. I mean, as necklaces go.

[*Beat.*]

Anyhoo! I'm outta here. Call me. And your hair's . . . I love it. No, I do. I do! God, I really do! Bitch.

[*Beat.*]

I totally do. Yeah. Totally!

[*A last smile. She turns and waves offstage. Only now do we see just how big her belly is. Noticeably great with child. She trots off and disappears into the shadows.*]

[*Silence. Darkness.*]

• • •

The Huntsmen (Scene 1)

by Quincy Long

characters

DEVON, male, teenager

FATHER, male, forties

• • •

[*A house in the suburbs. It's late at night.*]

DEVON   [*Sings, tentatively.*] *He's my hero and he's me / He's the zero you can't see / He's the nothing on your mind / He's the something you can't find*

[DEVON *enters the den. A desk, a lamp, a* FATHER. *The* FATHER *is working.*]

DEVON   [*Beat.*] Dad.

FATHER   [*Startled.*] Huh? Oh. Hey, sport.

DEVON   What are you doing?

FATHER   Same to you.

DEVON   Can't sleep.

FATHER   Uh-huh.

DEVON   You working then?

FATHER   Uh-huh.

DEVON   On what?

FATHER   Can't tell you.

DEVON   You always say that.

FATHER   It's always true.

DEVON   You can't tell me just a little bit?

FATHER   Not till it's over.

DEVON   Why?

[FATHER *gives a look.*]

I really want to know, Dad. Honest.

FATHER   I'll tell you if you tell me why you can't sleep.

DEVON   I don't know why.

FATHER   Alright. As a lawyer I'm an officer of the court. And as an officer of the court—

DEVON   I'm an officer too, you know. Sort of.

FATHER   Oh. An officer of what?

DEVON   Glee Club. At school. I'm like vice president.

FATHER   Well then, you know from awesome responsibility.

DEVON   What?

FATHER   You should be proud of that.

DEVON   And I'm in the Huntsmen too.

FATHER   The Huntsmen, huh?

DEVON   Yeah, it's a . . . Like a club that we have.

FATHER   What kind of club?

DEVON   Just a club is all. We had to memorize a poem in English called "The Huntsmen" and it turned into kind of a thing.

FATHER   Uh-huh So what's the poem?

DEVON   "The Huntsmen."

FATHER   I mean, let's hear.

DEVON   I can't. I mean, I can. But it's our thing.

FATHER   Okay. So what do you Huntsmen do?

DEVON   Stuff.

FATHER   Yeah...

DEVON   Just like build a fire. Tell stories. Sing songs.

FATHER   What kind of songs?

DEVON   [*Shrugs.*] Just songs.

FATHER   Hunting songs.

DEVON   I can't really say.

FATHER   Looks like we're at an impasse here.

DEVON   A what?

FATHER   I can't tell you. You can't tell me.

DEVON   I guess.

FATHER   Okay, I'm involved in a murder trial. Somebody was murdered. It's been all over the news so—

DEVON   Who?

FATHER A man. An old man.

DEVON Who did it? I mean.

FATHER The police say it was my client.

DEVON Wow.

FATHER Who says he didn't do it?

DEVON We don't. The Huntsmen. We're not like a gang or anything.

FATHER I'm glad to hear it.

DEVON We just... You know. Was there blood and everything when this old man... When he was murdered?

FATHER Presumably.

DEVON What.

FATHER I assume so. Yes.

DEVON Anyway, we... We meet in this place in the woods over by the country club.

FATHER Uh-huh.

DEVON In like a fort we built. Underground. With stuff we kind of borrowed from this new house over—

FATHER Kind of borrowed.

DEVON We took it back.

FATHER When?

DEVON We took it back, Dad, okay?

FATHER   Never mind. You built a fort.

DEVON   The Den, yeah.

FATHER   The Den, huh.

DEVON   I'm actually... Actually I'm pretty tired now.

FATHER   Oh.

DEVON   Yeah, I'm, I'm ready to go to bed, I think.

FATHER   Okay. Well...

DEVON   G'night.

FATHER   Sleep well.

[*The* FATHER *goes back to his work.*]

DEVON   [*Under his breath.*] *Well, they often call me Speedo / But my real name is Mister Earl*

FATHER   What?

DEVON   Did you ever do that, Dad? When you were a kid. Build a fort.

FATHER   Sure. Yeah. Old abandoned train yard. The pit of the roundhouse. Where they used to turn the engines around. We'd smoke cigarettes down there. Look at dirty pictures. Called ourselves the Playboys.

DEVON   The Playboys.

FATHER   Sound familiar?

DEVON   No. Yeah. Sort of.

FATHER   I, uh, stole this. A hunting knife from a sporting goods store.

DEVON   Did you get caught?

FATHER   No.

DEVON   Did you take it back?

FATHER   No, I didn't.

DEVON   What happened to it?

FATHER   Well . . . That knife I gave you for your birthday—

DEVON   That wasn't my birthday.

FATHER   Oh. Well, that was the knife.

DEVON   You said your dad gave it to you.

FATHER   No, I took it. And kept it. And lied about it. That's my big secret.

DEVON   [*Beat.*] We took this girl once.

FATHER   Girl? What girl?

DEVON   Just this girl. From school. She wanted to see our fort she said. So we took her out there. Just to show her, you know.

FATHER   And did you . . . Show her?

DEVON   Uh-huh.

FATHER   And then what?

DEVON   Nothing. Did he . . . This . . . Your client guy. Did he do it?

FATHER   He says not.

DEVON   What do you think?

FATHER   What I think is none of my business. It's my job to defend him.

DEVON   And the old man that got killed. Did the guy know him or—

FATHER   It was his father.

DEVON   Really?

FATHER   They didn't get along, apparently.

DEVON   So you think he did it?

FATHER   I didn't say that.

DEVON   You said they didn't get along.

FATHER   We don't get along occasionally. Do you want to kill me?

DEVON   Sometimes. I mean, I thought about it once. Imagined how I'd do it and say I didn't. That it was like an intruder or some accident. And they'd take me down to the police and question me hard and even give me a lie detector, but I'd practice my breathing and pass. Then I'd come home and do whatever. Take the car out on the road. Order-in girls.

FATHER   Girls, huh?

DEVON   You can like get them online.

FATHER   Like the girl you took to your fort?

DEVON   What?

FATHER   The Den. The girl. The Huntsmen.

DEVON   Oh. Yeah. She... She came down there. She wanted to, she said. She wanted to come. See what it was like. And so. You know. Somebody brought her down. And she came down. And she saw it.

FATHER   And then she left.

DEVON   Well...

FATHER   You let her go.

DEVON   Not right away, no. She... She stayed there for a while. Somebody had brought stuff. Stuff to drink. And we drank it and it got hot so we all kind of took our clothes off. And she took her clothes off too, you know. And we were sort of naked like... And it was dumb but I don't know. We're the Huntsmen so...

FATHER   So. What? You had sex with this girl?

DEVON   Not everybody.

FATHER   Did you?

DEVON   No. Yeah. Sort of. I tried to but...

FATHER   Okay.

DEVON   It was sort of weird because...

FATHER   Okay. These things are. Look, I was in a frat once.

DEVON   In college.

FATHER   Fraternity, yeah, and... And we had parties where... Sometimes things happened at those parties. Things like what you're talking about and—

DEVON   Did you do anything?

FATHER No. I... Well. I... Watched.

DEVON That's weird.

FATHER My other big secret.

DEVON I guess we're both pretty weird.

FATHER Yeah. Look...

DEVON Is that why you and Mom...

FATHER What?

DEVON I don't know. You know.

FATHER No, that was—

DEVON What?

FATHER Your mother is... Troubled.

DEVON But not you.

FATHER What?

DEVON Troubled. You're not.

FATHER No. Yeah. I mean... Look, I want to know what happened with this girl.

DEVON She... I don't know.

FATHER Did you take her home?

DEVON No. She... I... I left.

FATHER When was this?

DEVON What?

FATHER   When did this happen? How long ago?

DEVON   It was awhile ago.

FATHER   Awhile.

DEVON   A couple weeks, I don't know. Geez.

FATHER   But she's alright. The girl.

DEVON   Sure, I guess.

FATHER   You see her in school still?

DEVON   She's a picker. Her family. They move around a lot so . . .

FATHER   So you're saying she's not in school.

DEVON   Hey, I'm not some criminal, you know. Like you're in court trying to make me admit something I didn't do. That wasn't my fault even. I didn't bring her there. She didn't belong. She wasn't in the Huntsmen. She just came. And she laughed.

FATHER   Laughed.

DEVON   Yeah. At our machetes and stuff. Like the pickers, they have guns, she said. Real ones. Guys our age. And all we had are these stupid machetes from the Army Navy. I mean, wouldn't that make you mad?

FATHER   Maybe.

DEVON   So I think . . . I mean, she kind of had it coming to her. What happened. Don't you think?

FATHER   Sure. Oh yeah. Absolutely. What do you want me to say, Devon?

DEVON I want you to stand up for me. To say what I do and say and think is alright and not wrong all the fucking time.

FATHER Hey, you don't have to swear.

DEVON I want to swear.

FATHER Okay then, swear. Swear away.

DEVON Fuck. Fuck. Fuck you.

FATHER Feel better?

DEVON I'll feel better when I stop seeing her.

FATHER I thought you said she left school.

DEVON I said I keep seeing her.

FATHER Look, Devon. I don't...

DEVON In school. After school. At night. All night in my room. I CAN'T STOP FUCKING SEEING HER.

FATHER Hey. Hey. Don't. You're getting hysterical now. Just—

DEVON I didn't do it, Dad. I didn't do anything.

FATHER Do what, honey? What? You can tell me.

DEVON After...After it was over. The thing with her in the...In the Den. I left and I came home and I took a bath and tried to do my homework. And then I went to bed. And the next day...In school. She wasn't there. We didn't see her. But one of my friends. From the Huntsmen. He told me that her brother had been asking around because she hadn't come home that night. The night before. So me and my friend and a couple of the others we...We went to the

Den to see if maybe she was asleep or something because she got pretty drunk on the . . . On whatever it was she . . . What everybody'd been drinking. So we go out there. Look down there. And she's there. And it just looks . . . She's just asleep. Laying on her side like . . . And there was . . . There were all these empty bottles around. But when we like shook her, she wasn't asleep. She . . . She was blue like . . . Her color. And she . . . We didn't know what to do. We were so freaked. Then somebody said bury her. Just fucking bury her. 'Cause of she's dead . . . She died there. And there isn't anything we can do so . . . So we took the walls out. And let it kind of cave in on her. And scattered leaves and stuff on top. And said some things. That we were sorry. And we recited "The Huntsmen" over her and swore. Swore with blood we'd never tell anybody. And I guess because she was like a picker. And pickers move around so much. Nobody ever noticed. Until she's like here. I can see her. I mean, so real. But she's not real, Dad. It's not real.

FATHER   Hey. Hey. Come here. Come on. Come here.

DEVON   I don't know what to do, Dad. I don't. I don't know what to do.

FATHER   Okay. Okay. Okay. So . . . Here's what we do.

[*The* FATHER *picks up the phone.*]

DEVON   What? What are you doing?

FATHER   I'm picking up the phone. And I'm dialing, okay?

[*The* FATHER *dials.*]

DEVON   No.

FATHER   Yes. We ... This has to be done now. Right now. Before—

DEVON   But I can't.

FATHER   [*Into phone.*] Hello.

DEVON   I can't.

FATHER   [*Into the phone.*] I want to report ... Somebody here wants to report something. Something that happened. He'll tell you.

DEVON   Dad.

FATHER   [*Into the phone.*] It's my son. He'll tell you. He's the one who knows what—

DEVON   DAD, I CAN'T!

FATHER   [*Covering receiver.*] You have to, Devon. You have to do this. You were a witness to a crime and it has to come out.

DEVON   But I ... I ... It was me.

FATHER   What ... What was you?

DEVON   I killed her.

FATHER   You didn't kill her. She killed herself, Devon.

[*The* FATHER *hangs up the phone.*]

Devon. Look at me, Devon. What do you mean you killed her?

DEVON   She laughed. Laughed at me when I couldn't do it so ... So after the other ... The other guys did it and she passed out, I came back later to ... I don't know. Try again, sort of, because she ... She told me at school how she liked me.

Liked my sweater. So I get on top of her, but she doesn't want it now. Doesn't want it anymore. She wants to sleep, she said. But I'm ready now. I'm hard and everything. But when I try and kiss her she… She spits on me. Spits right in my face and screams at me to get off and I just I slap her. Hit her. With my… Hit her and hit her and… Then cave the fort in on her and…

[*Cries.*]

FATHER   Oh my God. Oh my God.

[*The phone rings. The* FATHER *picks up.*]

[*Into phone.*]

Yes. Oh. Yes, I called. But it's… Listen… Listen, I… I'm an attorney and I, uh, I'll have to call you back.

[*The* FATHER *hangs up the phone.*]

Oh Jesus. Jesus. Jesus. Jesus fucking Christ.

DEVON   [*To an unseen presence.*] I'm sorry.

FATHER   What?

DEVON   [*To an unseen presence.*] I'm so sorry.

FATHER   Who are you talking to?

DEVON   Her.

FATHER   You wish—

DEVON   I'm talking to her, Dad.

FATHER   Go to your room. Get changed.

DEVON   But—

FATHER   I SAID GO AND GET CHANGED, YOU FUCKING
             MORON.

             [*Beat.*]

             Sorry. I'm sorry. I . . . Look, we'll . . . You and I, we'll go
             down . . . To the police, we'll . . . Apparently
             you . . . Something happened. Something got out of hand.

DEVON   "Speedo."

FATHER   What?

DEVON   It's one of our songs we sang.

FATHER   Never mind about that now, just—

[DEVON *stands and sings "Speedo."*]

DEVON   *Well now they often call me Speedo / But my real name is Mister
             Earl / Well now they often call me Speedo / But my—*

FATHER   Hey.

DEVON   *My real name is mister—*

FATHER   HEY.

             [*The* FATHER *slaps* DEVON.]

             THE FUCK DO YOU THINK YOU'RE DOING?

DEVON   I—

FATHER   HUH?

DEVON   I don't—

FATHER   DO YOU THINK THIS IS KIDDING AROUND,
             BOY? SOME KIND OF FUN AND GAMES HERE?

DEVON   No.

FATHER   WELL, WHAT THEN? WHAT?

DEVON   I don't know. I—

[*The* FATHER *picks up the phone, dials.*]

FATHER   Just . . . just . . . just . . . Get yourself ready to—

[*Into phone.*]

Hey. Hi. Sorry to bother you so late, but we . . . My son and I, we, uh . . . We have a situation here. Apparently he . . . He saw something. Or was maybe involved with something, I don't know. Something he has to report to the police and he . . . He might be . . . Probably needs representation, you know, and . . . Thanks. Thank you. You're the best. No, no, we'll come down. We'll meet you at the station. We're leaving right now. Thanks. Thank you.

[*The* FATHER *hangs up, stands.*]

Okay, let's go, let's— Son . . . SON.

DEVON   *The Huntsmen rise / Beneath the sky / The ground beneath them cold / They raise their weapons / And their cry / Their spirits to make bold / The dogs are loosed / The line is spread / The slaughter is unfurled / The sky has seen / The earth is fed / The Huntsmen rule the world*

[*End of scene.*]

• • •

Determined to Prove

by Daniel Gallant

characters

NARRATOR, male, late 20s–early 30s

• • •

NARRATOR   One of the monologues most loved by high school
actors is the opening speech of Shakespeare's *Richard III*. It
begins "Now is the winter of our discontent" and includes
the boastfully immoral line "I am determined to prove a
villain." I was one of four in my high school Shakespeare
class to memorize and perform the opening monologue from
Richard III, but unlike my classmates, I used the speech as a
mantra. I ran it through my head to pump up adrenaline or
cool my nerves before a piano recital or a soccer game, when
energy and focus were most needed. I suffered horrendous
migraine headaches in high school. First I tried aspirin, then
extra-strength aspirin, then heavier prescription pills that
went under the tongue and tasted rancid. When all of those
remedies failed, a doctor nudged me toward a process called
biofeedback. During biofeedback, sensors monitored my
most stress-affected body parts—forehead, shoulders,
palms—and then displayed my stress levels cheerfully on a
monitor. One display showed a cartoon character in a Robin
Hood outfit who was stuck at the bottom of a mountain.
The more I managed to relax my body—through breathing
exercises, visualization, or boredom—the more progress
Robin Hood would make up his Sisyphean hill, the less the
veins in my head would constrict, and the shorter the
migraines would last. The tireless biofeedback technician

gave me soothing poems, statistics, song lyrics—but only one relaxation technique ultimately worked. And it worked like magic: *Richard III*. Richard came to my rescue then, and a hundred times after. Reciting that monologue brought a different personality into my body, and that new personality could confront a trying set of circumstances like my baseline personality could not. When I recited the words of a Shakespeare character who was confident and cool as ice, I could handle stressful situations with success and ease. Summoning the *Richard III* monologue from memory before a first date or an interview was like bringing forth a bodyguard, or the world's best wingman.

[*Beat; lights change.*]

Many first dates after high school, I met a girl named Josephine. And Josephine had never met a blouse low-cut enough to suit her needs, or a pocket that she couldn't pick. It took me barely a week to learn the downsides of having Josephine on speed-dial: they included phone calls at 3 a.m. insisting I escort her to South Jersey to nab raw materials for the construction of a hydrofoil sneaker. Every week, she'd launch new schemes. And I love schemes, because they're stories told in the present tense, with real-life humans as protagonists, heightened emotions, limited time frames, and uncertain outcomes. Josephine would scheme about creating the shoe of the future, the car of the past, an exercise regimen that allowed humans the swiftness of antelopes, while surviving on cantaloupes, and something about drinkable marijuana. A good 10 percent of her schemes came close enough to success to subsidize the other 90 percent. A few years back, my phone woke me with a call from Josephine at 4:15 a.m. I pick up the phone and I say "No" with great sincerity. However, she's already started in on the monologue portion of her scheme. By the time I'd woken up enough to

follow the logic, I heard her say: "The police are closing in—
they have my prints on file, matched 'em to the gun—and I
am still repaying college loans, so I need capital to start up in
another city. And perhaps to pay for an attorney." "How
much cash are we talking?" I ask. "I would love two-hundred
fifty thousand," she says. So I hang up, and back she calls,
and she starts in again. "You didn't let me finish," she says in
that husky voice that brings all parts of me to rapt attention,
"I just want your help in . . . netting all that cash. You get the
same amount if we're successful," and so then I was intrigued.
See, on a business level, I can interact with anyone—I've
negotiated deals with brutal felons, entered into contracts
with notorious offenders, shaken hands with colleagues
whose throats I'd prefer to wring. And this lady tells some
memorable tales. Her plan involved a swanky club in wooded
and serene Connecticut, a club whose common room held
court to careless, moneyed gentlemen with great enthusiasm
for expensive wagers. She assured me that the clientele loved
gambling, and that they would love her for reasons she
would temporarily augment with several makeovers. She had
a guest pass she had swindled from a partner in a previous
scheme. The guest pass specified a brief time period for us to
make our presence known within the club and plead our case
for membership. Josephine said that this scam was tailored to
the dramatic skills I'd honed in school. I was unemployed
and bored at that point, so I thought, what the hell.

[*Lights change to indicate a country club.*]

We left that afternoon. I changed into a ritzy outfit in the
car. Once at the club, she took the lead; I meditated in the
men's room, shifting my behavior and my personality into a
drunken, old-boy swagger. I breathed out my scrappiness
and desperation, and I breathed in manners of the over-
privileged upper crust. I made my way to one round table

circled by six comfy armchairs. Josephine had draped herself already on a plaid suit-panted, crew-sweatered man with husky shoulders...I crammed myself between two cohorts of her new friend, and I said, "So sorry to intrude, but I was trying to find out how much the Jets are up." "The Jets aren't up," the fatty athlete said. "They can't play football." "I know, man, that's why I'm drinking." He guffawed. "And by the way, don't use the sink," I said, all smiles, "don't use it, fellas, do not use the men's room sink." "You pissed in it?" the wrestler said. "It's all just water, right?" They snickered. Not that I stood any chance of garnering club membership now, but this crowd seemed to hardly care if I defaced club property, so long as it was done the honorable way. "You all aren't, uh...interested in wagers, are you?" It happened that they were. "You betting on the Jets?" somebody asked me. "There is no right answer to that question, not in this club. I will bet a little on the Jets, man, just a token." "Fucking coward." "No," I said, reproving him with buoyant humor, "I'm just being realistic with the team I love. A little for them, out of sympathy, or a little bit against them and I'm not a traitor. Where I will put money, honest money," I said, swagger now intensifying, "is on some sport I know not a thing about. Where I am fucking clueless. Gut instinct. So, women's basketball." "It's out of season," he said. "So you see how much I know. How 'bout canoeing." "Dude, that's not on cable. You don't bet canoeing." "I don't know, so give a sport to me," I said. "Man, we don't know what sports you know." I paused for drunk effect.

"I wager half a fucking million greenbacks, from my pocket, in a check, to split between you all, gents, on whatever sports-related challenge that the next one of you utters. If I'm right, you pay me half a million, all of you together." "Bullshit," they said in a single voice. "Write the check."

"Okay," I said. "I'm writing out a check…for half a million…with no name. Now you all gotta write your checks where I can see 'em too." Imaginary vodka really flooded through my veins now. My hand shivered as I scribbled numerals my bank account had never dreamed of. My small audience was scared, but proud, but drunk, but interested. We each wrote out our checks. "The first sports bet you all can throw my way," I said.

[*Beat.*]

"Hey! Acting! Ha!" This came from Josephine, who dangled fetchingly on someone's lap. "Ha! Acting is a sport! Acting and theater." They all stared back at her like she was splintered down the middle. I pretended even huger shock. My bottom lip danced with precarious aplomb against the downward tug of gravity. "Acting…isn't sports," I said with fever. They all began to laugh. One at a crusty time. They laughed at me, they laughed at her, they stuffed their checkbooks back inside their coats. "Looks like tonight is on the house. Big man is paying for my cab ride home." "It's not a sport…," I said again. "It is," they said as one. They laughed. "She said it is, it is." They slapped their sweaty palms together. "I don't know theater," I said. "That's right, you fucking jock," said Josephine. "You don't; I do. I do know theater. And it's competitive. And it's a sport." She cackled, and her new friends took it up. "You made the bet. You gave the word." They smiled with glee, and all fell silent. Predatory glances on me. Sleeves inched up as muscles flexed. "We're all men of our word. Here, we respect the fucking honor code." "You, my friend, you," said Josephine to me, with pinching cruelty, "you must recite"—(she laughed)—"a monologue, the whole thing, from whatever play I choose. Whatever play." "You're gonna let her do this to me?" I appealed to sweaty, hungry, overstuffed goliaths. "You made the call, my friend," they said. "Don't run away, unless you leave the check." "You, sir," said Josephine to me. "You must recite the first speech, man, from fucking Shakespeare's—" and they howled, "from fucking Shakespeare's fucking *Richard* fucking *III*. *Richard the Third*. The first speech in the first act." They all broke out cackling scandalously. One guy's whisky sour shattered in his hand; the livid, raunchy mess of them just curled up in hysterics. "You have gotta do it," Josephine said, almost unable to speak out between the tremors of her giggling comic frenzy, "in just sixty seconds. You have sixty seconds." "Sixty seconds?" The crowd laughed far above my auditory range. I did fret suddenly; I worried that perhaps Josephine had chosen to ally herself with wealthy lechers who would keep her in good money and away from prying legal eyes. Maybe she'd misjudged the situation or betrayed me, as revenge for my past mockery of all her crackpot schemes. Perhaps I was mere seconds from a mauling at the hands of human bulldogs on their precious turf…But she'd said Richard three, first act, first speech. She gave me sixty seconds. I breathed extra deep, and someone clicked his watch. I stared down at the man whose lap played host to Josephine, I said: "I don't like the position you have put me in, but I should tell you that

> *Now is the winter of our discontent*
> *Made glorious summer by this son of York;*
> *And all the clouds that low'r'd upon our house*
> *In the deep bosom of the ocean buried.*
> *Now are our brows bound with victorius wreaths,*
> *Our bruised arms hung up for monuments,*
> *Our stern alarums chang'd to merry meetings,*
> *Our dreadful marches to delightful measures.*
> *Grim-visag'd War hath smooth'd his wrinkled front;*

And now, in stead of mounting barbed steeds
To fright the souls of fearful adversaries,
He capers nimbly in a lady's chamber
To the lascivious pleasing of a lute.

[*Deep breath.*]

But I, that am not shap'd for sportive tricks,
Nor made to court an amourous looking-glass;
I, that am rudely stamp'd, and want love's majesty
To strut before a wanton ambling nymph;
I, that am curtail'd of this fair proportion,
Cheated of feature by dissembling nature,
Deform'd, unfinish'd, sent before my time
Into this breathing world, scarce half made up,
And that so lamely and unfashionable
That dogs bark at me when I halt by them—
Why, I, in this weak piping time of peace,
Have no delight to pass away the time,
Unless to see my shadow in the sun
And descant upon my own deformity.
And therefore, since I cannot prove a lover
To entertain these fair well-spoken days,
I am determined to prove a villain
And to hate the idle pleasures of these days.
Plots have I laid, inductions dangerous,
By drunken prophecies, libels, and dreams,
To place my brother Clarence and the King
In deadly hate the one against the other;
And if King Edward prove as true and just
As I am subtle, false, and treacherous,
This day should Clarence closely be mew'd up
About a prophesy, which says that G
Of Edward's heirs the murderer shall be.
Dive, thoughts, down to my soul . . .

[The final three words are delivered slowly, as though there's all the time in the world.]

Here . . . Clarence . . . comes!

The watch clicked off. According to the wall clock, I had finished with nine seconds left to spare, and I was greeted by much heavy breathing and some bitter looks . . . but Josephine played up her part with admirable intensity— "Fuck! Who the fuck are you?" Her huge friend said, "You missed the line about the horse," but Josephine, "reluctantly," gave way and handed me her check . . . and after that, the rest of them had little choice. When liquor and unthinking pride butt heads, the consequences tend to be expensive. They knew I was underhanded, but Ms. Josephine could imitate call girls and mindless floozies with admirable accuracy, so our victims did not give her credit for intelligence. They didn't smell conspiracy. The dumb broad lost their cash, and by tomorrow, they might very well forget. But we moved fast. I collected checks and narrowly escaped a showdown with the club's executor. Josephine and I left separately. She fell out of the women's bathroom window and I caught her, and we kissed, but that was habit or mistake, and I vowed never to let our lips interact again. The drive back was lovely and surreal. Halfway home, my cell phone rang. The club invited me to join. Josephine laughed till she passed out. The bumper on the car in front of us had one large, faded sticker. And I talk back to bumper stickers. I rolled down the window, and I shouted at that car in front, "Jesus may be your copilot, but Shakespeare is my fucking wingman."

[Lights down.]

• • •

What It Was Like

by John Guare

characters

NARRATOR, male, late 20s–early 40s

• • •

NARRATOR   Happiness. I had met the woman who'd become my wife on Nantucket in 1975 and it looked as if Adele and I might actually work out, or, more to the point, that I might not mess it up. I was finally living in my future. One day while walking along Hudson Street in Greenwich Village, where I lived, a flash of yellow crashed into me. A spandex-clad cyclist leaned over my body, sprawled on the pavement, and yelled down at me, "You broke the chain on my ten-speed Raleigh! You broke the chain on my ten-sped Raleigh bike! I wish you were dead! Die! Die! Are you dead?" He went off, pushing his lopsided yellow racer, screaming, "Die! Die!" I limped home. Nothing had happened, but suppose I had died? Worse—suppose something had happened to Adele? What would happen if I lost all this? How permanent was this unusual, precious happiness that she had brought to my life? What was the shelf life of our time together? I suddenly could imagine dying. The unimaginable became imaginable. But if I lost everything, what would I be left with? Everything seemed to be so perilous, life merely waiting to be broken by a yellow spandex flash out of nowhere. Is it all Mary Tyrone's last line in O'Neill's *Long Day's Journey into Night*: "And then I . . . was so happy for a time"? Things in the seventies were not so hot for little old New York. Like me and that cyclist, the city constantly careened on the brink of collapse. Basic services vanished. Garbage seemed to collect everywhere on the street. Gangs of thugs would set those piles of trash on fire. Lots of street crime. People exchanging mugging stories became the new small talk. "I gave him all I had. He waved his gun at me: "Is this it?" "Would you take a check?" Graffiti tattooed walls, windows, buses, billboards, parks. An English friend said the graffiti made each subway train zoom into the station with the force of an obscene phone call. On October 30, 1975, the *New York Daily News*' headline immortalized President Gerald Ford's response to this blight: FORD TO CITY: DROP DEAD. A massive, oppressive construction called the West Side Highway ran above and along the abandoned rotting piers that lined the Hudson River on West Street from Christopher Street to Fourteenth Street. In the round-the-clock darkness under the highway, trucks were parked, block after block of trucks, their rear doors hanging open, inviting anyone who desired to climb in, turning this underbelly into an ulcerous parking lot from hell. A sub-subculture of illicit sex, drugs, violence festered in the backs of these trucks. Were they abandoned? Where did they come from? You would never walk along the river at night unless you were feeling suicidal. Don't forget the unsolved Greenwich Village "bag murders"; butchered bodies in black plastic bags would float in the Hudson right off this hellhole. And just to keep you on your toes: a gang of wild neighborhood kids went around beating up people at random. Yet I was the happiest I'd ever been in my life. When I met Adele in 1975, I was living in the Village near the river on Bank Street in what had been John Lennon's apartment before he moved uptown to meet his fate in the Dakota. What an apartment! It consisted of two rooms, the first being the ground-floor length of the brownstone

building, windowless and very dark; the second room was all
light, a thirty-foot ceiling, banks of skylights, a spiral
staircase leading to the roof garden. An unnamed sculptor
decades before had built this dream studio on what had been
the brownstone's garden. Part of me loved living in the
shabby residue of John Lennon's fame. It made me
interesting. Another part of me refused to face the fact that
the apartment was unlivable. The studio room with the
thirty-foot ceilings and skylights was impossible to heat in
the winter. The drinks by my bed would freeze during a
January night. In the summer it would take a nuclear-
powered AC to cool this thirty-foot-high inferno. I asked the
landlord, "Why did John Lennon move out?" "He wanted
more room." And I said, "But that's why I'm moving in."
The rent for the time was outrageous. Five hundred dollars a
month. I took it. All that remained of John and Yoko was a
large bed in the center of the room with a number of posts
around it; attached to each post was a television set tuned to
one channel. In pre-cable days this meant seven TVs, seven
stations. My predecessors apparently would stay in bed
wearing headsets whose sound channels they would switch as
they switched (or didn't switch) their eyes. The first night I
moved in I heard scratching at the front door, which led up a
short flight of stairs onto the street. "John," the voice said.
"Who is it?" I asked brightly as I started to unlock the door,
sure it was some pal stopping by to see my new glamour pad.
The desperate voice mewled, "John, let me in. I've come
such a long way." Which friend was playing a joke? "No,
who is it?" "John, let me in, I love you." "Tell me who you
are." " John, I love you. Let me in." The creepy urgency in
the late-night voice was no joke. I didn't open the door. The
scratching and weeping continued all night. I opened the
door in the morning. Bouquets of wilted flowers lined the

doorstep with a card: "I love you, John." Almost every day in the four years I lived there I would find sprays of roses or chrysanthemums left at the door or elaborately decorated cakes with "John Forever" in frosting or long, yearning confessional letters that only John—the other John, the real John—would understand. They told me their secrets. In those pre-internet days, these pilgrims had not yet learned that the object of their obsession had moved uptown; 105 and one-fourth Bank Street (yes, one-fourth, not one-half) was still the requisite destination for their hajj. I'd say to the anguished spiritual travelers huddling outside my door, "He doesn't live here." "But we've comes so far. Australia. Japan. New Zealand. Oregon. Germany. Where is he?" Sometimes they'd get very angry. "Hey, don't get mad at me, I'm not hiding him. He doesn't live here. I swear to you. Yoko doesn't live here. No, I don't know where he went. Back off." "Let us in." "No, you can't come in." "We want peace!" "I want peace!" "We have to come in!" I understood that. I wanted "in" somewhere as well. I wanted peace as well. What was my life going to be? I inadvertently lived in a world that for so many others was the Mecca of desperate dreams. Why couldn't I be that John? Once, someone left a delicately painted, self-proclaimed official passport ensuring John free passage to anywhere in the universe. Why couldn't I have a passport like that to get me out of that place Wallace Stevens described so accurately, where one's desire is too difficult to tell from despair. I had a baby grand piano I loved to play, gleefully torturing my next-door neighbors John Cage and Merce Cunningham, who would pound on the wall for me to shut up. I'd leave my apartment, size up today's crowd of Lennonites, and then I'd trot up the street to do my day's errands—and watch out for yellow bikes. And then in the midst of all this, I met Adele. My next play came together out of incredible happiness and daily violence and insatiable yearning in this failing city that dreamed of success. Sometimes happiness gives you the security you need to go into the dark places. People always lament what the city used to be, or what a neighborhood once was. That's what I love about New York City—it's always being reborn, it's always reinventing itself. And it demands the same of you—that you keep readjusting to time. You can't live in the past in this city; it's just not there anymore.

• • •

acknowledgments

I would like to thank my publisher, John Cerullo of Hal Leonard Performing Arts Publishing Group, and my agent, June Clark, for their support of this edition and my position with Applause Books.

Furthermore, I'd like thank my professional colleague Rick Pulos, my graduate assistant Aimee Herman, and the administration of LIU— Dean David Cohen, Associate Dean Kevin Lauth, Assistant Dean Maria Vogelstein, and my chair Ralph Engelman.

I'd also like to express my gratitude to all the theatres around the country and their literary managers, as well as all the playwrights whose work I read, enabling me to compile this theatre series. A very, very special thanks to Michael Messina.

I follow in the footsteps of a wonderful project—The Best American Short Plays/The Best Short Plays series published by Applause Books, and I would like to thank all the previous editors of this series: the late Stanley Richards, Ramon Delgado, Howard Stein, Mark Glubke, Glenn Young, and anyone I may have left out who came before these fine editors, who've helped make this series a success since 1937.

A quote from the 1989 edition of The Best Short Plays edited by Ramon Delgado:

> From the beginning of this series the past and present editors have sought to include a balance among three categories of playwrights: (1) established playwrights who continue to practice the art and craft of the short play, (2) emerging playwrights whose record of productions

indicate both initial achievements and continuous productivity, and (3) talented new p1aywrights whose work may not have had much exposure but evidences promise for the future. An effort has also been made to select plays not anthologized elsewhere and, when possible, plays that are making their debut in print.... The value of these considerations is to honor the artistry of the established playwrights, encourage the emerging, acknowledge the promising, and offer a varied selection of new plays in one volume.

As the editor of this series, I plan to keep the tradition moving into the future.

—Barbara Parisi